Praise for *Wild West to Agile*

"Jim Highsmith is the Forrest Gump of software development. What made the 1994 movie so entertaining was how frequently Forrest found himself in the right spot as history was being made. Unlike Forrest, though, Jim's actions influenced that history.

"Jim tells us stories from his early-career invol‾ ‾ ‾ ‾ ‾ ‾ in the Gemini and Apollo space projects and then working as a leader to b methods. From there he outlines how approaches opment planted the seeds that became agile softwa

"Throughout, Jim played a part in bringing a ware development out of its Wild West beginnin stories Jim tells in this book are entertaining and ε to remember as we move into whatever the future holds for software development.

—**Mike Cohn**, co-founder of the Agile Alliance and the
Scrum Alliance; author of *Succeeding with Agile*

"Jim provides a unique perspective not just from the sidelines, but from out on the playing field. If you want to understand the shape of software development today, this is the book for you. If you want to understand how to navigate a turbulent career with grace and style, this is also the book for you. If you enjoy memoirs, ditto. Since I first encountered him in the 1990s, Jim has been my model of a steady, thoughtful leader. Enjoy his story."

—**Kent Beck**, Chief Scientist, Mechanical Orchard; author,
Extreme Programming Explained: Embrace Change

"A magnum opus from master storyteller, adventurer, nonconformist, and adaptable agile maven Jim Highsmith. With this braided narrative, Jim defines what it means to be truly agile, both personally and organizationally. A must-read for a fascinating first-person perspective and invaluable insights into the past, present, and future of agility. I haven't enjoyed a book as much in a very long, long time."

—**Sanjiv Augustine**, Founder and CEO, LitheSpeed

"The phrase 'been there, done that' has rarely been as true as it is for Jim Highsmith and his long and varied career in software. Jim is a great storyteller, and this book tells great stories about many of the leaders of our industry. Enjoy the ride!"

—**Rebecca Parsons**, Chief Technology Officer, Thoughtworks

"The evolution of the software industry from its humble beginnings is captured in a way that only Jim Highsmith can. His coupling of the historical evolution of the software industry with his own personal experiences helps to bring greater insight to the reader as he explains the driving business factors that led to the creation and evolution of the agile software movement. This is not just a walk down memory lane. As an industry leader, Jim clearly demonstrates the next evolution for business and how the software industry is leading the change. Well done, Jim!"

—**Ken Delcol**, Former Director, Product Development, Sciex;
Advanced Program Manager, MDA

"*Wild West to Agile* is an exhilarating ride through the landscape of IT history. Accompanied by personal stories and humorous anecdotes, Jim Highsmith shares his reflections on the good, the bad, and the ugly of agile software development. By knowing the heroes of days gone by, and understanding what came before, you can prepare yourself for a better future in the technology business."

—**Jurgen Appelo**, creator of unFIX; author of
Management 3.0 and *Managing for Happiness*

"More than 70% of agile transformations fail, and many more fall short of expectations. In his book, Jim reflects on decades of learnings on technology innovation and encourages business leaders to embark in the *ultimate transformation journey*: the company-wide adoption of an agile mindset to achieve sustainable business success."

—**Marcelo De Santis**, Chief Digital Officer, Thoughtworks

"What happened over the last six decades in the software field? How did our methods, methodologies, and mindsets evolve? Who played a key role along the way, and where are we headed today? Only a veteran practitioner, industry legend, master storyteller, and agile pioneer like Jim Highsmith could tell this tale with such detail and depth."

—**Joshua Kerievsky**, CEO, Industrial Logic; author, *Joy of Agility*

"It is not often you get to read a front-lines view of the explosive software industry, running from 1966 to 2023—nearly 60 years of being an eyewitness to history! Not just witnessing history, but also driving it. This is an eminently readable narrative by a figure in our history."

—**Alistair Cockburn**, co-author, the Agile Manifesto

"More people every day join the digital workforce to enjoy the agile paradise, but they have not experienced a single real day of being inside a waterfall project or experiencing hardcore command-and-control management delivered in inhuman facilities in dark basements.

"What they enjoy today is the result of courageous battles against powerful executives fought by thought leaders like Jim, who believed that a better status quo was possible. Jim's braided approach in Chapters 1 to 6 sheds light on this past and will help the newcomers more meaningfully value the status quo they enjoy today.

"The last chapters of the book contain valuable keys for unlocking future challenges for both digital practitioners and analog C-executives who are willing to unlearn so that they can have a seat at the table in the future."

—**Ricard Vilà**, Chief Digital Officer, Latam Airlines (Chile)

"An entertaining and insightful book full of nostalgia and advice from a true leader in this space. This book has firsthand experiences and stories of the real struggles of becoming an adaptive organization. Coverage of topics such as the implementation of EDGE is a valuable addition."

—**Linda Luu**, Enterprise Strategy, IBM;
co-author, *EDGE: Value-Driven Digital Transformation*

"Since I just retired from the company I founded 15 years ago, Jim's memoir comes a day late for me. *Wild West to Agile* would have been the perfect vehicle to help this 'courageous executive' address the biggest challenge that I was facing at the time of my departure: the need to evangelize the agile mindset to the next generation of employees, whose focus is primarily on the pedantic pursuit of agile methods.

"Jim has been there and done that, and in *Wild West to Agile* he gives us an educational and entertaining ring-side seat to his historical travels and his many contributions to the software development industry. I'm honored to have played a small part in Jim's matriculation as an agilist and grateful for the mentoring he provided as I was transitioning out of the laboratory and into this century's most exciting business opportunity—creating valuable software for humanity."

—**Sam Bayer**, Founder and former CEO, Corevist

"This is a valuable retrospective on a journey from Apollo to SpaceX, through the evolution of technologies from vacuum tubes to billions of transistors on a chip, from the perspective of a leader in software methodologies and a signatory of the Agile Manifesto. Jim Highsmith's work with other experts on adaptive approaches to business and technology has turned agile software development from a great idea into an essential tool for business survival in the modern world for all successful technology companies."

—**Jeff Sutherland**, inventor and co-creator of Scrum and Scale;
signatory of the Agile Manifesto

"I began working with Jim when we both joined Exxon in the early 1970s. He and I were in the same systems group. I was a business guy by education; Jim was an engineer who was already moving forward in the software development world. I eventually became a manager in the accounting department and Jim a key player in implementing a new, quite complex financial system, which was an arduous task in those early days. Jim spent many days and nights as the driving force during implementation. A brilliant software developer, he had the dedication and work ethic to 'get the job done,' and was highly effective at working with all involved, from the accounting folks to the division executive."

—**John Fahlberg**, executive leadership coach; previous CFO, COO,
and CEO of early-stage growth companies

"Jim Highsmith is truly a pioneer who inspired and led the evolution of software development through the past six decades. *Wild West to Agile* is an enlightening and entertaining trip down memory lane, built on the stories and the people who were lucky enough to collaborate with Jim on that journey."

—**Gary Walker**, Former Manager, Software Development, MDS Sciex

"I thoroughly enjoyed *Wild West to Agile*, which chronicles Jim Highsmith's fascinating career. When I met Jim in the late 1990s, I felt I had finally met someone who was talking about software management in a way that made sense. His stories of success and failure are engaging and show how he constantly evolved to better ways. Highly recommended."

—**Todd Little**, Chairman, Kanban University

"Do you like listening to family elders tell their history? If you're a member of the software development community, here is your opportunity to hear its wild and wonderful history from a leader who's spent six decades affecting it."

—**Gil Broza**, author, *The Agile Mindset*

"Jim Highsmith was literally in the middle of the maelstrom that was the birth and evolution of agile software development. His perspective and stories are fascinating and telling. This book is a must-read for those who prefer to learn from history, rather than repeat it."

—**David Robinson**, Digital Transformation Partner, Thoughtworks; co-author *EDGE: Value-Driven Digital Transformation*

"I have hoped for a book like this, an accurate historical accounting of the software development world, for quite some time. And Jim has certainly delivered. Any serious agilist, or serious software professional, needs to breathe in Jim's words. You won't be disappointed."

—**Scott Ambler**, author

Wild West to Agile

Wild West to Agile

Adventures in Software Development Evolution and Revolution

JIM HIGHSMITH

✦ Addison-Wesley

Boston • Columbus • New York • San Francisco • Amsterdam • Cape Town
Dubai • London • Madrid • Milan • Munich • Paris • Montreal • Toronto • Delhi • Mexico City
São Paulo • Sydney • Hong Kong • Seoul • Singapore • Taipei • Tokyo

Cover image: ShutterOK/Shutterstock

Author photo: Janet Meyer Photography

Many of the designations used by manufacturers and sellers to distinguish their products are claimed as trademarks. Where those designations appear in this book, and the publisher was aware of a trademark claim, the designations have been printed with initial capital letters or in all capitals.

The author and publisher have taken care in the preparation of this book, but make no expressed or implied warranty of any kind and assume no responsibility for errors or omissions. No liability is assumed for incidental or consequential damages in connection with or arising out of the use of the information or programs contained herein.

For information about buying this title in bulk quantities, or for special sales opportunities (which may include electronic versions; custom cover designs; and content particular to your business, training goals, marketing focus, or branding interests), please contact our corporate sales department at corpsales@pearsoned.com or (800) 382-3419.

For government sales inquiries, please contact governmentsales@pearsoned.com.

For questions about sales outside the United States, please contact intlcs@pearson.com.

Visit us on the Web: informit.com/aw

Library of Congress Control Number: 2023934207

Copyright © 2023 Pearson Education, Inc.

All rights reserved. This publication is protected by copyright, and permission must be obtained from the publisher prior to any prohibited reproduction, storage in a retrieval system, or transmission in any form or by any means, electronic, mechanical, photocopying, recording, or likewise. For information regarding permissions, request forms and the appropriate contacts within the Pearson Education Global Rights & Permissions Department, please visit www.pearson.com/permissions.

ISBN-13: 978-0-13-796100-9
ISBN-10: 0-13-796100-6

1 2023

Pearson's Commitment to Diversity, Equity, and Inclusion

Pearson is dedicated to creating bias-free content that reflects the diversity of all learners. We embrace the many dimensions of diversity, including but not limited to race, ethnicity, gender, socioeconomic status, ability, age, sexual orientation, and religious or political beliefs.

Education is a powerful force for equity and change in our world. It has the potential to deliver opportunities that improve lives and enable economic mobility. As we work with authors to create content for every product and service, we acknowledge our responsibility to demonstrate inclusivity and incorporate diverse scholarship so that everyone can achieve their potential through learning. As the world's leading learning company, we have a duty to help drive change and live up to our purpose to help more people create a better life for themselves and to create a better world.

Our ambition is to purposefully contribute to a world where:

- Everyone has an equitable and lifelong opportunity to succeed through learning.
- Our educational products and services are inclusive and represent the rich diversity of learners.
- Our educational content accurately reflects the histories and experiences of the learners we serve.
- Our educational content prompts deeper discussions with learners and motivates them to expand their own learning (and worldview).

While we work hard to present unbiased content, we want to hear from you about any concerns or needs with this Pearson product so that we can investigate and address them.

- Please contact us with concerns about any potential bias at https://www.pearson.com/report-bias.html.

For their inspiration, encouragement, and support

Grandkids: Zach, Ellie, Ruby

Daughters: Nikki, Debbie, and goddaughter Amy

My life partner, Wendie, who kept me sane by periodically prying me from my writing desk.

Contents

Foreword

I STILL REMEMBER WHEN I first saw Jim, in the late 1990s on a stage at a software conference in far-away Wellington, New Zealand. As someone immersed in Extreme Programming, I didn't expect much from someone steeped in the traditional software engineering processes of the time. Yet I experienced a talk full of refreshing thinking, giving credible reasons and citing experiences that resonated with my own sense of modern software management.

Jim's conference biography only hinted at his experiences thus far—a programmer from the early days of computers, who went deep into structured methods, but also saw their weaknesses. The decade before this talk, he'd been actively exploring a new route, one that had a lot of similarities with my very different community.

After that time in New Zealand, our paths crossed more often, although it became a running joke that we rarely met in the country in which we both lived. Jim's book *Adaptive Software Development* was an influence on many people in my circles. A few years later, we were together in Snowbird writing the Manifesto for Agile Software Development. Since then, it's been a mixed couple of decades. The approach we advocate has come further than we thought it would, but it continues to run into obstacles, often caused by the common human inclination to favor surface impressions over deeper understanding. Jim has helped tackle this challenge head on, rethinking the dreaded project management triangle, teaching managers to live with ambiguity, and mentoring new generations of software developers to work in this new style.

Jim's history in the software industry has put him at the forefront of a wave of changes, and I've enjoyed learning about his full story as I've read drafts of this book. It's a personal book, one that can only be written by someone who values adventure but also understands that you need the right training and equipment to get down from the mountain safely. Reading this memoir of someone who worked in the heart of Monumental Methodologies but recognized their limitations and cut a path out of them, I'm learning about many things that influence our current world. I've always felt that understanding history is important, because it's hard to understand where we are unless you understand the path that we took to get here. Jim's memoir is an entertaining and astute odyssey through this history.

—**Martin Fowler**, Chief Scientist, Thoughtworks

Foreword

I'VE SPENT MOST OF MY CAREER—which included five different C-level roles encompassing six different business models—leading and advising businesses on designing new operating and engagement models to drive digital transformation and achieve enterprise agility through the adoption of fundamentally different ways of working, thinking, and being. Like Jim, what I've learned—sometimes quickly, sometimes slowly—is that "Waiting for something to happen and relying on your ability to adapt is one thing, but building a sustainable enterprise having a greater *capability* to adapt is even better." I can assure you, Jim never waited for something to happen: He was a true adventurer and pioneer throughout his career.

This book is an extraordinary trip down memory lane! Jim meticulously describes the evolution of software methods, methodologies, and mindsets through the eras of software development that occurred during his extraordinary six-decades-long career. A prolific storyteller, Jim guides us through this journey from the perspectives of both his personal experiences and the experiences of the adventurous pioneers he encountered along the way, and through the lenses of technical innovation and management trends during these periods.

Jim's last book, *EDGE: Value-Driven Digital Transformation*, which he co-authored with David Robinson and Linda Luu, helped leaders unleash the promise of agile development. It also helped leaders build the capabilities to transform and demanded that one develop the capacity to embrace and lead change. This book, *Wild West to Agile: Adventures in Software Development Evolution and Revolution*, will help all of us who are interested in learning about how agile practices evolved to the pillars of agility: to consistently deliver customer value, to foster enterprise benefits, and to build a sustainable enterprise. Agile methods and methodologies will continue to adapt and evolve, but the need for enterprise agility will not lessen.

What strikes me most about this book is Jim's commitment to preparing for the future by learning from the past. Not only does he honor the pioneers of software development, but he does so in a way that gives both my generation and younger generations insights into the events that we lived through, events that we may have missed, so that the seeds of agility planted and germinated decades ago will continue to flower in the future.

Finally, I would be remiss if I did not note the underlying thread that is interwoven through Jim's braided narratives. This entire journey—beginning with the Wild West era of software development through the Agile era to today's Digital Transformation era—*is entirely empowered by people*. Thank you, Jim, for sharing these beautiful stories and honoring the people who were a part of this amazing journey.

—**Heidi J. Musser**, Board Member, Board Advisor,
Executive Consultant, Vice President and CIO,
USAA, *retired*

Preface

WHY *WILD WEST TO AGILE*? As I retired and began writing a family-centered memoir for my grandkids, I realized I was taking a trip back through time in all-embracing ways I'd not done before. These reminiscence trips through my outdoor and career adventures were both revealing and thought provoking. Every now and then, I would stop and ask younger colleagues if they knew of Tom DeMarco or Jerry Weinberg or Ken Orr. They didn't. They knew about Azure and Ruby, and agile practices, but little about software development history. Technology blazes forward, leaving little time to contemplate the past.

I wanted to write about the history of software development, embellish it with my personal experiences, and introduce the people, the pioneers, who strived to make the world a better place, by building better software. Pioneers—whether 1800s fur trapper Jim Bridger, Apollo astronauts, structured software developer Ken Orr, or agile methodologist Kent Beck—displayed adventurousness, adaptability, and nonconformity. I wanted to resurrect experiences shared with colleagues of earlier generations and offer a sense of perspective to colleagues of a more recent generation.

COVID-19. Lockdown. Retirement. Building project completed. Languishing. What next? These were the thoughts running through my mind as 2022 got under way. As I began to remember, research, and find old emails and documents, the idea of turning a family memoir into a book began to take shape. I had the idea of organizing the book around different eras of software development and writing about my work, stories, experiences, and observations during each era. So, little by little this book evolved from a few fuzzy narrative chunks. I wanted to explore how and why the software industry evolved from the ad hoc code scribbling of the 1960s to the blizzard of methods, methodologies, and tools available in 2022.

Both my career and software development in general were hugely impacted by changes in information technology (IT). One simple illustration: An iPhone with 64 gigabytes of memory has 250,000 times more bytes of memory than the IBM 360 mainframe computer that I worked on in the early 1970s. In 2021, a gigabyte of memory cost about $10. In the Wild West era, although a gigabyte of memory was technologically[1] impossible, the cost for that gigabyte would be nearly $734 million![2] We need to remember that methods, methodologies, and mindsets all evolved to solve the problems of each era, and were both enabled and constrained by the technology of that time.

As I explored this history, *Wild West to Agile* evolved into a work of braided, creative nonfiction. Nonfiction, as the name suggests, is the opposite of fiction. I've always wondered why this genre was named the "non" of something else. Books about technology and science are usually nonfiction and, regrettably, sometimes tedious to a non-researcher. Enter "creative" nonfiction, whose writers use literary craft elements of character, story, structure, tension, and plot to make nonfiction readable and enjoyable. Simply put, they are "true stories, well told."

Braided narrative is the name bestowed on a nonfiction (or fiction) subtype. One braid tells the author's personal story, while another explores an environmental or social justice issue, or a historical event. These two story lines weave together over time, each enhancing the other to create a cohesive whole.

Wild West to Agile weaves together several braids. The first includes the overall evolution and various revolutions occurring in software development over four distinct eras. The second describes my personal and client experiences during each era. The third pays tribute to the adventurous, innovative pioneers. The fourth and fifth braids are technology innovations and management trends.[3]

Writing in this braided narrative genre provided two benefits: scope and stories. A book that purported to be about "the" history of software development would be far beyond my interest or capability. Limiting the scope to events I participated in narrowed the coverage substantially. My career was exclusively involved with business systems (except in my early years

---

1. The maximum memory available for the popular IBM 360/30 was 64K.
2. https://ourworldindata.org/grapher/historical-cost-of-computer-memory-and-storage?country=~OWID_WRL
3. These braids are further explained in Chapter 1.

as an electrical engineer). I wasn't involved in scientific or engineering computing, never wrote compilers or operating systems, never wrote complex algorithms, never worked on Unix systems. What I did work on were business systems, such as those used for accounting, finance, order processing, inventory management, and transportation. What I did work on were methods and methodologies that improved software development. What I did work on were technical, project management, organizational, and leadership issues.

Terminology was a challenge. Today's popular terminology was probably not yesterday's. Should I use the term *software development*, *software delivery*, or *software engineering*? Controversy over terms was, and remains, rampant. Is software engineering really engineering? Is software development a subset of software engineering or a superset? And on and on. My first inclination was to jump into the definitional fray, but then I rethought this decision: "That's the road to lunacy!" So, considering my own personal preference, I used *software development* as a broad term and threw in a few software engineering labels when it felt appropriate. In *Wild West to Agile*, my definition of software development encompasses a complete range of activities—from product and project management, to requirements, design, programming, testing, and deployment.

Another conundrum was topic timing. For example, the term *object-oriented programming* first appeared in the mid-1960s, but had limited use until the 1990s, when the market expanded rapidly. Technical debt followed a similar path. My guideline was to delve into topics during their market expansion period.

I was lucky, fortunate, and humbled to collaborate with two generations of software development pioneers. In the early eras, I was colleagues with people like Ken Orr, Tom DeMarco, Tim Lister, Ed Yourdon, Larry Constantine, and Jerry Weinberg. As 1999 turned the corner into this century, I added agilists Alistair Cockburn, Pat Reed, Kent Beck, Mike Cohn, Ken Schwaber, Jeff Sutherland, and Martin Fowler to this list.[4]

My goals for this book are as follows:

- Document the evolution and revolutions of software methods, methodologies, and mindsets.
- Remember and honor the pioneers of software development.

---

4. More about each of these people in later chapters.

- Prepare for the future, by learning from the past.
- Give my generation a vehicle to reminisce about events we lived through.
- Give younger generations a peek into events they may have missed.

Additionally, I wanted my grandkids to know more about me, to understand my career and explore its purpose.

Finally, a word about my lens into software development history. "Perspective is the point of view that a person sees a historical event from. . . . Every source has a perspective."[5] I've approached this history from my perspective, which of course includes my age, education, work experience, and geography, but also race, gender, sexual preference, and religion. A software history written by a New Yorker would look different from one written by a Silicon Valley alum. The lens of a marginalized person—female, BIPOC, LBGTQ+, or a person with a disability—would be different from mine, very different. I can only write from my perspective, my lens, but I can also acknowledge and support the blossoming goals around diversity, equity, and inclusion.[6]

The braids of this book weave together to tell a story. For mountaineers, a tightly braided climbing rope binds them together into a collaborative, self-organizing team. There are many kinds of braids that bring people together.

Register your copy of *Wild West to Agile* on the InformIT site for convenient access to updates and/or corrections as they become available. To start the registration process, go to informit.com/register and log in or create an account. Enter the product ISBN (9780137961009) and click Submit. Look on the Registered Products tab for an Access Bonus Content link next to this product, and follow that link to access any available bonus materials. If you would like to be notified of exclusive offers on new editions and updates, please check the box to receive email from us.

---

5. historyskills.com, https://www.historyskills.com/2019/03/22/what-s-the-difference-between-perspective-and-bias/
6. More about diversity in the Afterword.

Acknowledgments

HOW DOES ONE WRITE an acknowledgments section when the time span is six decades? My solution was to hack away at it and hope I didn't leave anyone out. I owe much to many.

A special thanks to my consulting clients who, over many years, have courageously endeavored to try new methods, methodologies, and mindsets.

The best products come from collaborative efforts. The content, structure, and flow of this book were greatly enhanced by the invaluable contributions of Heidi Musser, Amy Irvine, Martin Fowler, Barton Friedland, Freddy Jandeleit, Pat Reed, Ken Collier, and Mike Cohn.

Thanks to my industry colleagues, some of whom I have worked with over a span of years: Sam Bayer, Donna Fitzgerald, Jurgen Appelo, Josh Kerievsky, Ken Schwaber, Kent Beck, Anne Mullaney, Sanjiv Augustine, Scott Ambler, Linda Luu, Kevin Tate, Jerry Gordon, Morris Nelson, Lynne Nix, Steve Smith, Gary Walker, Jeff Sutherland, Chris Guzikowski, Mac Lund, Ken Delcol, Larry Constantine, Israel Gat, Tom DeMarco, Tim Lister, Ken Orr, Martyn Jones, Michael Mah, Ricard Vilà, Todd Little, Dave Higgins, John Fahlberg, Karen Coburn, Gil Broza, Alistair Cockburn, Ed Yourdon, Jerry Weinberg, and Wendy Eakin.

Although I retired from Thoughtworks in 2021, a number of Thoughtworks colleagues contributed to this book: Chad Wathington, Rebecca Parsons, Angela Ferguson, Mike Mason, Neal Ford, Roy Singham, David Robinson, Marcelo De Santis, and Xiao Guo.

Thanks to graphics designer Mustafa Hacalaki, who provided just the style and tone I wanted for the book's graphics.

Thanks also to the wonderful staff at Pearson who shepherded me through the editing and production process—executive editor Haze Humbert, developmental editors Adriana Cloud and Sheri Replin, copy editor Jill Hobbs, and the rest of the production team.

About the Author

 **Jim Highsmith** retired as Executive Consultant at Thoughtworks, Inc., in 2021. Prior to his tenure at Thoughtworks, he was director of Cutter Consortium's Agile Project Management practice. He has nearly 60 years' experience as an IT manager, product manager, project manager, consultant, software developer, and storyteller. Jim has been a leader in the agile software development community for the past three decades.

Jim is the author of *EDGE: Value-Driven Digital Transformation* (2020; with Linda Luu and David Robinson); *Adaptive Leadership: Accelerating Enterprise Agility* (2013); *Agile Project Management: Creating Innovative Products* (2009); *Agile Software Development Ecosystems* (2002); and *Adaptive Software Development: A Collaborative Approach to Managing Complex Systems* (2000), winner of the prestigious Jolt Award. Jim is the recipient of the 2005 international Stevens Award for outstanding contributions to software engineering.

Jim is a co-author of the Agile Manifesto, a founding member of the Agile Alliance, co-founder and first president of the Agile Leadership Network, and co-author of the Declaration of Interdependence for project leaders. Jim has consulted with information technology organizations and software companies worldwide.

1

The Adventure Begins

Beginning

HIGH ON THE north ridge of Mt. Jefferson in the Oregon Cascades, near the top of a 25-foot ice chute—a left cramponed foot with two small front-points in the ice, an ice ax with its pick buried a quarter-inch deep in the ice over my head, right foot scrabbling for purchase on a rock nubbin, and my rear extremity hanging 800 feet above the Jefferson Park glacier—I asked myself, "Did I pick the wrong mountain to climb?"[1]

The previous day, in July 1987, my two climbing partners and I drove three hours from Portland to the trailhead, then hiked four miles to establish a base camp at tree line. Up at 4 a.m. the next morning, sleepy and cold after lacing up icy boots, we started the 4,000-foot ascent. Just after mid-day, we encountered the ice chute. Above the chute and just 500 feet from the summit, we abandoned the climb—wanting to complete the challenge, but mindful of losing daylight. As it was, we got back to the car around midnight after a harrowing descent across a rock-strewn glacier, where we packed up camp, and continued the descent, briefly losing the snow-covered trail in fading light.

Later, reflecting on this trip, I realized adventure was becoming a cornerstone of my life, both at work and at home. The term *adventurous* means "eager to go to new places and do exciting or dangerous things,"[2] but also

---

1. A version of this story opened my first book, *Adaptive Software Development* (Highsmith, 2000).
2. Reprinted by permission of Pearson, *Longman Dictionary of Contemporary English*, 2014. www. ldoceonline.com/dictionary/adventurous.

willing to take a calculated risk without being foolhardy. This expresses my approach to adventure. I'm not a free-soloist who climbs without a rope or protection[3]—I want a safety factor. Still, there is a risk of my protection popping out or a sudden rockfall. So, my adventures might be considered risky, but not foolhardy.

My sense of adventure wasn't just about hanging from ice chutes; it was also about adventuring in the exciting wilderness of software development. In 1980, Ken Orr called with an unlikely job offer that changed my work life. I had only worked in large, traditional companies that offered a safe and comfortable working environment. Ken offered the uncertainty of a startup. I was a software development guy. Ken offered the position of sales and marketing vice president. I would be commuting from Atlanta, Georgia, to the office in Topeka, Kansas. I had just begun to use structured development methods. The new job would include teaching them. The job was too exciting to turn down—risky, but not foolhardy.

While these events suggest an adventurous spirit drove my work and play, it took several years for me to appreciate its implications. For a time, work and play took independent paths, eventually merged, and then evolved into a consistent theme of exploration. Adventurousness supplied an initial idea about *how* I was approaching life, but at this early point I hadn't thought much about the underlying *why* of my career. That, too, would evolve.

My career began after I graduated with a bachelor's degree in electrical engineering from North Carolina State University in 1966. My undergraduate curriculum barely mentioned the word "computer," and we designed circuits with individual transistors (about the size of the tip of a little finger), capacitors, and resistors. Wide use of integrated circuits, which in 2023 can contain more than 50 billion tiny transistors and are each 10,000 times smaller than the width of a human hair, was still in the future. While I had heard of the Fortran language, during my college years I never had a programming course and there wasn't even the whiff of a computer science curriculum.

Having worked my way through college with summer and part-time jobs in construction, I needed a full-time job immediately after graduation. The salary for my first engineering job was the outlandish amount of $6,800 per year. My two-bedroom furnished apartment in Cocoa Beach, Florida, one block off the ocean, cost a mere $135 per month.

---

3. Free-soloists tend to push their limits one too many times.

Now, almost six decades after I first entered the field, I can look back on a career encompassing software development, software methodologies, management, and writing. I have identified four major "eras" of software development and five braids (see Figure 1.1), or themes, that wove these eras together. Sometimes we get so caught up in the *now* that we don't connect to the *then*. This book gave me the opportunity to reflect on connecting then and now, to explore the history as a way to prepare for the future.

In each era, *Wild West to Agile*'s first braid explores the evolution of software development methods, methodologies, and mindsets. As individual methods (diagrams, practices) evolved into methodologies (combinations of methods that define a software delivery process), the need to articulate a mindset (guiding values, principles) became paramount. The second braid of this book contains my experiences and growth, from working on the Apollo mission, to programming early business systems, to managing software projects, to helping spark and promote the agile movement. Not only do I want to create a narrative of *what* happened, but I also want to offer some insights into *why* things happened. For example, the Year 2000 (Y2K) scare raised the question, "Why had those idiots [including me] created a two-digit year field?" And why were data flow diagrams appropriate for the 1980s? And why did the agile movement evolve when it did? Conceivably, understanding the *why* of these events will help prepare you for the future.

WILD WEST TO AGILE BRAIDS

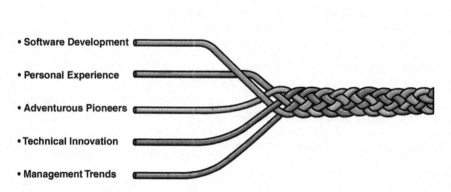

- Software Development
- Personal Experience
- Adventurous Pioneers
- Technical Innovation
- Management Trends

Figure 1.1 *Wild West to Agile braids.*

The third major braid introduces the pioneers who drove forward into the unknown of each era. Who were they? What did they contribute? Were there traits common to these pioneers and innovators? In this braid, I also reflect on my own evolution and adventures into uncharted territory. Finally, two other braids influenced methods, my experiences, and the pioneers—the explosion of technology innovation in computers, and progressive management trends.

I was lucky enough to be in the right place at the right time to work at the leading edge of several eras. According to complexity theory (which we will get into later), perhaps I was *attracted*[4] to these times and places by previous decisions and actions. In the early 1980s, I was recruited from corporate life into the thick of the structured methods era by Ken Orr, who had a tremendous influence on my career. Participating at the cutting edge of software development was too exciting a prospect to pass up.

In the 1990s, Larry Constantine introduced me to a consulting gig that propelled me into Rapid Application Development and a 30-year friendship with Sam Bayer. Late in the 1990s, I met Martin Fowler in New Zealand, where we were speaking at a Software Education conference. Martin later introduced me to Kent Beck, which eventually led to my participation in the Snowbird, Utah, meeting that birthed the Agile Manifesto. All of these people, and many others, will pop up in later chapters of this book, as they influenced both software development and my career.

Career overview

Like many kids of my era, my career started with afternoon newspaper delivery (by bicycle) and then construction jobs during college. After graduating from engineering school, I worked on the Apollo program, designed computers for an equipment manufacturer, and then had a systems analyst job in Tampa, Florida, while pursuing a master's degree in business.

After several engineering jobs, I decided to broaden into management rather than dive deeper into engineering, so in 1970 I obtained a master of science in management degree from the University of South Florida in Tampa. Later in the early 1970s, I obtained a Certified Public Accountant (CPA) cer-

---

4. Complexity theory uses the term *strange attractor* to indicate the fuzzy goal of a chaotic system.

tificate in Texas.[5] During this time, IT professionals typically reported to a chief financial officer and having a CPA was helpful in career advancement. I never practiced public accounting but gaining accounting skills was worthwhile. With a background in engineering, I could communicate with engineers and technologists. With a background in business and finance, I could communicate with managers and executives. This dual ability impacted my entire career.

An Emerging Nonconformist

There was a cultural divide in the 1960s (just as there is today)—the nonconformist hippies and war protesters versus the conformist status quo. While in engineering school in 1963, I visited my parents in Atlanta. My dad, a civil engineer, invited me to his downtown office to observe engineers at work. I dressed up in a suit, proper shoes, shirt, and a tie—the works to look professional. But when my dad saw my pale-yellow shirt, he freaked out: "Where is your white shirt?" It didn't take much to be a nonconformist in those days.

From graduate school, it was off to Houston, for six years as a business systems analyst and accounting supervisor at Exxon (see Figure 1.2 for a career braid overview). Then to Atlanta, taking a couple of systems jobs until I ended up at a power company as systems development manager. At this point my career careened off in an entirely new direction, as I became vice president of sales and marketing for a start-up, structured development consulting and training firm, Ken Orr and Associates (KOA). Leaving KOA because of the commute from Atlanta to Topeka, I began a nearly 30-year stint as an independent consultant, punctuated by two brief full-time jobs. One of these brief interludes was to jump into the CASE tools fray with Optima. I started as a product manager and then became vice president of consulting.

Although an independent consultant, most of my agile-related work has been associated with the Cutter Consortium, an IT research and consulting company, as director of agile project management and fellow. In the final decade of my career, I worked for a worldwide software delivery and IT consulting firm, Thoughtworks. I had a great run.

---

5. At that time, obtaining a CPA in Texas required experience with either an accounting or industrial firm.

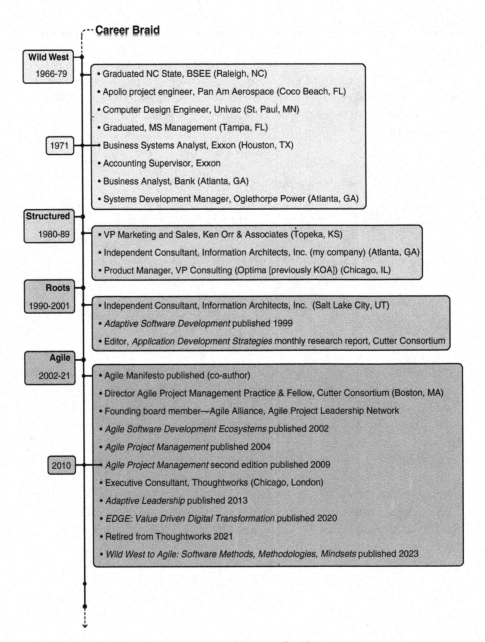

Figure 1.2 *My career braid.*

The word *metamorphosis*, from the Greek, means to "transform"—literally, to "form differently." "Metamorphoses," a poem written by the Roman poet Ovid, chronicles a series of stories based on Greek myths in which the characters undergo personal transformations. In 1912, Franz Kafka wrote *The*

Metamorphosis,[6] a novella about a salesman transformed into a monstrous bug and the consequences of that conversion. The software industry—in fact, the entire technology realm—has been transformed repeatedly over the last six decades by the individuals driving change. By providing insight into my personal transformation, I hope to illustrate what drove others as well. We are all caterpillars, struggling to become butterflies.

In reflecting for this book, I realized my driver, in both career and personal life, was seeking adventure. My first career adventure was working on the Apollo moon mission. My first climbing adventure was on a 25-foot, gently sloping slab of granite in the mountains of North Carolina. My metamorphosis had begun.

Software

What defines software? First, it is, well, *soft*, as illustrated by the 1970s-era story "Weighing Software." Misunderstandings about software persist to this day. You can literally kick hardware. You can't even see software (although you can see the results from it). This confusion has not just flummoxed the public at large; business leaders have floundered because they poorly understood technology in general and software development specifically.

Weighing Software

A software group at a southern university was working on the flight avionics software for an Air Force fighter jet. One critical spec for any airplane is weight, so of course there was a weights engineer on the project. One day the engineer asked the manager of the software group, "How much does your software weigh?" The reply was "It doesn't weigh anything." The aghast engineer blurted out, "Fifteen million dollars and it doesn't weigh anything!" ($15 million was a lot back then). He stomped off, muttering to himself.

A few days later, the weights engineer returned with a stack of punch cards and said, "These cards represent the weight of your software, so all I have to do is weigh these cards to get the weight of your software, correct?" To which the software manager responded, "Sort of, but you have to weigh the holes in the cards."

---

6. Or *The Transformation*, depending on the translation from German.

I've always looked for an analogy that would help people bridge this intangibility gap. Think of the analogy between writing the words in a book and writing software code. *The Lord of the Rings* trilogy contained about 575,000 words. Rounding up a single *Lord of the Rings* book to 200,000 words, and assuming there are 3 lines-of-code (LOC) per word,[7] there would be 600,000 LOC per book. Considering a moderate-size software system of 30 million LOC, this translates to about 150 books. Autonomous car software will have hundreds of millions of LOC.

Imagine you were tasked with a project to write a series of 150 novels. How would you organize the staff? How many staff would you need? How long do you have? What roles would you have—writer, senior writer, plot planner, character developer, consistency editor, content editor, copyeditor, style reviewer, graphics designer? How would you assign roles/people to teams? How would you coordinate between teams? What organizational structure would you use—by role groups (an editorial group, for example), or by cross-functional teams (all required roles for a book)? Who makes which decisions? Do your readers want the entire series at one time, or a sequence of books parceled over time? How will you interact with potential readers to see if your effort is on track? What level of planning do you need for the 150 books? Is the current planning level different for book 1 than for book 150? Thinking about leading, organizing, and managing this 150-book project gives you some idea of the scale and complexity of managing a large software development effort. Furthermore, the answers to all of these questions will change over time.

Software development

From day one of my software career, I've struggled with the question, "What do you do?" Today, with the ubiquity of technology, the question may be easier to answer, but I still find it awkward. It's similar to when people ask what I do for fun. It can also be challenging to explain why dangling off a vertical rock face by two fingers is fun.

From apps on your smartphone, to the operation of the James Webb Space Telescope 1 million kilometers from Earth, to rapid gene sequencing in biotechnology, software runs the world. However, you can hold a smartphone in your hand, you can see the golden wings of the Webb, and you can

---

7. This is the key assumption, and it is highly computer language dependent. Three LOC per word is a guesstimate, but good enough for the purposes of this example.

observe the rows of gene sequences—combinations of AGCT[8]—scroll by on your monitor. But you can't see software; it is an abstraction.

Software is to hardware as words are to actors. A script of words tells an actor what to say and how to move about. A script of code tells a computerized robotic arm in an automobile plant where to attach the next part to an assembly. You don't see what drives the actor to move, you just see the movement. Likewise, you don't see what drives the robotic arm, you just see the movement.

"Our business is not what's in the brown boxes, it's the software that sends the brown boxes on their way."
— Former Amazon CEO Jeff Bezos

Software instructions tell a computer which tasks to perform. Software can be categorized into various types, from operating systems (Unix, Windows, Linux) to applications (Google Maps, Microsoft Word). Based on a computer's hardware design logic, computer-specific machine code interfaces higher-level languages to the hardware. At the core, a "gate" controls the flow of electric current through a circuit. It has two states—on and off. The gate consists of transistors that alter the current flow by the arrangement of AND, OR, XOR, NOT (and a few others) logic gates, giving a computer its capabilities. Machine languages, such as binary, are derived from the gate structures. Luckily, few developers today need to know machine language because a line of code today might translate into hundreds or even thousands of lines of machine language code.

Software development is script writing—but for a computer, not an actor. But think of the script for an entire movie. Movies have themes (good versus evil, family drama, romantic comedy), characters, plots, action sequences, conflicts, and plot twists. Software development has desired outcomes, the feature requirements, data design, and coding in a specific language (COBOL, Java, Python). Making a movie is a collaborative effort; so is software development. At its core, software development is about people—their creativity, organization, knowledge, motivation, and skill.

---

8. Adenine (A), guanine (G), cytosine (C), and thymine (T).

Software development eras

To organize the history of software development, I divided six decades into four eras. Although I named the eras and delineated their timeline based on my experience, they mirror what was occurring in the industry. Two of the eras are further divided into periods. The eras of software development are illustrated in Figure 1.3, while Figure 1.4 provides a timeline of specific methods and methodologies.

- Wild West (1966–1979)
- Structured Methods and Monumental Methodologies[9] (1980–1989)
- Roots of Agile (1990–2000)
  - Rapid Application Development (RAD)
  - RADical Application Development
  - Adaptive Software Development
- Agile (2001–2021)
  - Rogue Teams (2001–2004)
  - Courageous Executives (2005–2010)
  - Digital Transformation (2011–2021)

The Wild West era was, as the name suggests, *wild*. Software engineering[10] was in its infancy and the knowledge of how to "do" software development negligible. By the mid-to-late 1960s, early business applications concentrated on accounting—general ledger accounting, payroll, fixed assets, and accounts payable—all internal applications whose value proposition was productivity and cost reduction. Software enabled businesses to do necessary things faster. During this era, software was an arcane art. Companies hired "magicians" to write code for them. My most rewarding project during this era was working on the Apollo moon shot mission—an unforgettable experience. In the Wild West era, in my own searching, I worked for seven companies in 14 years, spread out in four dispersed locations from Florida to Minnesota to Texas and Georgia.

---

9. I first used the term "Monumental Methodologies" in *Adaptive Software Development* (Highsmith, 2000).
10. In this era, the term *software engineering* was used. My use of the terms *software development* and *software engineering* is explained in the preface.

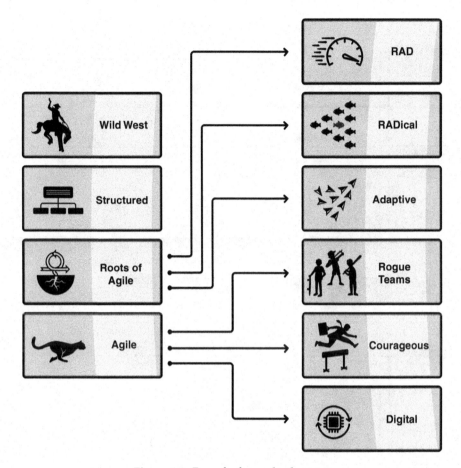

Figure 1.3 *Eras of software development.*

The Structured Methods and Monumental Methodologies era spanned the 1980s. By the late 1970s, structured techniques were becoming popular with individuals who wanted to move beyond the "code and fix" ad hoc approach to development. Structured methods—utilizing techniques such as data flow diagrams, Warnier-Orr diagrams, entity-relationship models, and structure charts—edged into mainstream status. So-called waterfall life cycles were combined with these structured methods into Monumental Methodologies, adding phases, extensive documentation, and process to the mix. I was heavily involved in teaching, consulting, learning, promoting, writing about, and selling structured methods and methodologies during this decade.

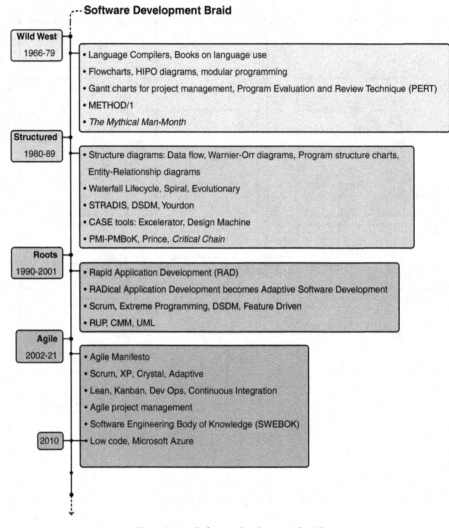

Figure 1.4 *Software development braid.*

During the Roots of Agile era, rebellion against the prescriptive meth-odologies—and their lack of flexibility and speed—began. First with Rapid Application Development (RAD), then with newcomers like Scrum, Extreme Programming, Dynamic System Development Method (DSDM) in Europe, and Adaptive Software Development—the seeds of the agile revolution were sown. By the end of this era, the Internet revolution demanded new thinking about software development. I began this era immersed in structured methods, but by the end I had turned 180 degrees to embrace what were to become agile methods.

The Agile era has now prospered for more than two decades, beginning in 2001. That February, I joined 16 other individuals at the Snowbird ski resort in Utah to discuss the future of what was then referred to as "lightweight methodologies." And the rest, as they say, is history. The outcome was the Manifesto for Agile Software Development, a document whose values underpinned two decades of advancements.

> Agile's Impact on Software and Beyond. These [Agile] principles have penetrated virtually every industry and market. They are prescribed by consultancies and business schools as the antidote to a variety of enterprise ailments. And they are regularly dissected through books, management seminars, and online forums. Not bad for a project the founders intended only to galvanize the software sector—and some were unsure would succeed even in that.
>
> Time, it seems, continues to prove the naysayers wrong. While many management buzzwords die a quick death, Agile has proved remarkably persistent. Google Trends data shows interest in terms like "Agile" and "Agile certification" has remained on a steady upward track worldwide since 2004. Agile has also been the focus of recent articles in publications as diverse as *Forbes, CIO, Global Healthcare,* and *Harvard Business Review* exploring its applicability across functions from marketing to human resources. (Thoughtworks, 2018)

Six decades of change

The software development braid shown in Figure 1.4 provides examples of the changes that have occurred over six decades. The overall magnitude of these changes will be illustrated by examining the following issues:

- Person-to-computer interaction—from punch cards to virtual reality
- Computer performance—exponentially increasing speed, memory capacity, storage options, coupled with plunging unit costs
- Organizational structure—from hierarchical and static to team-networks and flexibility

- Software development life cycle—from serial phases and documentation to iterative phases of delivering incremental value and rapid learning

These trends are described in this chapter and will be reexamined in later eras.

IN SAINT PAUL, MINNESOTA, in the late 1960s, I dipped into investing—tech stocks were on the move—and briefly considered becoming a stockbroker. From then until the mid-1990s, I would call a broker and place a verbal order, based on my analysis of published "paper" information. Then the broker placed the order using punch card input sheets or a character-based terminal (depending on the decade), called me on a landline phone with the results, and snail mailed a paper confirmation. In the mid-1990s, Internet brokerages like Schwab created a different model. The broker didn't enter the order; I did. Stock and market information was now instantaneously available online.

Figures 1.5 and 1.6 illustrate the evolution of human–computer interfaces over six decades. The first figure shows the 1960s version: punch cards input, 144-character printed results. Oh, and a big honking computer with tape-drive storage in between input and output. Input to output speed was measured in hours, many of them.

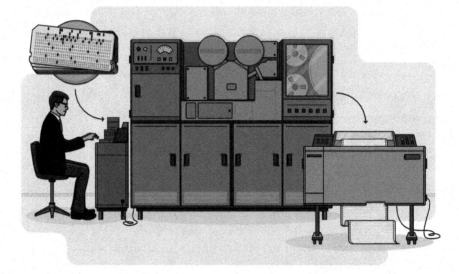

Figure 1.5 *Person–computer interaction in the Wild West era.*

Figure 1.6 *Person–computer interaction in the Agile era.*

Fast forward six decades to Figure 1.6. A family living room contains laptop computers connected to the Internet, Netflix movies streaming on their TV, a tablet PC, a game controller, a virtual reality headset and controllers, Wi-Fi, and a digital robot cat—all available instantly. Rather than a big computer behind a wall, processing and data storage take place in the cloud, floating around in cyberspace somewhere. This increasing personalization and connectivity of computer technology has had a major influence on software development's evolution.

COMPUTER HARDWARE TECHNOLOGY and software advances drive each other. To understand the evolution of software methods, we have to understand the technology of each era, as shown in Table 1.1. Computing performance has increased at an exponential rate. For example, processing speed from the Wild West to Agile eras ballooned from 1 megahertz to 5 gigahertz. The increased performance in each of these areas—processor speed, storage, and connectivity—has enabled an expansion of person-to-computer connectivity unimaginable to early pioneers in the field.

Table 1.1 *Computing Performance over the Eras*

Tech Area	Processing Speed	External Storage	Connectivity	Person–Computer Interface
Wild West **1966–1979**	From kilohertz to megahertz Intel 8080 (1974): 3.125 MHz	From magnetic cores to random access IBM "Minnow" floppy disk drive (1968): 80 KB	Leveraging the phone network ARPANET (1969): 56 Kbps	Wild West of concepts Pong Arcade Game (1972)
Structured **1980–1989**	From 16 to 32 bits Intel 80386 (1985): 40 MHz	The sprint to GB CD-ROM (1982): 550 MB	Increasing speed Ethernet 2.94 Mbps (1983)	Increasing mobility Osborne 1 (1981)
Roots **1990–2000**	From megahertz to gigahertz Intel Pentium Pro (1995): 200 MHz	From kilograms to grams IBM 9345 hard disk drive (1990): 1 GB	Introduction of wireless WWW (1993): 145 Mbps	Apple iMac (1997)
Agile **2001–2021**	From single chip to distributed Intel Core I7 (2008): 2.67 GHz	Transition to cloud Amazon Web Services launches cloud-based services (2006)	From speed to compression Bluetooth 3.0 (2009): transfer speed 23 Mbit/s	Interaction via touch Apple iPod and iPhone (2007): Introduction of a touch phone

In the early days, in the 1960s and 1970s, computers were housed in big, specialized rooms, and their interaction with people was impersonal. Today, individuals have access to thousands of applications on their personal devices. Software development has been profoundly impacted by the technologies of personal touch and customer focus. Table 1.1 shows how computing technology performance has exploded over the years (a comprehensive table including references appears in the Appendix).

Extremely costly computing performance led us to optimize machine performance over people performance. By the Agile era, this was reversed: Now knowledge and innovation, not bits and bytes, drove business performance.

As we journey through the four eras, we will see how strides in technology impacted software development and, in turn, people's experience with computer technology. We will also see that software development methods and methodologies evolved to solve the business problem of the day.

TWO ADDITIONAL INDICATORS OF CHANGE can be seen in the evolution of both organizational structure and software development life cycles.

First look at the traditional organizational diagram at the top of Figure 1.7. It screams functional, predictable, precise, and hierarchical. Then examine the bottom diagram of Jurgen Appelo's unFIX organizational model.[11] It's Lego-like, crew (a type of team) oriented, flexible, and networked—just the ticket for success in the 2020s. Similarly, Figure 1.8 on page 19 shouts out the differences between the linear, limited feedback, prescriptive waterfall life cycle, and my adaptive life cycle's iterations, distinct learning loops, and product vision. These stark contrasts are indicative of six decades of transformation.

Observations

As I dug into my memory bank for this book, I realized a common thread ran through both my work and my play: I was fundamentally an adventurous person. I made adventurous career pivots, from the safety of working for big companies to the turmoil of working for start-ups. I climbed mountains, cycled century races, raced sailboats, and skied black diamond runs. Pushing new concepts such as RAD and the agile movement was equally risky.

Risk and nonconformity energize each other, and most adventurers are nonconformists. As a curious person, every time I drive in the mountains, even today when my climbing days are over, I look up and plot which route up I might try. But I'm also a nonconformist—not in the sense of being different just to be different, but in the sense of being authentic to myself even when outside the norm. I like to shake things up and try the unexpected. I once acted as substitute teacher at a workshop for a friend. The class talked about collaborative teams, but at work if someone on one team wanted to talk with someone on another team, they had to talk with their respective supervisors first. When the men went to the restroom or lunch, they had to wear jackets. Why, with their staunchly conformist culture, they were interested in RAD and collaboration methods I taught will forever be a mystery—I couldn't get away from there fast enough. Jerry Weinberg, whom you will meet later in this book, had a quote for any situation, including one for nonconformity: "Within IBM at that time, growing a beard without getting fired was an indisputable mark of technical genius" (Weinberg, 1985) .

Adventurous. Nonconformist. Adaptable. These actions form the core message to explore further during each software development era.

---

11. More about the unFIX model in Chapter 8.

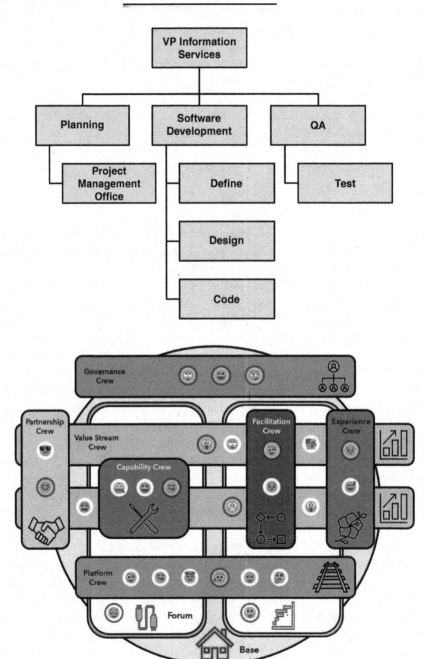

Figure 1.7 *Organizational charts then and now. (Bottom image courtesy of Jurgen Appelo.)*

WATERFALL LIFE CYCLE

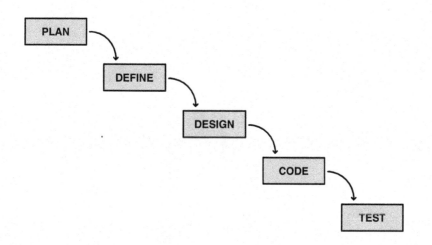

AGILE PROJECT MANAGEMENT LIFE CYCLE

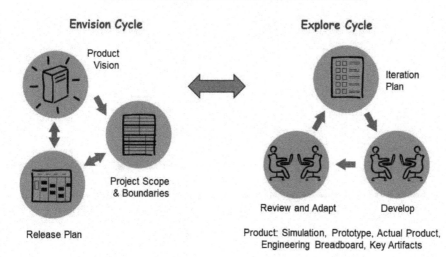

Figure 1.8 *Evolving software development models.*

2

Wild West

(1966–1979)

Wild West

"A SMALL STEP for man, one giant leap for mankind," said Neil Armstrong, venturing onto the lunar landscape for the first time. Upon college graduation in 1966, I had several electrical engineering job offers—Westinghouse in Pittsburgh, Pennsylvania; IBM in Poughkeepsie, New York; and Pan American World Airways Aerospace in Coco Beach, Florida, working on the Apollo moon landing program. My selection process was not difficult. Pan Am had a contract with the Air Force to manage the missile flight operations at Cape Canaveral (not at the Kennedy Space Center, a National Aeronautics and Space Administration [NASA] facility), so I jumped at the chance to be a tiny part of Apollo.

Apollo

My first assignment was looking over engineering drawings and calculating component and system mean-time-to-failure (MTTF) and mean-time-to-repair (MTTR). One time, I flew to the primary downrange missile tracking station on Ascension Island in the middle of the Atlantic Ocean to oversee a computer memory upgrade and test. What I remember most about the trip was the discomfort of flying in an Air Force C-130, losing an engine in-flight, overnighting in Antigua, and the happy hour at the officer's club on Ascension when drinks were 10 cents.

Figure 2.1 *Apollo downrange tracking ship.*[1]

In the early 1960s when Apollo was being designed, global communications was iffy, so five ships were retrofitted with radars, telemetry, inertial navigation systems, and a fully functioning, but smaller, mission control center mirroring the one in Houston. These ships were to be deployed to the Pacific Ocean to acquire and track the command module as it returned to Earth. I worked on two of these ships, like the one shown in Figure 2.1.

"Work" was somewhat of a misnomer for my job. In reality, I reviewed and approved others' work. The number of entities involved in the Apollo mission was startling to a newbie like me. As you would expect, there were multiple contractors for the ships themselves, for everything from anchor chains to computers. What I did not expect was the contract management flotilla—NASA, NASA prime contractors building things, other contractors to monitor the primary contractors, and the Air Force, with the same menagerie

---

1. Photo courtesy of CPC Collection/Alamy Stock Photo

of which Pan Am was a part. For a computer test, for example, there might be a contractor running the test and several observers, each of whom supplied their own hierarchy with reports about the success or failure of the test.

Patrick Air Force Base (AFB), near Cocoa Beach, was the primary launch site for the Mercury and Gemini missions (and military vehicles like Titan), while the launch complex for Apollo was being constructed on Merritt Island, north of Patrick AFB. My office was located at Patrick. One morning, as a friend and I walked into work, we saw tourists standing around the life-sized missile display in front of the building (Figure 2.2). We were dressed for the times in white shirts, thin dark ties, and—the sure sign of an engineer—pocket protectors jammed with pens. We walked over to one of the missiles, looking seriously up and down and around, and started yelling, "Ten, nine, eight, ..." as we ran in the other direction. Wow, the tourists took off! We laughed all the way into the office.

By the time I arrived, the Mercury program was completed, Gemini was under way, and Apollo was getting ready for early test launches of the Saturn rocket. My next-door neighbor was an Air Force camera operator, and

Figure 2.2 *Missiles outside Patrick Airforce Base.*[2]
(Courtesy of Air Force Space and Missile Museum.)

2. https://afspacemuseum.org/sites/patrick-air-force-base-florida/

he invited me to accompany him to watch launches from extremely close up—almost hair-scorchingly close. We were about a mile in front of the news media cameras. I made it to the top of a Saturn rocket on the launch pad and got to look inside the Apollo command module (but unfortunately did not go in). During the first Saturn test flight (at the Patrick site), the ground shook so violently that three separate power feeds to the primary computer facility shut down—they were down for the first 2 to 3 minutes of the flight.

The ships had C-band and S-band radar, telemetry for data downloads, and inertial navigation (secret at the time, used on nuclear subs, and predating the Global Positioning System [GPS]). The computer was a reduced-size, hardened military computer used on Navy ships. It had a red "battle" button so it could run past its temperature limits (and literally burn up) while a battle was under way. This 8-bit machine had a 32-bit word length and an eye-popping 36K of memory (36K was the maximum at the time). At sea, our programming interface was punched paper tape (on land, punch cards). There was a control panel with 3 or 4 columns across and about 10 to 12 rows down—each intersection was a button that signaled currently unneeded programs to roll out of memory so others could be read in.

Consider trying to program complex orbital mechanics calculations to acquire a tiny command module as it came up over the distant horizon given the memory and processing speed constraints. Besides radar and navigation data, another calculation input was ship flex data.[3] The command module acquisition calculation was so sensitive it required ship flexure data in the calculation—all programmed in 36K.

For six months, I was on temporary duty at a shipyard in New Orleans, where two ships were being built. We went out on sea trials—down the Mississippi River to the Gulf of Mexico to test the systems by trying to find airplanes. In an actual mission, the command module would enter the atmosphere at 24,000 miles per hour, then slow down by using retro-burn engines to less than 350 miles per hour. Our target planes flew right over the ship at several hundred miles per hour. The first few tests we couldn't even find the planes.

The entire Apollo program was huge, and its success was a testament to a big vision, creativity, collaboration, learning through failure, engineering expertise, and management talent. It was a fun, but busy time, and it was

---

3. Obtained by measurements in a narrow tunnel between the radars through which a laser was beamed to measure the ship's flex.

great for me to play even a small part in this event. Looking back, it was an exciting way to begin my career adventure. However, by the first manned Apollo flight, the ships had been repurposed due to advances in communications.

BEFORE CONTINUING WITH MY CAREER stops, a couple of leading-edge projects, the state of software methods, and establishing a management context for the entire six decades, I first need to set the technology stage for this Wild West era.

Technology and the world

Apollo was an electric piece of the wider world during the early part of the Wild West era, which included events like the Beatles, the Vietnam War, flower children, antiwar protests, President Richard Nixon and Watergate, and rising inflation. While the global geopolitical and social changes were significant, business leaders continued much as before. The economy was hit by oil crises in 1973–1974 and 1979, whose major impacts included rapid wage and price inflation, which slowed business growth. The combination of these conditions inspired the term *stagflation*. Retail sales sank, and corporate profit margins suffered.

Some big businesses suffered. In particular, manufacturing titans like General Motors and Ford lost ground to European and Japanese car makers, whose vehicles offered both higher mileage ratings and lower costs. But there was another emerging trend. New companies like Apple (1976), Starbucks (1971), Microsoft (1975), and Nike (1964) showed smaller, nimble companies might have a future.

The 1950s had laid the groundwork for 50 years of corporate myopia. The economy boomed, people had jobs, prosperity seemed inevitable, and the future appeared to stretch out into a grand undertaking (unless, of course, you were female, BIPOC [Black, Indigenous, and people of color], LBGTQ+, or a person with a disability). Corporate executives planned for the future as if the progression was predictable and linear. Some things did change, however, so businesses had to adapt, but within acceptable limits. This assumption of predictability infused everything from business planning to project management. "Plan the work and Work the plan" was the corporate mantra. This predictability and internal focus led to trends like management by objectives (MBO) and cost and schedule as the primary objectives of project management. Even into the mid-1980s, big corporations had large planning departments.

In the late 1960s and all of the 1970s, IBM dominated the mainframe business computer market. Prior to that time, IBM offered different lines of computers depending on how much processing power a customer required. Unfortunately, these computers, which had designations like 1620 and 7064, were incompatible, so upgrading from one size to the next was difficult and expensive. The IBM 360/30, released in 1964, was the first of the 360 series of computers having, among many innovations, a common operating system. Magnetic tape drives provided external storage for these early systems.

Beginning in the 1970s, IBM began delivering random-access disk drives with its 360 computers. A small configuration of 2314 disk drives, with 146 MB of storage, sold for $175,000[4] (today that much storage would cost about ½ cent, not adjusting for inflation). Commensurate with the development of disk drives, IBM introduced an early database management system, called Information Management System (IMS). Random-access drives and IMS introduced new complexity, and new opportunities, into software development.

The rise to prominence of minicomputers began in the 1970s and extended into the 1980s, led by Digital Equipment Corporation (DEC), which released the PDP-8 in the late 1960s. DEC developed ever more powerful minis, driving Data General, another major manufacturer, to release its Eclipse superminicomputer in 1980. The intense development effort of the Eclipse was documented in a Pulitzer Prize–winning book, Tracy Kidder's *The Soul of a New Machine* (1981). Still, IBM mainframe computers dominated business computing during this entire era.

Interactions with computers during this time were primitive and impersonal (as illustrated in Figure 1.5). Large mainframe computers resided in specially constructed rooms with raised floors, overhead wire bins, and serious air conditioning.[5] Computer operators input card decks, mounted and dismounted tape and disk drives, and gathered and distributed printouts. Because disk storage was so expensive, most systems used a combination of storage forms—magnetic tape for high-volume data, disks for lower-volume data. Online, time-sharing systems were available on minicomputer systems

---

4. 2314 drive performance and cost in 1970, IBM Archives, www.ibm.com/ibm/history/
   exhibits/storage/storage_2314.html.
5. No one worried about energy costs or environmental impacts in those days.

using Unix and some mainframes, but were primarily reserved for academic and engineering applications.

Software was poorly understood by business executives. They could see the mammoth computers, but the software was hidden. In addition, most of the vendor-supplied software during this time was included in the price of the hardware—software appeared to be free!

WANTING TO DESIGN and build rather than audit, I quit Pan Am and relocated to Saint Paul, Minnesota, to work for Univac Federal Systems Division, which manufactured computers for the Navy and Apollo ships. I was involved in designing gates and registers for computers and early communication modem design. After two engineering jobs, I began to see myself as more a generalist than a specialist and decided to pursue an MBA degree, attending night school at the University of Minnesota for the prerequisite accounting and economics courses. I had anticipated the cold weather in Minnesota but driving to work one morning, after hacking ice off the car windows, with a windchill of minus 78 degrees proved too much. Having braved the cold for one winter, I decided to high-tail it out of there.

Back to the warmth of the South in Tampa, I graduated with a master of science in management degree from the University of South Florida in 1970. For my master's project, I developed a simulation application for analyzing barge traffic from Tampa to ports along the Mississippi River. While I was working as an intern for a local company, the model proved useful, and managers were pleased with the results. The simulation utilized a package called the General-Purpose Simulation System (GPSS). This software was new, so none of my professors could help. I learned how it worked from incomplete manuals and trial and error. Since this was still the punch card and printout era, with slow turnarounds, I spent many evenings in the school computer center. However, there was a flaw in my analysis, which one of the managers caught in my final presentation. One of the data tables contained bad data, throwing off the final results a bit. The bad data was given to me, but I should have been more diligent in reviewing it. In projects to follow, I made sure someone on the team was as detail oriented as I was big picture oriented—I sought to ensure the team had the diversity of skills required to do the work and optimize team performance.

Esso Business Systems

In 1970, fresh out of graduate business school, I moved to Baytown, Texas, just east of Houston, to work in the Esso[6] refinery as a business systems analyst. But the job wasn't just analysis: It also included design, programming, testing, documentation, and—at crunch times—mainframe computer operator.

One leading-edge project I worked on would in the future be called a management information system (MIS). A study team consisting of young gung-ho, mostly MBA types did the analytical work to identify management's needs. John Fahlberg,[7] a colleague from that period, was on the team and reminded me of details in a 2022 call. John's first recollection was our regular Friday night retreat to the top-floor bar in the then-new Galleria Hotel, where we commiserated about long work hours and management, *of course*. When our report was presented and approved, I was a team of one who wrote the software system, which consisted of COBOL[8] and Mark IV (a high-level reporting language) code that extracted data from various operational systems and generated the new reports. The system was a big kluge, but it worked, and the executives benefited from the data. The information included barrels of refinery products produced, staff levels, maintenance activities, costs, and other financial analyses. It was the first time, at least in the Baytown location, data was extracted from multiple operating systems and consolidated for management. Previously, managers received transaction data from operating systems, but no cross-system data in a consolidated manner.

I was still new to programming, with no formal training, and I'm sure my COBOL programs were a maintenance nightmare. We did have a few pattern-like models, such as updating a primary file with transaction files—all of which contained serial data stored on magnetic tape. This was an era in which the last record in files had to contain all 9s as an end-of-file indicator.[9] The only interaction tools at the time were punch card input and printed reports. Turnaround for running and testing programs was usually overnight. It often took several iterations to get a clean compile, at 12 hours

---

6. Esso became Exxon while I worked there.

7. John went on to become the CFO at Target and CEO of several Silicon Valley start-ups.

8. COBOL: Common Business-Oriented Language.

9. Without the 9s record, file read processing would abort when it tried to read past the last record.

per try. In addition to programs, linking a series of programs together with needed data files and tape drives required knowing IBM's arcane Job Control Language (JCL).

> *"JCL is a clumsy and cumbersome system that is hard to learn, full of inconsistencies, and avoided by anyone with an iota of common sense and access to an alternative."*
>
> —Mainframes.com

Testing in those days was a trip. Testing tools were nonexistent. Once you had a clean compile, test data was developed and key-punched into cards, JCL was modified, and the test was run. Of course, if the file was greater than 80 characters, first you ran a program to combine multiple cards into an extended file format. Not surprisingly, many transaction files were 80 characters in length. If you were lucky, the test results were printed and analyzed. If you were unlucky—which was most of the time in the beginning—execution terminated, resulting in a core dump. This 144 characters per line printout of the entire computer memory in hexadecimal[10] looked like "01 A9 34 5A D2 88 88" and went on for page after page. Figuring out where your program started and then tracing the execution path was loads of fun!

In those days we had a vision of what management wanted, but the technology was severely limiting.

A Wild West Story

At Esso, my colleague and early mentor, Ed, was in his 60s. His desk, shelves, and floor overflowed with punch card decks. Instead of the stacked books of a university professor, every surface in his office was covered with computer printouts. Ed was responsible for maintaining accounting systems. He had a box of "secret" one-time "card" decks that he would tweak each year to complete year-end financial books. There was no backup for Ed. If he wasn't there, the books didn't close! None of us had any backup in those days. It really was the Wild West of IT.

---

10. The hexadecimal (hex) numbering system used in computing has 16 symbols (base 16) rather than the standard decimal (base 10) system. The 16 symbols are 0–9 and A–F.

I managed the implementation of a new accounting system scheduled to replace both the software application and the entire account coding system (another team developed the software). Because of the new coding system, the operational systems, such as payroll, would begin using new codes during the month. As a result, when we turned the old month-end system off, and switched the new one on, there was no going back. The project involved modifying and integrating many subsystems, which pushed the implementation to a nine-month project.

My innovation as the project manager was to build a test program that compared the outputs of the existing subsystems (payroll, accounts payable, cost allocation) with the outputs of the new or modified ones. My comparison program was complex, since it involved mappings for all the data in the operational systems feeding data to the accounting application. As different subsystems (for example, the maintenance cost system) became ready and started generating new codes, the testing program would map the new codes back to the old, and compare them with the correct mapping—and we would find tons of errors. It was my first insight into how critical, and hard, testing was.

As we neared our dreaded conversion date, working nights and weekends, we often helped the operators in the computer center, mounting tape drives, making card deck corrections on the fly, and rerunning the system. In subsequent years, developers were banned from operations due to audit "separation of duties" controls.

One evening toward the end of the project, the team returned from dinner, and I parked my car in a director's reserved spot. I worked all night and completely forgot about the parking. The next morning, one of my colleagues informed me I was in big trouble and needed to go see the director post haste. He was a gruff, traditional executive, so I was nervous as I entered his office, apologized, and told him my story of working all night. He surprised me by being gracious: "Anyone who works 24 hours straight gets to park anywhere they damn well please. Just leave your car where it is." He also thanked me and the team for our hard work.

Closing the accounting books for the month, even with the new system, took three nights.[11] The morning after the first day, things weren't looking good: The dreaded, and complex, cost accounting system, named BUPS

---

11. Computing resources were costly, so balancing loads over a 24-hour period was necessary. Therefore, jobs for many operational systems such as accounting were run overnight.

(Burden, Utilities, and Plant Services),[12] wasn't working correctly. There were only two or three people who knew this system well enough to troubleshoot it, so we took a small conference room to hash out solutions. My manager at the time was an old-school micromanager, and he walked into the room and started trying to "fix" things. Having worked two days with almost no sleep, I had little tolerance for his interference, but I did have enough sense not to confront him directly. I went to my friend, John Fahlberg, who was on my manager's level. "Get him out of there before I lose it," I tried to say somewhat civilly. John, being the suave guy he was, guided my manager out of the room and convinced him to let the team fix the problem—which we did shortly thereafter.

The project was a huge success, and everyone was relieved after nine months of 60- to 80-hour workweeks. My friend John planned a party for the team and their significant others. Ignoring his boss's suggestion to keep the cost of the party down, he put on a first-class event, replete with surf-and-turf entrees. Considering the enormous number of overtime hours put in by the project team, this was a minor concession.

While my title on this effort was Project Manager, I knew nothing about project management, except perhaps what a Gantt chart looked like. As with programming, I'd had no formal education and there was little material on the topic available. But I knew other team members had programming experience, knew their systems, and didn't need me micromanaging. We had a deadline, lots to do; the team just needed an overall game plan. It was the Wild West of project management, but I was starting to develop an inkling of management *style*.

During this period, most systems users were clueless, and most of us computer pioneers were marginally less clueless. A project with the refinery maintenance department provided a couple of clues. Managers there wanted a rudimentary system to keep track of maintenance tickets. Like a good analyst, I talked to several maintenance people who currently performed the task manually, wrote down a few specifications, and then developed and tested a system in Mark IV in about three months. I showed the various reports to the managers, which they liked, and then showed them the input forms

---

12. This was a state-of-the-art cost allocation system that allocated administrative costs, based on various factors such as people count, square footage of warehouse space, and many more, to production units, which were eventually reflected in product (e.g., gasoline, heating oil) costs. However, before allocation to the production units, admin costs were allocated among the admin groups—for example, accounting costs to IT, and the reverse, and around and around it went! This single system took 3–4 hours to run on our IBM 360 computer.

they would need to fill out and get keypunched. "Cease" was the response. "You mean we have to fill out these forms?" I tried to explain that producing reports required input data. They were not happy and ended up abandoning the effort. The knowledge on both sides about computers and how to make them effective was in its infancy.

The successful accounting system implementation led to my first management job—promotion to supervisor of an accounting group responsible for payroll, accounts payable, and materials accounting, among other areas. I was 28 years old, and the next youngest person in the group was 45, and they were all unionized. In this role, I learned the difference between being in IT and being on the business side of the IT–user interface. In IT, we were always asking for business users' time to learn about what they did, so we could build systems to support their efforts. Due to the long IT project timelines, there wasn't always daily stress—until the end, of course. On the business user side, there were daily stresses of making deadlines for payroll, accounting closes, and invoice payments. I've never forgotten the different dynamics of these interactions.

Once, when a staff member complained about a rude, disrespectful vendor demanding immediate payment (it wasn't overdue), I called the vendor vice president. I said if his staff were ever rude again, they would never do business with Exxon in the future! Of course, I had no such authority, but he didn't know that, and my staff loved it. This episode added another bit to my nascent management style—you treat everyone with equal respect.

In the early 1970s, there were seven Exxon refineries: four large and three smaller ones. The business systems group in the large ones had developed systems independently and the accounting system mentioned earlier was an initial step in instituting commonality. This reconciliation of differences wasn't easy, as each location had its own way of doing business and was reluctant to change.

To assist in rationalizing IT systems throughout the refining department, the position of business systems coordinator was established in the Refining Controller's office in Houston.[13] As in many companies at that time, IT reported to the controller. Later, as IT became an integral part of businesses, IT organizations would report to a chief information officer (CIO), who then reported to the chief executive officer (CEO). Accepting the coordinator's job,

---

13. Because the most important applications at that time were accounting and finance oriented, most IT departments reported to the controller (now we use the term chief financial officer [CFO]).

I worked to consolidate business systems, of which the accounting system was an excellent start. Consolidation of the software systems eventually led to consolidation of the refinery's computer facilities—a major accomplishment in those days.

Since we were in the controller's organization, one of my infrequent tasks was consolidating quarterly refinery financial reports. One day, I received a call from my counterpart at the corporate level who consolidated reports from all the divisions—refining, exploration, production: "Congratulations, your numbers are off by only a billion dollars." "Well," I said, "it was only one digit."

This was an influence job, not a managerial job, as the business systems supervisors in each refinery didn't work for me. Even so, I needed their help in planning how to bring the refinery IT systems into a modicum of commonality.

Exxon to Oglethorpe

In 1976, after nearly six years with Exxon, I moved to Atlanta, where, after a couple of short-term jobs, I ended up at Oglethorpe Power Company as software development manager.

During a brief stint in an Atlanta bank, where computer operations staff deposited piles of computer printouts on the president's desk each day, I worked on their first international banking system. This project included a trip to Citibank in New York City to investigate its state-of-the-art international banking system running on a DEC superminicomputer. Combining what I learned at Citibank with the knowledge I had gleaned in my discussions with our international bankers, I wrote a proposal for moving forward with new international banking systems for processing foreign exchange, letters of credit, and other international banking transactions. I liked working with international staff, as they were laid-back as bankers go.

But others were not so laid back, as I learned when confronted about my adherence to standards and procedures in a conservative bank. It seems my travel and proposal costs had exceeded my budget by more than the 10% limit. I hadn't even known I had a budget, but I received a dunning letter from a guy in accounting. I would have ignored it were it not for the five to six pages copied from an accounting book and stapled to the letter, which suggested I bone up on my cost accounting. I invited the guy to my office for a chat.

"What is that on my wall?" I asked, pointing to a framed document.

"It looks like a CPA certificate," he replied.

"Do you have one?" was my second question.

"No."

"Well, until you do, don't send me more pages from accounting books!"

Although my proposal on developing an international banking system was well received, by that time my nonconformist side conflicted with a banking career, so I quickly moved on to a less rigid culture.

OGLETHORPE POWER was a newly formed power generation, transmission, and distribution cooperative serving power companies in rural Georgia (in my undergraduate program, I majored in power systems engineering). My software development manager job was like a start-up position, as I got to build my staff and implement methods.

My department manager had worked for Andersen Consulting[14] in the past, so we adopted that firm's Method/1 methodology, which was advanced for the times. While Method/1 was intended as a project management tool for software projects, it didn't include specific development methods. For example, it contained tasks like "Define a file format" and "Complete a file layout form," but had no methods for actually defining them.

I had taken a few courses in structured techniques from Yourdon, Inc., and wanted to incorporate them into our company's development process. In a structured techniques discussion with one of the Andersen consultants, he suggested we look at the Warnier-Orr approach in addition to the Yourdon one. Subsequently, I brought Ken Orr in to teach us about his methodology and methods. While these methods were initially created by Frenchman Jean-Dominique Warnier, Ken Orr added to the original ideas and popularized them in the United States. The diagrams showed constructs such as hierarchy, sequence, repetition, and alternation. The methodology focused on starting with the outputs and working out the flows that produced those outputs. This emphasis on outputs rather than inputs was a concept that stuck with me, eventually extending to the concept of outcomes in the Agile era.

My staff embraced the Warnier-Orr approach, and we delivered several applications using it. We also purchased and used Ken's software package called Structure(s), a precursor to computer-aided software engineering (CASE) tools. One member of my staff got excited. An experienced

---

14. Arthur Andersen was primarily an accounting firm. The Andersen Consulting group grew and was eventually spun off as Accenture.

programmer, he remarked, "This is the first time I've ever written a COBOL program that didn't have a compiler error the first time through." This system was our first complete life-cycle use of the Warnier-Orr techniques. It was successful and well designed. However, it sowed a tiny seed of doubt in the back of my mind: "It sure took a longer development time than I expected."

During 1978, my writing career began with a published article, when "Solving Design Problems More Effectively" appeared in *Management Information Systems Quarterly*. Interestingly, this paper was not about software development, but rather about a process for group problem solving. During the 1970s and 1980s, I published other articles in *MISQ*, *Auerbach Reports*, *Datamation* (Highsmith, 1981), and *Business Software Review* (Highsmith, 1987).

Software development

In the early Wild West era, software processes, tools, reference books, and training were scarce. I learned from the IBM COBOL manual and rushed frequently into Ed's (from Esso) office to ask questions. Most of my knowledge acquisition came through experiences—both good and bad. Owing to his quiet style Ed was difficult to communicate with, but his experience made him an invaluable early mentor to me.

In the Exxon business group, there was a programmer who transferred in from technical systems. His technical programming had been in Fortran,[15] so he wrote his first business application, a payroll system, in COBOL, but used Fortran-like data names. Fortran programmers were accustomed to using data names like "EMPRT2" because of language restrictions,[16] rather than COBOL data names like "Employee-Pay-Rate2." His COBOL programs using Fortran data names caused untold maintenance headaches when he moved on. More Wild West.

One infamous, insidious, and even dangerous COBOL statement epitomizes the nature of this era—the ALTER statement. Think of a program statement—Go To CALC-Pay-Status. Okay, so far. Now comes the fun part.

---

15. Fortran (FORMula TRANslator) was an early computer language used for scientific and engineering applications.

16. Variable names in Fortran were limited to six digits, a–z and 0–9. In a large system, this limitation led to bizarre variable names. In addition, COBOL was a file-oriented language, designed for business systems. Fortran was a variable-oriented language designed for scientific and engineering calculations. IBM offered PL/1 as a one-language solution to replace both Fortran and COBOL, but it was not widely used.

Three pages down on the program printout (remember, only paper output in those days), an ALTER statement, based on some variable, modifies the initial GO TO destination to something like Go To ALT-CAL-PAY-STATUS. Wow. Now think of a COBOL program of 1,000 statements containing 50 of these ALTER-GOTO constructs and the difficulty in following the logic. You needed at least 25 fingers to keep up. Maintenance of these programs was a nightmare—usually passed along to the next poor soul.

During the time of serial tape files, prior to random-access databases, we used techniques like assigning a single data field multiple data types depending on a variable such as the record type. Field 4 might be used for "color" if the record type was "commercial" and for "size" if it was "retail." Date fields were often two digits, which precipitated the Y2K problem 30 years later. Why? Why would programmers create these maintenance nightmares?

Today, cell phones have 128 MB of memory and access to inexpensive terabytes of cloud data. The first Intel chip, introduced in 1971, had a clock speed of a little less than 1 megahertz.[17] Today, chip clock speeds can exceed 5 gigahertz.[18] In the Wild West era, computer speeds were glacial and memory was exorbitantly expensive. As programmers during this period, we needed to save every byte and hertz we could. We had to know which COBOL statements were fast and which were slow. This contributed to the overuse of ALTER statements, because they were fast.

During this period, development tools included flowcharts and hierarchical input–output (HIPO) diagrams. In the mid- to late 1970s, data flow diagrams and other structured methods emerged.[19]

In 1978 I read Tom DeMarco's (1978) book, *Structured Analysis and System Specification*, and attended a Yourdon class on structured analysis taught by Steve McMenamin.[20] I was an instant convert to this systematic approach to uncovering and documenting requirements. This "engineering" approach fueled my enthusiasm. When I accepted the job as software development manager at Oglethorpe, I knew incorporating these methods was part of my mission.

---

17. In this context, hertz is not a car rental company, but rather a frequency measure of cycles per second. One megahertz (MHz) equals 1 million Hz; 1 gigahertz equals 1,000 MHz or 1 million Hz.
18. In 2022, Oakridge National Labs supercomputer exceeded 1 petahertz (1×10^{15} Hz).
19. These diagrams are explained in Chapter 3.
20. More on these topics in Chapter 3.

Management trends

My pursuit of a management degree arose from curiosity and a growing sense I wanted a better understanding of management and leadership as a context for software development. General and project management trends shaped software development in the early years, as well as in following eras.

Inflexible cultures were the norm during the Wild West era—hierarchical, command-control, focused on planning and execution of those plans. Great strides were being made in engineering, and its assumed predictability crept into management thinking. Businesses were universally measured in financial terms—as always, driven by Wall Street. Software project success was measured by completion and cost. Just getting software delivered was considered a success, but schedule was also essential for projects. Cost was certainly important, but was secondary to getting systems up and operating.

Businesses operated on the premise—correct or not—that the world was nominally predictable and if plans failed to materialize, the problem was execution, not planning. Good managers and executives got things done—end of story. The nascent IT world was less predictable, which put IT executives in the hot seat because little allowance was given by general management for the still experimental nature of computers and software.

Looking at how management evolution impacted software development, four factors appeared important: industry evolution, work type, management style, and worker category.

As the industrial age blossomed in the early twentieth century, researchers like Frederick Winslow Taylor introduced the term *scientific management*, extolling the virtues of precise measurements and rigorous, prescriptive job duties. The view of the organization as machine became embedded in the management culture, and optimizing those machines became a key management goal.

Later, management theory began to change based on the work of individuals like Douglas McGregor and Peter Drucker. We hear about GOATs (greatest of all time) in various categories—but who would take the prize in literature? While it might depend on whose list you use, the general consensus is *In Search of Lost Time* by Marcel Proust.[21] If there is a GOAT in management theory, it could well be Peter Drucker. In his time, Drucker wrote 39 books and coined the term *knowledge work* in 1959. Called the father of modern management, he defined *management* as follows: "Management is

---

21. Depends on which Google list one concurs with.

a multi-purpose organ that manages business and manages managers and manages workers and work" (Drucker, 1954). This succinct definition helps us assess changes over time as work changes, workers change, managers change, and managers of managers change. Drucker's coining of the term *knowledge work* signaled that the very nature of work was changing.

"Organization as machine"—this imagery from our industrial past continues to cast a long shadow over management. Managers assumed stability was the normal situation and change was the "unusual state," writes Rita McGrath in a 2014 *Harvard Business Review* article. McGrath identifies three ages of management—execution, expertise, and empathy. "If organizations existed in the execution era to create scale and in the expertise era to provide advanced services, today many are looking to organizations to create complete and meaningful experiences" (McGrath, 2014). These management style categories bring another dimension to our discussion of the software development eras.[22]

Unfortunately, I never found further McGrath material other than her *Harvard Business Review* article. Moreover, there is debate about the empathetic style.[23] Even so, I liked the words McGrath used to categorize management periods. While the label command-control has often been applied to traditional management, none of the recent style names has emerged as "the" term. Names such as leadership-collaboration, adaptive leadership, Agile leadership, Management 3.0, savant leadership, and others have all appeared in the last two decades. So, I will nominate McGrath's "empathy" as the best name for modern management.

KLAUS SCHWAB, CEO of the World Economic Forum, proposed a way of looking at the evolution of work. Schwab's four ages are centered on the advances of science and technology:

- First: The Age of Mechanical Production
- Second: The Age of Science and Mass Production
- Third: The Digital Revolution
- Fourth: The Imagination Age

---

22. McGrath's styles are revisited in Chapter 8.
23. "Easily one of the most debated topics currently, the trend of increasing empathy in leadership has two very opinionated sides" (www.business.com).

As the Age of Science and Mass Production[24] got under way, organizations got bigger and needed a way to manage multilayered organizations, from ground-level supervisors to executives. Practices such as standardized processes, quality control, and specialization of labor were widely applied. Optimization—efficiency, consistency, measurability, predictability—was the goal. This approach, dubbed command-control management, defined the Execution Age. This was the age in which industrial workers were performing physical work.

With the Digital Revolution, computer technology evolved from mainframes to minicomputers to personal computers, broadening access to computing power. Concepts from other disciplines such as psychology and sociology began to creep into management theory, but this age primarily brought expertise into play, characterized by the concepts of reengineering, Six Sigma, and MBO.

Software development would add its own terms in this period—namely, *waterfall* and *Monumental Methodologies*. As the use of technology, including software, medicine, computers, materials, and computing devices, exploded, so did the need for knowledge workers. As knowledge work expanded, employees rebelled against existing manager–subordinate relationships, which drove early agilists to focus on building person-centric workplaces. In recognition of this change, *Adaptive Software Development* (Highsmith, 2000) used the term "leadership-collaboration" management, in contrast to the earlier "command-control," to characterize practices of this age.

Schwab doesn't set the time frame for the fourth industrial age, nor does he explicitly name it the Imagination Age, although there are references to imagination and innovation in his work. He defines this age by the *velocity* of change, the *breadth and depth* of change caused by the rapid evolution and integration of technology, and the *systems impact*, referring to international sociological systems. To prosper in this era, we will need to define "work" yet again, understand the differences between knowledge workers and innovation workers, and know how to lead, organize, and manage in an empathetic way that encourages imagination and creativity.

The Imagination Age is the period beyond the Digital Revolution, where creativity and imagination become the primary creators of economic value, as technologies such as artificial intelligence, biotechnology, robotics, quantum computing, and robotics become integrated into our world.

---

24. I didn't describe the First Age because it wasn't relevant to software development.

> *"We stand on the brink of a technological revolution that will fundamentally alter the way we live, work, and relate to one another. In its scale, scope, and complexity, the transformation will be unlike anything humankind has experienced before."*
>   — Klaus Schwab, January 14, 2016

Eventually, workers were classified into three types: industrial, knowledge, and innovation. As the nature of work changed, the types of workers required changed, which in turn changed the way managers and executives (managers of managers) viewed and interacted with the workforce.

REMEMBER HOW YOU MIGHT have felt about the certainty of the future before the COVID-19 pandemic. And now? The ripple effects of the pandemic are unknown and largely unknowable until they fully play out. Many of these changes were emerging before 2020, and the pandemic just accelerated them. As uncertainty has increased, people have begun to theorize ways to model uncertainty and devise tools and methods to manage it.

Stephan H. Haeckel, who worked at the IBM Advanced Business Institute, published a *Harvard Business Review* article in 1993 and went on to further explain his ideas in his book *Adaptive Enterprise* in 1999 (Haeckel, 1999). His message: Organizations needed to move from a plan-and-execute to a sense-and-respond approach to the future. Sense-and-respond enables organizations to sense the outside world, respond quickly, and use feedback to initiate the next cycle. Organizations dedicated to plan-and-execute become so plan obsessed that deviations from the plans are considered mistakes rather than opportunities.

Why didn't Kodak respond to the digital camera threat? Did digital cameras appear overnight, or did Kodak miss market cues? Why did Netflix oust Blockbuster? Didn't the latter pick up on Netflix's rising market share of movie rentals? Sensing, in our fast-moving business and technology environment, can be extremely difficult. What is noise? When does accumulated noise raise to the level of alarm? In her latest book, *Seeing Around Corners: How to Spot Inflection Points in Business Before They Happen* (2019), Rita McGrath provides insight into this difficult question. In attempting to sort through and analyze streams of data, you need context—what arena are you playing in?

Dave Snowden devised a way to think about uncertainty in a context that supports decision making. In 1999, Snowden introduced the Cynefin model derived from his study of complexity theory. Snowden's model has been embraced and widely used by the agile community. With each category of change, Snowden proposed a practice type to use. His model identifies five categories, or types, of change:

- Obvious, for which best practices suffice
- Complicated, for which good practices are used
- Complex, for which emergent practices are best
- Chaotic, which requires novel practices
- Disorder, for which practices might be unknown

As economies, businesses, and technologies evolved from somewhat complicated in the 1980s to complex, and then to chaotic in the 2000s, Snowden's framework helps us understand the role that combating uncertainty played in the transition from structured to agile development. In this book, I will use the Cynefin model as an indicator of strategic, high-level changes in the business and technology worlds. At the tactical, project, and product levels, I will introduce the exploration factor (EF) in Chapter 6. These two "methods"—Cynefin and EF—provide tools for managing uncertainty.

Table 2.1 summarizes the changes in these factors over the four software development eras and helps us understand why methods and methodologies evolved as they did. During my evolution from structured to agile methods, these frameworks helped me put useful context around my work.

Table 2.1 *Management and Work Evolution*

Key Factors and Thinkers				
Software Era	Management Style (McGrath)	Work Type (Schwab)	Worker Category (Drucker)	Type of Change (Snowden)
Wild West	Execution	Science and Mass Production	Industrial	Obvious/ complicated
Structured	Execution/ expertise	Digital Revolution	Knowledge	Complicated
Roots of Agile	Expertise	Digital Revolution	Knowledge	Complex
Agile	Empathy	Imagination	Innovation	Chaotic/disorder

TOWARD THE LATTER HALF of the Wild West era, I began to delve into project management practices. While project management had a long history, practices relevant to software development emerged only in the 1950s and 1960s. Gantt charts (task and schedule) were used successfully on projects such as the Hoover Dam in the early 1930s. Other large projects in these early years included the Manhattan Project to develop nuclear bombs in the 1940s. Bernard Shriever, while in the U.S. Air Force, was credited with originating the term *project management* in 1954.

The cornerstone of modern project management techniques was the Program Evaluation Technique (PERT), popularized by the Navy's successful use building Polaris submarines. PERT and Critical Path Method (CPM), invented in 1958 at Du Pont, began to be used in the U.S. aerospace, construction, and defense industries. The use of work breakdown structures (WBS) began in the early 1960s. The Project Management Institute (PMI) was founded in 1969 to do research into and promote project management practices. The most famous project undertaken in the 1960s was the Apollo Project (1963–1972), in which NASA successfully led six missions to explore the moon. Even though I had an exceedingly small part in the Apollo mission, this experience provided me with a happy quip: "My first project was a success."

Era observations

The 1960s and 1970s set the stage for subsequent eras in software development. Computer performance began to realize exponential improvements. Random-access storage devices multiplied. Core memory evolved from workers manually feeding wires through sets of tiny toroid "doughnuts." Person–computer interactions began their steady evolution.

Through the early years of this era, we might label software development as "ad hoc," but pioneers worked on early methods they envisioned turning into an engineering discipline. By the end of the era, structured methods and project management methodologies began to bring better organization and control to bear on the process of delivering working software; we might label them "advanced ad hoc." The next era would build on this base.

In the Wild West era, optimizing computer resources took precedence over optimizing people resources.[25] The costs of computer processing cycles, core memory, and external memory were enormous compared to those today.

---

25. Thanks to David Robinson, my *EDGE* book co-author, for this concept.

Hardware began its Moore's law[26] performance improvement march. In early years, computing power was expensive compared to personnel costs, which led to compromises, some of which caused problems for years (such as the Y2K issue). Today, in a world mired in the digital revolution, the situation has reversed: People costs are high compared to computer resources.

Although software development was in its infancy in the Wild West era, valuable solutions were delivered. Some of these systems, modified repeatedly, still exist today. Systems were primitive by today's standards, but they worked.

---

26. In 1965, Gordon Moore, the co-founder of Intel, observed what became known as Moore's law: "The number of transistors in an integrated circuit doubles about every two years."

3

Structured Methods and Monumental Methodologies

(1980–1989)

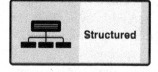

WANT TO DEVELOP software really fast? How about one minute? Based on such exciting concepts as total data independence (the output has nothing to do with the input); the notion that management is not interested in information, only in being happy; and a one-minute life cycle whose speed leads to happiness, Ken Orr wreaked havoc on the state of software methods in the early 1980s. His self-published 1984 satirical novella, *The One Minute Methodology*,[1] was funny as well as prophetic. Ken's book reflected his style, discussing serious issues without being too serious.

The greatest metamorphosis in my career happened in the early 1980s, initiated and sustained by my relationship with Ken Orr. Ken was a well-known software development luminary. He was my friend, colleague, and mentor. He and I worked together in various capacities in the 1980s, corresponded and talked during the 1990s, and worked closely in the first decade of the 2000s as fellows of the Cutter Consortium on its Business Technology Council. Sadly, Ken passed away in 2016.

Ken received undergraduate degrees in mathematics and physics and a master's degree in philosophy. He went on to be the director of information systems for the state of Kansas prior to founding Ken Orr and Associates (KOA). Ken had an easygoing manner but was also intense in promoting

---

1. This book was self-published in 1984 and republished by Dorset House in 1990.

better software engineering. His philosophical inclination peppered our conversations.

Ken was a visionary. He excelled at creating a clear vision that generated excitement in those around him. An astute industry observer, Ken articulated where it had been and where it was going. We didn't always agree, but we always had great fun discussing a wide range of topics.

Ken could talk for an hour from just four slides, keeping an audience spellbound. As a fellow speaker, you never wanted to follow him to the podium. He was a philosopher, a keen observer, and a critical thinker who could converse for hours on any software topic, from programming to architecture.

He was one of the prominent proponents of structured methods. When we discussed "competitors" like Tom DeMarco or Ed Yourdon, Ken would always caution, "Our real competition isn't these guys. Our real competition is apathy, those who aren't using any methodology." I carried this thought with me as the agile movement unfolded. The real competition in the early agile movement wasn't Scrum versus Extreme Programming versus Crystal; the real competition was apathy about using any agile approach.

In early 1980, Ken called me and asked if I would come to Topeka and be vice president of marketing and sales for KOA, then a tiny company with annual revenues of a little more than $1 million. My wife and I didn't particularly want to move to Kansas, and I had a great job at the time, so the decision was a difficult one.

But it turned out to be one of my career pivot points. My decision came down to the answer to a single question: "Did I want to look back later and wish I'd taken Ken's job offer?" My answer became a solid "no." Taking this position led to five significant life changes:

- A role switch—from software development manager to vice president of sales and marketing. This also meant a switch from a comfortable skill set to one barely touched on in my master's program a decade before.

- A company style switch—from a "safe" large company with traditional command-control management to a small start-up utilizing a nontraditional, flexible management style.

- A travel switch—from a desk-bound job with infrequent travel to a road warrior job that entailed weekly travel. At the time, my wife was a relatively new flight attendant for Delta Air Lines, so her schedule included working weekends. Once, I flew to Memphis on Friday evening where she had a layover. We had dinner and I flew home while she continued her trip.

- A location switch, from Atlanta to Topeka. I continued to live in Atlanta, which meant a 5-hour, door-to-door trip to the Topeka office (plane and car). It meant being away from home four days a week.
- A change from learner to teacher of structured methods.

In retrospect, this pivot was certainly an adventurous one and launched my nonconformist journey into a higher gear.

The KOA office was on the opposite side of the railroad tracks from downtown Topeka. The small, stand-alone building was surrounded by grasslands, not other buildings. We affectionately dubbed it the "Little House on the Prairie."[2]

Ken had great ideas—he was a veritable fountain of great ideas. He would pop into my office multiple times a day with just one more idea—which I would dutifully jot down. Soon overwhelmed, I needed an "idea" strategy. So a few days later when he came into my office, I said, "Ken, when you pop in here with new ideas, I'll jot them down. However, I don't plan to act on any until you have popped in with the same idea three times." That strategy worked for us.

As in many small start-ups, I wore at least three hats. I oversaw a *huge* marketing and sales department of three people including me. I did everything from making cold calls via telephone to designing marketing brochures to staffing booths at conferences. I had two salespeople, each of whom covered half the country. As a point of comparison, Ken had a friend in Chicago who was a sales representative for IBM whose sales territory was just 15 floors of Sears Tower.

I also taught workshops, did consulting, and developed new workshops. I didn't want to get completely away from the technical side of things, and Ken didn't want me to. Since we were selling a technical product, it was appropriate for me to keep my hand in.

---

2. Also, the name of a book by Laura Ingalls Wilder and a family-oriented TV series that aired from 1974 to 1983 and starred Michael Landon.

Lastly, I worked closely with Ken and others to develop our version of a Monumental Methodology we called Data Structured Systems Development (DSSD). It had the requisite volumes of documents, but we managed to keep it to four 4-inch notebook binders. My typical workweek, if there was such a thing, might go this way:

- Arrive at the Topeka office at 9 a.m. on Monday morning, usually before my staff (commuting from Atlanta).
- Make a few sales and customer calls.
- Referee between my two salespeople, who for some reason couldn't stay out of each other's territory and constantly bickered.
- Fly to San Francisco for a day to talk with our biggest client, who had 6 to 10 of our consultants working there full time. Work with the consultants to get the status of their projects, but mainly give them a home-office ear to bend.
- Work on a class on structured planning I envisioned.
- Draft an article for our monthly newsletter.
- Fly home, ideally on Thursday, but often on Friday afternoon.

It was a blast! (Except for one cold, snowy Sunday at midnight when my car refused to start in the Kansas City airport parking lot.)

With my marketing and sales hat on, I learned about pressure in a sales job. At a large West Coast company interested in a significant purchase of DSSD methodology, training, and consulting, I sat around a conference table with several IT managers, a purchasing agent, and one of their lawyers. The thought interjecting itself into the back of mind was "I have to close this sale if we are going to make payroll next month." I'd worked under time pressure before, but this was the first time I was under serious sales pressure.

DAVE HIGGINS SPENT much of his career working with KOA; in fact, he was Ken's chief associate. Because they were a lot alike—both took software development seriously—their opinions conflicted occasionally. Sometimes Dave would leave, but he would always come back. I spoke with Dave in 2022 and asked him about the methodology wars during the Structured era.

This was what he remembered:

"First of all, when we got together with Yourdon practitioners and others, we quickly recognized there were more similarities than differences. We were all trying to establish and document the best practices of the times. We were moving from an undisciplined state towards an effective software engineering discipline. Software's malleability created challenges in turning discipline into engineering."

As we talked, the topic of advances in computer interfaces came up:

"That era linked 'green'[3] screen terminals to people. Remember era keyboards had Return rather than Enter keys. Manual typewriters didn't have word-wrap capability; you had to manually advance to the next line by hitting the carriage return. Technology turns many problems into nonproblems but creates others as well."

Era overview

The Structured era consisted of three phases, which overlapped considerably. The Methods phase brought a number of entrants into the structured revolution. In the Monumental Methodologies phase, structured methods were integrated with project management practices into software life-cycle management methodologies containing development phases, detailed tasks, and documentation requirements. As these Methodologies grew into Monumental ones, the next evolution was, of course, to automate the graphics diagrams and the requisite documentation. This last phase was dubbed the Computer-Aided Software Engineering (CASE) Tools phase.

These three phases are described in this chapter together with examples of structured methods, several customer stories, a glimpse at technology and management advances, and an in-depth look at a concept—the waterfall life cycle—which was to dominate thinking for the next couple of decades.

The wider world during the early 1980s was grappling with high inflation and a recession, the Iran hostage crisis, and a political shift toward conservatism as liberal peanut farmer Jimmy Carter gave way to Republican Hollywood actor Ronald Reagan as U.S. president. The movie *Raiders of the Lost Ark* wowed the public, but not the Oscars voters. The later 1980s saw the Berlin Wall fall and the rising popularity of Madonna. New computer technologies emerged and blockbuster movies and MTV reshaped pop culture. It was a time of change, but the rate of change was still moderate—still in the Cynefin complicated phase, where good practices dominated, edging into the complex phase, which required a different set of practices.

---

3. "Green screen" refers to the character color on the black background of IBM terminals.

Working in the early 1980s in Portland, Oregon, I met Jerry Gordon, who introduced me to mountain climbing on the slopes of Mt. Adams in Washington. After that, in addition to working, I spent a couple of weeks every summer mountaineering and rock climbing in Washington's Cascade Mountains.

> **My First Mountaineering Adventures**
>
> Our (I convinced my wife to go along) first outing was to Mt. Adams in southern Washington. The route was strenuous, but not technical. The first day we made it to the "Lunch Counter," where we camped in bivy sacks, no tents. The second day, we ran out of steam before reaching the summit, but it was a great introduction to climbing.
>
> Our second outing with Jerry was a climb of Mt. Hood in Oregon. Up at 2 a.m., at a temperature of 5°F, in a high wind with blinding snow—we trudged up the mountain in the dark, finding temporary respite in the abandoned Silcox Hut. Shortly after resuming the climb, my wife turned to me and said, "I'm not having fun!" She descended with a wedding party headed down from a summit wedding. She loved the outdoors, but technical climbing not so much. Jerry and I tried again on the second day, and I reached my first mountain summit. The gorgeous scenery, lush vegetation at the lower elevation opening at the tree line to wide expanses of rock pinnacles and glaciers, the physical stamina needed to hike thousands of feet of elevation, and the technical skills with ropes, crampons, and ice axes all captured my imagination for the next two decades.

Software methods

In 2011, Marc Andreesen, cofounder of Netscape, authored an article in *The Wall Street Journal* titled "Why Software Is Eating the World." Software may be eating the world, but it can run amok as well.

> During the late 1980s, the Therac-25 medical device malfunctioned, delivering lethal radiation doses to patients. An investigation found that the machine's operating system had been kludged together by a single, ill-trained programmer who had created a condition conducive to operator mistakes.

The Year 2000 (Y2K) bug, created in the 1960s and 1970s, caused havoc in the 1990s as organizations worldwide poured billions of dollars into software remediation.

Software developers and software development needed to evolve to meet the challenges of our faster-moving, complex world. We needed to make software both more valuable and safer. Software engineers strived for legitimacy, and eliminating debacles was one goal of the Structured era.

Structured methods for requirements, design, and programming built on the enthusiasm of the 1970s. As the 1980s got under way, the leading company in structured development consulting and training was Yourdon, Inc., founded in 1974. Ed Yourdon, Steve McMenamin, Tom DeMarco, and Tim Lister were all software development pioneers who worked at Yourdon, and with whom I was privileged to be friends over the years.

Structured methods comprised a series of diagrams and methods that together brought both discipline and techniques to software development. The diagrams were a graphic way of depicting processes that occurred in organizations: order processing, inventory control, accounting. The diagrams were a way to document one's thinking about what could be automated. The methods outlined a series of analytical diagrams and documents designed to lead from the need to automate a business function to a physically implemented system.

DeMarco's (1978) method for requirements analysis[4] outlined four phases using data flow diagrams (DFD), as shown in Figure 3.1:

1. Analyze the current physical business process flow.

2. Convert the current physical flow to a current logical flow.

3. Examine the current logical flow, propose an improved business flow, and create a future logical flow.

4. Create a future physical model.

---

4. Tom's book, and a Yourdon workshop, provided my introduction to structured methods and methodologies. I still have my original 1978 copy of the book.

DATA FLOW DIAGRAM

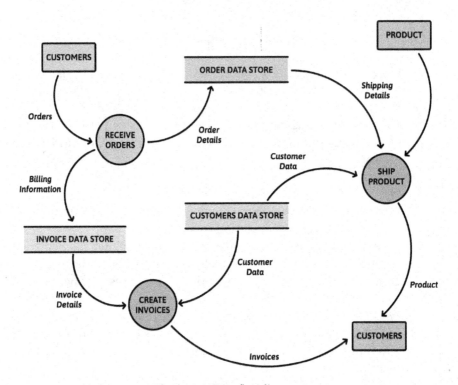

Figure 3.1 *Data flow diagram.*

The initial step in structured analysis was to document the "as is" business process using DFD by interviewing the system user. The analyst's notes might read something like this: "John in accounts payable receives invoices, makes sure the vendor has an account, assigns account number, makes a copy, and sends the original to the payment group." The analyst would sketch out the flow and then try to streamline the process, revising the diagrams as appropriate. The logic and calculations—calculating pay amount, for example—were documented using a logic diagram, decision tree, or flowchart. DFD included bubbles; arrows between bubbles, indicating flow; and data stores.

The data stores were depicted as open-ended, narrow, rectangular boxes. As the analyst reviewed invoices, they would jot down the data fields and assign them to the data store. When the physical DFD had been analyzed and transformed into a logical DFD, the analyst would then create a new logical DFD, potentially adding new processes and data that improved on the manual system. The final process step determined which parts of the new logical DFD would be automated. At the time, businesses were heavily investing in automating internal business functions such as accounting, order processing, and inventory control.

Finally, all the information would be gathered into a specification package. While this transition from physical to logical to physical might seem like excessive work, it was really a thought process to go through. I usually worked on a single DFD, modifying it as appropriate for each phase. Others would take the process too literally and end up with a morass of DFDs. Ken Orr once visited a customer project team who showed him conference room walls covered with DFD. "What do you think?" they asked Ken. "I think you are lost," he replied.

In browsing through DeMarco's 1978 structured analysis book, I was struck by the "agile nature" of this passage:

> The human mind is an iterative processor. It never does anything exactly right the first time. It is particularly good at taking an imperfect implementation of a given task and making improvements to it. This it can do over and over again, coming up with better results each time. (p. 79)

Tom's quote was an early indication that iterative development might be preferrable to prescriptive, serial development.

This early work occurred before the wide use of database management systems (DBMS) and random-access disk storage. As their use increased, entity-relationship (ER) diagrams (Figure 3.2), developed originally by Peter Chen, were used to model database requirements. Remember, during this time frame, businesses were heavily investing in automating internal business functions like accounting, order processing, and inventory control.

ENTITY-RELATIONSHIP DIAGRAM

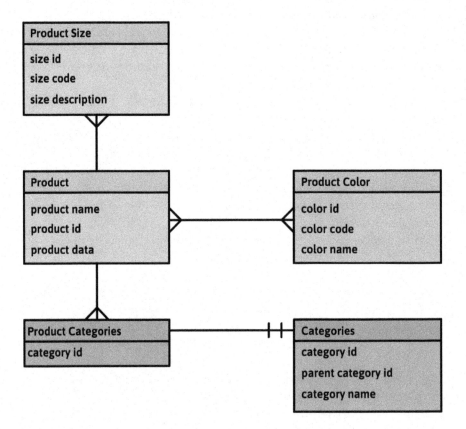

Figure 3.2 *Entity-relationship diagram.*

Along the way, there were silly method arguments. For example, should analysts use circular or rectangular bubbles on DFD? There were also differences in perspectives among the various structured methods. As you can assume from the name, DFD focus on the business process flow first. DFD show flow steps as circles and data stores as rectangles, but the priority is flow. Ken Orr's DSSD approached analysis differently by focusing on the desired system outputs first, and only then the process flow to generate those outputs.

Both system charts and program charts are similar to the one in Figure 3.3. Many diagrams were used for logic, including Warnier-Orr diagrams like the one shown in Figure 3.4.

PROGRAM STRUCTURE CHART

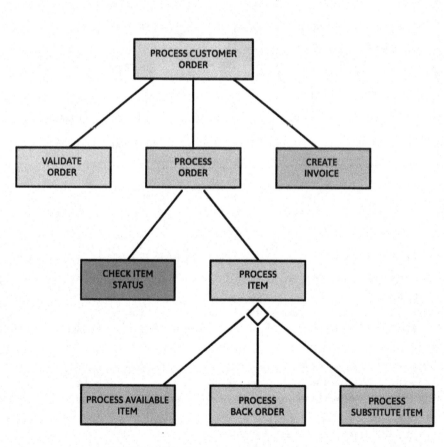

Figure 3.3 *A program structure chart.*

WARNIER-ORR DIAGRAM

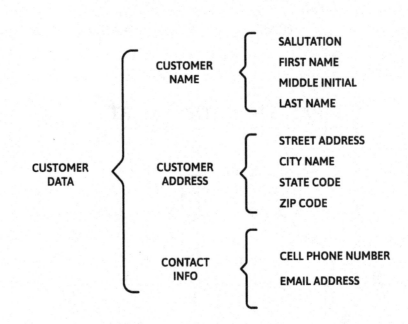

Figure 3.4 *A Warnier-Orr diagram.*

Output first (Orr) or process first (Yourdon)? In the end you needed both, although the output-driven analysis appealed more to me. During the 1980s, I taught workshops and consulted on a variety of methodologies. There were many more similarities than differences, as with agile methodologies today.

These structured approaches still required a laborious translation from requirements to design, and from design to code. Programmers were not always well versed in how to use the diagrams. Analysts and designers often thought the transformations were obvious. In the early years, the debate over this issue was muted because all the roles were instantiated in single individuals. Later, with the movement to waterfall life cycles, larger projects, and siloed development groups, these gaps proved more troublesome.

Software developers were dealing with a new way of interacting with users via terminals and learning transaction processing with random disk access. Going from batch updates to serial tape files, now they could perform near-instantaneous single transaction updates. When redesigning its systems for this new transactional environment, an organization I worked with had an accounting system backup procedure that used the primary file from the previous midnight, so staff had to reenter all the transaction data that had been created since then. Obviously, the accounting staff didn't like this procedure much.

Methods, methodologies, and mindsets

Have you encountered fuzziness around the words *method* and *methodology*? To be candid, I have probably contributed to the fuzziness a time or three. In scientific research, the researcher's methodology—the strategy—and steps to collect data—the methods—are often defined early in both the process and the subsequent published paper.

A software **method** defines the detailed steps to deliver artifacts identified by your chosen methodology. Refactoring is a technique for improving the quality of code. You could have a high-level process in a methodology called "Review your code and make improvements." Refactoring might then be one technique or method to accomplish that process.

A software **methodology** defines your strategy. It divides software work into activities or steps, each of which may include the definition of specific deliverables (a requirements document) and artifacts (DFD). Software development life cycles (SDLC) define the highest-level sequence of processes, which bear names like waterfall, spiral, and iterative.

Confusion arises at the dividing line. For example, Extreme Programming comprises 12 practices including simple design, testing, and refactoring. Since there are several ways to go about refactoring, is it a method or a methodology? Scientists define these terms early in their research, so I will do the same: In this book, I will use the term *methodology* when it covers several development phases. Traditional examples would be Method/1, STRADIS, and DSSD; agile examples would be Scrum, Extreme Programming, and Crystal.[5] *Methods* might then include DFD, refactoring, or data modeling.

A **mindset** is an attitude, a set of beliefs we use in making sense of the world. Our mindsets cause us to think about issues from a certain perspective, to have feelings about events, and to act accordingly. In software development, a person with a cautious mindset will interpret an event differently from a person with an adventurous mindset.

---

5. All of these methodologies are explained later in the book.

As we traverse the evolution and revolution of software development, we need to remember that methods, methodologies, and mindsets all evolved to solve the problems of each era, and were both enabled and constrained by the technology of that time. In my experience, I've seen every methodology succeed, and also every one fail.

CSE/Telco

Two of my engagements, the first with a Chicago Stock Exchange (CSE) and the second with a telecommunications company (telco) in Florida, illustrate software development issues encountered during the Structured era.

In the mid-1980s, I frequently traveled to Chicago to consult at a stock exchange, advising my client on DSSD. In addition to working closely with the software development group, I wandered over to the enterprise database group from time to time. The manager of the latter group complained when the development group would not support his creation of an enterprise data model (too pie in the sky), and the IT vice president usually sided with the development manager. The data manager and his staff grew so frustrated that they wasted time building a customized data dictionary rather than purchasing a readily available application. On several occasions, I sat down with the data manager and shared my observations.

"Your group has no credibility with the dev manager. You keep pushing this elaborate corporate data model, but the dev manager is under pressure to deliver systems today. I suggest you offer data design assistance to dev teams on their current projects to build credibility. Your staff would gain both credibility and understanding of system-level data that could be useful in higher-level data models."

Of course, his pride, ego, and sense he was "right" wouldn't let the data manager take my advice. Eventually he left the organization in frustration. This schism between software development and data organizations would continue for years to come, presenting itself in numerous ways.

One tidbit from my time working at the exchange was the use of Warnier-Orr diagrams to model logic, rather than the more widely used structure charts or flowcharts. When orders were received from brokers, the algorithm for routing them was extremely complex, taking 17 pages of Warnier-Orr diagrams. They were efficient, visual, and excellent diagrams for collaboration with users.

ON ANOTHER OCCASION, I taught a workshop for a telco in Tampa, Florida. Representatives from multiple districts were designing a common equipment maintenance system. The consolidated system was to be used by all locations, but they also needed the ability to generate locally relevant reports. They had approached the design by first asking themselves, "What data entities and attributes do we need?" and then modeled the results using entity-relationship diagrams.

I asked the participants, "Do you think all the reports can be generated from this data model structure?"

"Of course," was the reply.

I had them organize into district groups and had each group lay out several high-priority reports for their location. They then determined whether the 18 or so reports could be generated from their data model. The total number of successful reports: ZERO. While I had assumed there would be some disconnect, I was surprised at the result, and they were mostly in shock. There were benefits to designing backward from outputs to database to inputs.

Structured pioneers

If you perform a search for the key phrase "software pioneers," the results will undoubtedly be skewed toward what I'll call engineering applications: algorithms, languages, operating systems, and real-time control systems. Names such as E. W. Diijkstra, Niklaus Wirth, and Admiral Grace Hopper are frequently mentioned. Contrasting business systems with engineering systems, people and work I consider pioneering include Ed Yourdon, *Design of On-Line Computer Systems* (1972); Tom DeMarco, *Structured Analysis and System Specification* (1978); Chris Gane and Trish Sarson, *Structured Systems Analysis: Tools and Techniques* (1980); Ken Orr, *Structured Requirements Definition* (1981); Larry Constantine, *Structured Design* (with Ed Yourdon, 1975); and Steve McMenamin[6] and John Palmer, *Essential Systems Analysis* (1984). It may be an oversimplification, but the technical or engineering pioneers built the tools, and the business pioneers applied those tools to analyze, design, program, and test business systems.

TOM DEMARCO WAS a major contributor to the structured methods era, an early advocate for the people side of development, and a thoughtful voice

---

6. My formal introduction to "structured" was a Yourdon analysis class taught by Steve McMenamin.

in the evolution of information technology. You don't often get to be friends with your heroes, as I did with Tom later in the 1990s. Tom changed software development, first with technology (DeMarco, 1978) and then with people (DeMarco, 1987). He was also both a captivating speaker and an insightful conference facilitator. I had several email exchanges with Tom for this book, posing a series of questions to him.

What were you involved with prior to Yourdon and your *Structured Analysis* book?

Managing a large online banking system. We had a presentation by SofTech that showed their data flow techniques, and I was taken with their graphics, which I hadn't encountered before.

How did your structured ideas come about and evolve?

I started my career at Bell Labs working on a distributed real-time system that meant the flow of data gave a much stronger hint than the flow of control about what the system was trying to accomplish. I was early to understand that, but wasn't yet inclined to develop graphics to make the idea communicable.

What was the state of software development then, and what encouraged structured development?

This seems harsh to say, but software development at the time was all about code and debug. There was no real concept of design, though we were all aware that some people's code was a lot prettier and more understandable than that of others. And there were some people who wrote code that was totally incomprehensible, so a lot of us were thinking backward about the problem: What would you do to MAKE your code incomprehensible? We were coming up with ways to do just that in order to create a list of no-nos.

One area of my focus at Bell Labs[7] had to do with comments. I had proposed that if comments weren't allowed in the code, people would be inclined to write better code.[8] So instead of

```
ADT turnip, 1 * increment the relay matrix index
```

---

7. Bell Telephone Laboratories (1925–1984) was a hotbed of innovation in the early years of computing. Bell Lab researchers are credited with the development of the transistor and the laser. In the computing realm, they developed the Unix operating system and the programming languages C, C++, SNOBOL, and others. Nine Nobel Prizes have been awarded for work at Bell Labs.

8. Kent Beck would advocate for writing readable code and eliminating most comments in his Extreme Programming work decades later. There are a few good ideas in software development that arise generation after generation. Unfortunately, there happens to be a greater variety of bad ideas.

you would (just to preserve your sanity) be naturally led to write

```
ADT RelayMatrixIndex,1
```

It seems obvious now, but getting rid of comments made a huge improvement in our code. The "turnip" example was from actual code I encountered in which all data names were vegetables.

This led inevitably to a startlingly new concept of functions. In place of a long section in the middle of a program that would need a lot of explanation, you could define a function with a highly descriptive name and call it in the main line of code. That meant the main line could be easily understood without comments. Prior to that, functions were used only to describe code that might be reused; we instead used them to make top levels of routines more comprehensible.

Who were your influencers?

My main influencer was Ed Yourdon. We had worked together at Mandate Systems years before Ed formed Yourdon, Inc. And it was Ed who got me thinking of the idea of a "picture specification," since he was into picturing anything that would hold still for it. Why not the specification?

What did you observe as the major benefits of structured development?

The shift from left-brain thinking to right-brain thinking. We were all enchanted at the time by Julian Jayne's book, *The Origin of Consciousness in the Breakdown of the Bicameral Mind*. (Again, it was Ed Yourdon who first put that book into my hands.) The major idea we took from it was using left-brain methods for an inherently multidimensional problem was the tragic flaw of our then approach to software development.

How did people/organizations misuse structured techniques?

Some systems are data flow intensive, and others are data structure intensive. I mean some systems are most appropriately described by calling attention to the view of the data items themselves as they make their way through, while others are better described by calling attention to the relationships among data items. A typical database system has flows into and out of the repository, which doesn't tell you much. Distributed and real-time systems, on the other hand, have little data structure but lots of flow. Applying data flow methods to a database system is, in my opinion, a misuse. The great strides forward in database design were happening almost at the same time as structured methods were coming of age. And lots of people chose their methods—either one or the other—with little regard to how well the chosen method worked for their particular system.

Any general observations from the Structured era, roughly the 1980s?

It was, oddly enough, a renaissance for technical writing. The software industry had moved through the $10 billion a year mark with almost nothing written down about how the work ought to proceed. (Typical of the sixties were programming books like the ones written by Daniel McCracken, mostly just explanations of language instruction sets.) Suddenly, there were books you could go to for insight. Again, Ed Yourdon was early in this trend. Ed wrote at typing speed, and he was the fastest typist I ever encountered. We shared an office at times and when he started typing, it was like sitting next to a machine gun. And the text he turned out was highly readable, often amusing, and full of insight. He set a standard for the rest of us.

What influenced your change in emphasis from technical practices to the people practices you wrote about in *Peopleware* (DeMarco and Lister, 1987) and *Slack* (DeMarco, 2001)?

On a flight to Sydney, Australia, with Tim Lister, we were working together on our first Peopleware session. We were actually drawing OHP (overhead projector) slides at our seats. One of us observed—neither of us remembers who said the words for the first time—that the major problems of software development are more sociological than technological. That became our mantra, our "Battle Hymn of the Republic" we sang together for the next few years. It's something I think is every bit as true today as it was then, only I now think it applies much more broadly, to subjects more diverse than just software.

Slack stemmed from a similar observation, that the rule bases of organizations had been allowed to evolve instead of being designed, and their evolution tended to lead them into appealing but destructive dead ends like overtime, burnout, impossible deadlines, death march projects, and prescriptive methodology.

Both works have a common theme: Getting out of people's way can be a recipe for huge improvement.

LARRY CONSTANTINE ORIGINATED the fundamental design concepts of coupling and cohesion still in use today. But his resume goes far beyond that achievement. Upon graduating from Massachusetts Institute of Technology (MIT) with a management degree, Larry worked as a programmer in its Nuclear Research Institute. He became an assistant clinical professor of psychiatry at Tufts University and wrote a book on family therapy in the mid-1980s. Under the pen name Lior Samson, he has published 16 fiction titles. I didn't know Larry as well as other pioneers of the times, but he had several impacts on my career, as I will describe in later chapters. I posed a series of questions to Larry in an email exchange.

What was your early career and how did it result in your later structured ideas?

I started working on these ideas in 1963 at my first full-time programming job at the MIT Laboratory for Nuclear Science, where I worked under Harry Rudloe, who had a disciplined but nonformal approach to programming in preplanned subroutines. The real core arose from working at C-E-I-R, Inc., in D.C. later in 1963, where the concepts of coupling and cohesion evolved in lunchtime bull sessions with Ken MacKenzie, Dave Jasper, Bud Vitoff, and others. Modeling with diagrams came later, after my return to MIT in 1965, and evolved rapidly once I launched my first company, Information & Systems Institute, in 1966.

The core of structured design (but not the branding) was more or less complete by the time my firm sponsored the National Symposium on Modular Programming in 1968—now recognized as a founding pivot point in modular programming. My paper was the first published complete outline of the core concepts and theory, but I had been writing about the ideas for several years. The *IBM Systems Journal* piece in 1974 of course launched the "movement" with branding insisted on by IBM.

What was the state of software development then, and why did that encourage structured development?

People cut code. Pretty much. Some would flowchart tricky algorithms, some would do some form of system-level process flow, but most considered that a waste of time. There were no CASE tools, only IBM plastic charting templates [see the example in Figure 3.5].

The idea of mapping out the structure of a system before starting to program was around, but little practiced.

Who influenced your thinking?

Besides the troika at C-E-I-R, I would have to mention James Emory, who also got me teaching at the Wharton School before I even graduated from MIT. At MIT, I had been immersed in systems thinking—so all of the classic writers in that area, including Jerry Weinberg later. Ed Yourdon played a huge role in the propagation of the ideas, and they might never have seen the light of day were it not for his entrepreneurial wizardry and co-authoring with me. He was brilliant and a great friend.

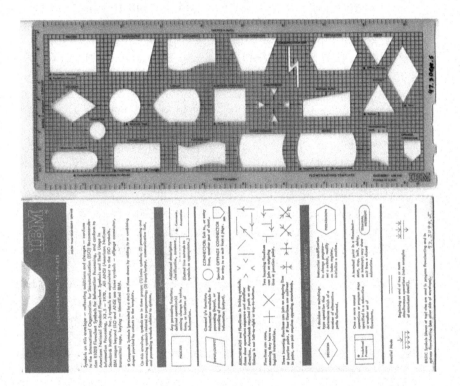

Figure 3.5 *1970-vintage programming template.*[9] *(Image courtesy of Division of Medicine and Science, National Museum of American History, Smithsonian Institution)*

---

9. www.si.edu/object/ibm-gx20-8020-1-um010-flowcharting-template%3Anmah_694227.

What were the benefits of structured development?

All that's been hashed over so many times. How can you cut code until you know how it's organized? The biggest contribution was actually in the underlying theory, which has been validated in hundreds of studies since. Coupling and cohesion. That's what it's about, not diagrams or process or practices. Keep component parts tight, compact, and independent; figure out how to connect them correctly; build. Agile, RAD, OO [object orientation], functional—the theory is the same.

How did people and organizations misuse structured techniques?

The whole "waterfall" brouhaha was a crock. Ed [Yourdon] and I conceived that model as a form of "training wheels" but it took off with management and then became the straw man to attack with the arrival of object orientation and agile. To correct the record, OO and agile did not evolve out of the failure of SD (structured development). SD did not fail; it was a documented success in countless projects, large and small, over the decades. Some organizations fell into a tyranny of diagrams, especially after the arrival of CASE, but the models were always intended to be just tools, ways to externalize, refine, and document thinking. Interestingly, DFDs have been the big long-term winner and are still taught and used all over the world.

I agree with Larry's assessment. Structured methods, RAD, and agile methods all successfully delivered software applications, especially in their time. It was when these methods became subsumed by large, formal methodologies that problems arose. Some ideas like coupling and cohesion and DFD are still in use today.

While structured methods were developed in the 1960s, their popularity increased in the late 1970s and 1980s, just as the seeds of agile took root in the 1990s, then flourished in the 2000s. Indications of this evolution for structured methods can be seen from Larry's early publications.[10]

---

10. Constantine, 1967; Constantine, "Control of Sequence and Parallelism in Modular Programs," 1968; Constantine, "Segmentation and Design Strategies for Modular Programming," 1968; Constantine, "The Programming Profession, Programming Theory, and Programming Education," 1968; Constantine, "Integral Hardware/Software Design," 1968–1969; Constantine and Donnelly, October 1967; Constantine, Stevens, and Myers, 1974; Constantine and Yourdon, 1975.

Information Architects, Inc.

After 2½ years, tired of commuting halfway across the country each week, I told Ken Orr I would continue to teach workshops and consult with customers as an independent contractor and be a sales agent for KOA's products in the Southeast. I pursued other work under my newly formed company, Information Architects, Inc. We—that is, one employee and me—moved into the Georgia Tech start-up incubation center, tempting the fates as a software entrepreneur with a marketing and sales application. I funded the start-up from my consulting work but had to abandon the endeavor when other funding failed to materialize.

One of my consulting gigs was to audit a project for an insurance company in Atlanta. My cohort in this review was a former large company IT manager. The company's internal insurance processing systems were running on a Honeywell mainframe and needed a serious upgrade. The company had a variety of life and casualty products and a network of independent sales agents. It was time for a major overhaul.

IBM sold a comprehensive insurance processing system, so the decision was made to convert the IBM software to Honeywell hardware—a major undertaking. To reduce the conversion costs, the IT manager decided to sell the converted software to other companies running Honeywell computers. Although the firm presold (before conversion) a couple of installations, 90% to 95% of insurance companies used IBM hardware, so the potential market for the converted system was tiny. Our project review objective was to recommend whether or not the company should abandon the project and to propose further action in either case.

After several years and significant millions of dollars, progress had eluded them. Testing went on and on. I started the review with the CEO of the firm.

"What was your involvement and how are you monitoring progress?" I asked.

Well," he replied, "I approved the budget for the project, which has been greatly exceeded by the way, but I haven't been involved otherwise. You need to talk with my product line VPs."

So, I interviewed the vice presidents. And guess what? They hadn't been involved, either. They suggested I speak with the managers, who suggested I talk with their supervisors. And down the hierarchy I went, until I was talking with insurance clerks and programmers who didn't really understand the project's goals and were frustrated. Typical of the time, the users wanted to modify the system to fit their processes, rather than adopting the package processes, so the dev team was bogged down with modifications. Of course, the modifications reduced the benefits of the packaged software, and the management hierarchy had no clue about what had transpired. Priorities were being set by the clerks and the programmers.

We recommended the developers immediately stop the customization, involve management, task one of the senior IT managers with managing the project, and cancel the project if it could not be completed in three months. In our audit report we also raised the bigger question about hardware. If nearly the entire insurance industry employed IBM computers, our client needed to seriously consider a hardware swap, Honeywell to IBM, rather than a software conversion. Future purchased applications would probably utilize IBM hardware.

After the client made some personnel changes in IT and elevated a manager to the chief information officer (CIO) position, it decided to pull the plug on the software conversion effort and initiate the hardware conversion. I worked with the client for more than a year on this effort.

This story illustrates four IT trends during this era. First, the use of software application packages supplied by vendors was increasing. These often replaced first-generation, internally developed applications. For standard internal systems for accounting, order processing, inventory management, and the like, vendors provided solutions at a lower price, with faster implementation, and less risk—usually.

At another client, the human resources department became so frustrated with the IT department they purchased an HR application without IT involvement, then turned to IT for the application's implementation. "Sorry" was the reply. "It looks like a fine application, but it runs on a type of computer we don't have." This incident was indicative of the ongoing struggles between IT and business users, and the latter's response of doing it on their own.

Second, companies turned around and "customized" the package software, or had the vendors do it, losing much of the benefit. Every time the vendor enhanced their software, the customization had to be redone. Even if the new features weren't needed, companies needed to keep the packages up-to-date so they could deploy the next updates.

This customization craze even extended to methodology. I helped a large insurance company in the Midwest integrate Warnier-Orr technical practices into Method/1. Just as we were ready to publish the new notebooks full of processes and forms, you guessed it—Andersen came out with a newer version of Method/1! There were no word processors in wide use then, so the manuals had to be completely retyped.

Third, management remained reluctant to delve into IT, other than grousing about the cost. Executives didn't understand the technology or its impact. This disconnect was partially caused by the software's intangibility. Executives understood building a new manufacturing plant—that was tangible, and they could monitor the progress with their own eyes. Software, not so much.

Fourth, as package software companies began to sprout, IT executives began looking through their portfolio of application assets, thinking, "We could become an exciting software company, too." Most of the investments that arose from this thought process resulted in abject failure. Just because someone could run an internal IT department, it didn't mean they could survive the rough-and-tumble software product wars. Just because they could develop software, it didn't mean they could build marketing, sales, sales support, and customer service organizations. IT shops were relatively risk averse; software companies weren't. This fad fizzled out quickly.

Technology

The tech device synonymous with the 1980s was the Sony Walkman, a portable cassette player that enabled users to listen to music anywhere and anytime. It was the first of the portable music devices along the road to the iPod and then the iPhone. The Walkman weighed in at nearly a pound, three times as heavy as the first iPod, and each cassette contained 36 songs compared to the iPod's 7,000 songs.[11] Devices used for portable music were winners for the next four decades.

While mainframe computers remained the mainstay of business computing and minicomputers became more powerful, new devices initiated the trend to provide computers to individuals. Tom Watson Sr., CEO of IBM from 1914 to 1956, is reputed to have said in 1943, "I think there is a world market for maybe five computers." Some think Watson was misquoted, but accurately quoted or not, no one in the 1940s through the 1970s even dreamed about the proliferation of computing devices to come—except pos-

---

11. Comparative capacities can be tricky because they vary by year, model, song length, and more, so numbers should be considered relative to each other rather than absolute.

sibly Dick Tracy, ace comic strip detective (1931–1977), who communicated via his watch-phone. Every time I answer a phone call on my Apple watch, I imagine Tracy.

IBM released its landmark Personal Computer/2 (PS/2); Compaq launched its IBM-compatible luggable (28 pounds). I lugged mine onto airplanes way too many times. Graphical user interfaces (GUI) appeared on the Apple Macintosh and Lisa computers, and the Mac sported the first mouse. The object-oriented programming (OOP) language C++ garnered attention, and Windows was launched by Microsoft, although it remained a real clunker until the 1990s.

Early User Interface Hassle

In the late 1980s, in Atlanta, my wife and I shopped for a living room chair. We looked for style, color, price, and comfort, which meant visiting a variety of stores. Finally, we found just the right one and informed the salesperson. She completed the sales slip and entered the transaction into the company sales system. We wrote out a check (you know, a small rectangular piece of paper that was filled out to pay bills in olden days) and asked about loading the chair into our car.

"I'm sorry, but you need to come back tomorrow and pick up the chair," she said.

"But the chair is right there, we can easily load it now," I replied, becoming frustrated.

"I'm really sorry," she repeated. "But our inventory control system prints out picking tickets overnight and I can't release the chair until I have one."

If this story indicates the way computer systems treated paying customers in the 1980s, you can imagine what internal users faced. This lack of a customer-friendly design was caused by a focus on internal users, technology limitations, and the newness of interactive design guidelines.

Figure 3.6 shows the prevalent person–computer interface in the 1980s.[12] Both business systems users and software developers were able to advance

---

12. Symbolic of the generational divide, when my graphics designer first sketched this figure, he included a mouse. "No mice in this era" (for business systems that used character-based screens).

Figure 3.6 *Person–computer interface in the Structured era.*

from punch cards and printouts to nongraphical, character-based terminals. This sped up turnaround dramatically. Connectivity from the computers (mainframe) to the terminals was wire Ethernet[13] cables spiderwebbed in massive cabling boxes throughout the computer center and beyond.

Monumental Methodologies

Structured methods did bring discipline and graphical tools to software development. These were thinking and organizing tools. DFD were useful during an era when automating business processes to increase efficiency and reduce costs was important. Entity-relationship diagrams provided a great tool for graphically analyzing and documenting data structures.

These graphical diagrams and methods were incorporated into Monumental Methodologies (MM) that grew into tomes of documentation. Attempting to go from the undisciplined Wild West to a more disciplined, formal approach, MM overshot and focused on the wrong things—processes and documents. We—and that group includes me—mistook formality

---

13. Ethernet is a wired computer networking technology commonly used in local networks to connect computer devices. It was introduced commercially in 1980 and standardized in 1983.

for discipline. In attempting to better organize and manage software projects, formal processes, phase reviews, and documentation added a level of bureaucracy that overshadowed the benefits of structured techniques. As a friend once quipped, "Anything worth doing is worth overdoing." Our overdoing flourished. But those who used MM as rules floundered. Those who used them as guidelines to adapt to their situation did much better. This rules-versus-guidelines approach would continue to be critical to effective methodology implementation.

The evolution of MM was driven by several factors. First, the emergence of software engineering[14] was in part based on the desire to elevate the software field to a legitimate, professional level. Other engineering disciplines such as civil engineering had gained professional status based on rigorous certification processes to become a "professional" engineer. Software engineering proponents wanted a similar level of legitimacy.

Second, general management was still mired in the execution era, in which the command-control style flourished. Assuring "control" was a key management performance measure. IT projects were generally viewed as out of control. Business managers often knew little about software development and assumed it must be akin to building a warehouse; they assumed they could accurately predict the future and, thereby, control outcomes. Because they lacked a good handle on the value of IT systems, even though business productivity increased, business executives focused on "out of control" cost and schedule overruns.

A third factor was the increasing interest in project management, in part driven by the Project Management Institute (PMI). Since many project management practices evolved from those in the construction industry (e.g., ships, manufacturing plants), project managers were schooled in serial, waterfall processes.

A fourth factor was the advent of waterfall life cycles for software, as shown in Figure 3.7 later in this chapter. Waterfall lifecycles were a watershed moment in software development (pun intended), with concepts and problems I will address in detail shortly.

These four factors encouraged the formation and expanded use of waterfall, control-oriented, process- and documentation-heavy MM. Monumental certification came from the Software Engineering Institute's Capability Maturity Model (CMM). Implementation of these methodologies was

---

14. The name "software engineering" emerged at a 1968 NATO conference.

generally top down from management to development staff. Aside from employing structured techniques, developers considered the documentation and process a burden, not a help. Management dictated MM use and development staff excelled in finding ways around the processes.

During the 1990s, I worked with a company in Florida that sold financial software to medium-size companies in the United States and Europe. Its European customers required the company to maintain International Organization for Standardization (ISO)[15] certification. Following the required documentation, process, and sign-off practices ensured little progress, so staff found ways around them. The periodic ISO audits would find issues, requiring hours of work responding to the audit—a nightmare of going around in circles. Although ISO guidelines allowed modifications to the approved practices, the company was reluctant to modify them since it would require additional ISO review.

The most monumental of the MM was information engineering (IE), an approach founded by James Martin and Clive Finkelstein. IE was the ultimate top-down, long-range planning approach to IT. It advocated a lengthy strategic planning process, followed by enterprise data models that supported all the identified systems, packaging those systems into projects, and finally, after 2 to 3 years, you would begin implementation. IE was an anathema to most structured methodologists. Nonetheless, IT and senior business executives, yearning for control and understanding of their rapidly growing IT budgets, attended IE workshops in droves.

Waterfall

A 1970 paper by Winston Royce is generally credited with starting the "waterfall" trend. In reality, Royce was an advocate of iterative development for anything more than simple projects. Given the serial "hardware" mindset of the time, it's easy to see how his serial waterfall diagram took hold, even though he explained its dangers in his paper.

Larry Constantine commented, "Ed [Yourdon] and I conceived that model as a form of 'training wheels' but it took off with management." When I queried Larry about the concurrent thinking about waterfall life cycles, he was not aware of Royce's paper. Since waterfall-like stages were becoming widely used in management practices at the time, their growing use in software development wasn't surprising. It's also interesting that Larry and

---

15. Reflected thinking about quality control.

Ed considered waterfall approaches to be "training wheels" for budding software developers and not for use in serious projects.

Waterfall thinking extended far beyond software, making the transition to iterative methods difficult. Figure 3.7 shows the software waterfall life cycle and organizational structure diagrams associated with this technique. The waterfall life cycle was greatly influenced by the surrounding ethos of the times—functional organization hierarchies and serial approaches to project management. Waterfall fit right in. IT was organized into functional groups aligned to the waterfall structure—requirements groups, design groups, programming groups, and more. Over time, these groups became isolated from the other groups, with each working well within its designated group, but erecting barriers between them. Analysts feuded with designers, programmers feuded with testers, and everyone outside IT feuded with IT.

A waterfall assumption was that documentation was sufficient to communicate between groups. The belief was that documentation, or drawings, could be complete and accurate with no need for further explanation.[16]

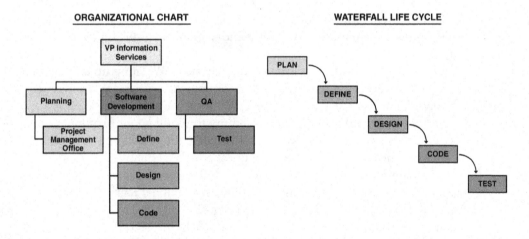

Figure 3.7 *Waterfall life cycle and hierarchical organization charts.*

---

16. I saw a conference presentation in the 1990s that addressed requirements accuracy and completeness issues. I could never find the study or who did it, so a big caveat accompanies the following memory: The average requirements document was less than 20% complete and less than 10% correct. I think these numbers are too low, but they are nevertheless startling.

I received a phone inquiry in the early 1990s. "We need a requirements definition class," said the development manager.

Rather than just recite what was included in my class, I asked, "Why do you need the class?"

"Well," said the manager. "We want to outsource development to India and need to make sure the specs are complete."

"How complete are your specs today?" I asked. "And, how complete do you think they should be to outsource programming?"

"I would estimate we are about 50% complete today and I would like to get over 80%."

"Well, a couple of industry studies and my observations would indicate your percentages are significantly overestimated. One final question: How long does it take for new hires in your firm to learn enough about your environment to be productive?"

"Our environment is pretty complex, so about six months," was the reply.

"If the accuracy and completeness of specifications are in the 20% to 25% range, at best, and it takes six months when the people are sitting in your office to learn the context for a set of specifications, then how will you convey this context information to the staff in India and answer the inevitable list of questions?"

He mused, "I hadn't considered those issues." We hung up and I never heard back. I knew producing a better requirements document wasn't going to solve his problem.

These kinds of incidents influenced my thinking about functional silos, the effectiveness of documentation, and the need for collaboration. I carried these growing concerns into the next Roots era.

The communications issues inherent in the waterfall life cycle gave rise to solutions—matrix management and cross-functional teams. Project managers reported to the project management office, but also managed a project team (and usually several in IT organizations). In the 1970s, matrix management became popular, and it expanded in the 1980s, particularly in project management. In a matrix organization, an individual employee could have two (or more) managers. On a software project, project team members might come from functional organizations, such as analysis, database design, programming, testing, and project management. Team members reported to the project manager for work tasks and results, and to their functional manager for human resources items such as performance reviews, pay increases, and training.

It's not difficult to see how this organizational approach ran into trouble, especially as the Agile era began. IT departments were chronically short of project managers and database administrators (DBA), so project managers supervised several projects and DBAs acted as subject-matter experts (SME) for multiple teams. Developers might be assigned to several teams, plus ongoing maintenance. These organizational solutions caused accountability nightmares: "I couldn't complete task Y because the DBA was busy on another project." Allegiance was to functional groups, not to project scope, schedule, and cost, much less to customer values.

Departments outside of IT adapted their work to conform to the serial, waterfall mindset. Legal departments created contracts based on the serial delivery of specific documents. Accounting departments established standards for classifying operating versus capital costs based on the serial model. Purchasing and human resources departments followed suit.

The reliance on waterfall development in software began to change in the late 1980s with the introduction of Barry Boehm's spiral model and Tom Gilb's evolutionary model. Gilb used the term "evolutionary" to describe an iterative approach with small, well-planned development cycles. Boehm's spiral model explicitly incorporated the concept of driving development based on risk. Both life cycles are iterative, and they address uncertainty by taking smaller steps and testing the results. Each step's deliverables are included in an overall project plan, which is then usually revised at each subsequent iteration.

The waterfall life cycle had a hidden flaw that a few individuals had exposed. Each stage in a waterfall life cycle has a box (process) and an arrow to the next process. However, in the middle of each arrow there needs to be a triangular box with the words, "Here lies magic," as shown in Figure 3.8. The transitions between requirements to design to programming are not algorithmic, and MM and CASE tools floundered on this rarely discussed flaw. Maybe they should have been called Monumental Mythologies.

Transforming design into code is not a defined, automatable process; it is an empirical one requiring "thought." Overcoming this flaw requires magic. Agilist Ken Schwaber later noted this difference in his investigation of empirical versus defined processes. Defined processes are algorithmic; empirical processes are not. Tom DeMarco touched on this issue in our discussion: "Using left-brain methods for an inherently multidimensional problem was the tragic flaw of our then approach to software development."

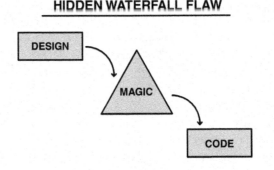

Figure 3.8 *Hidden waterfall flaw.*

Trying to impose an algorithmic conversion to an empirical process leads to disaster. For this reason, I've advocated using the term *reliable* for agile methods rather than the term *repeatable* used in defined processes. Magic would be a great help, but only for Harry Potter.

I may be going out on a definitional limb here, but this "magic" triangle may define the core difference between software *engineers* and software *developers*. In the translation of customer needs to a software application, technology has provided the means to shrink the "magic gap" dramatically—from compilers as the main 1970s tool to complete platforms like Azure (from Microsoft) today. I think software engineers believe that at some point in time, the magic gap can be eliminated; software developers don't think it can. I'm with the developers, which is one of my reasons for preferring that term in this book.

So, serial thinking was not an invention of software management, but it permeated managers' thinking at the time. Unfortunately, it was also an impediment to agile implementations that organizations had to address.

Management

During the 1980s, management style began the transition from execution to expertise. As knowledge work increased in biotechnology, computers, materials science, medical technology, and in every other field, the need for knowledge workers increased. The Digital Revolution was upon us, and with this burgeoning class of workers came the need to modify how to manage them. The "get a job and stay there" career model was breaking down. Knowledge workers began to have more loyalty to their profession than to their employers and with multiple employment opportunities, they began to move away from traditional careers. The rapid rise of new technology companies and the prospect of big paydays from stock options helped fuel the changes. With the shift from the expectation of a lifelong career with the same company to the 21st-century gig economy where "jobs" were tied to a project, changes in employer–employee relationships were occurring.

DURING THE STRUCTURED ERA, project management (PM) was increasingly used in software development. I began to read about and study PM and to integrate what I had learned with what I had experienced. I started teaching a rudimentary PM workshop associated with DSSD as increasingly PM practices were baked into Monumental Methodologies.

At the time, the most famous book related to software development was *The Mythical Man-Month* by Fred Brooks (1975). Brooks was the manager of the IBM operating system (OS) development for the IBM/360 line of computers, probably the largest software project to date. After analyzing performance on several OS projects, he reached his most famous conclusion: "Adding people to a late project just makes it later." Noting managers tended to repeat such errors, he quipped his book was called the Bible of Software Engineering "because everybody quotes it, some people read it, and a few people go buy it." That sentiment could be applied equally to today's agile methodology implementations.

The PM practices used during the Wild West and Structured eras were best suited for tangible products, initially construction-type projects, for which a serial approach worked. The fact that software was more malleable didn't impact how projects were managed, and frankly software development in its infancy wasn't overly malleable itself. Project managers focused on tasks, rather than on people and team dynamics.

In the 1980s, project managers incorporated practices such as risk and issue management. The first *Project Management Body of Knowledge* was published in 1987 by the PMI, which led to a PM Monumental Methodology to accompany those for software development. Shortly thereafter, in 1989, the PRINCE methodology was published and became the standard PM methodology in much of Europe.

One important new project management theory emerged from a novel, *The Goal: A Process of Ongoing Improvement*, by Eliyahu Goldratt (1984). His theory of constraints showed that there was always one primary "bottleneck" to value generation, and reducing or eliminating it would increase throughput. Of course, eliminating the first bottleneck would uncover the next one. This principle meant people performing non-bottleneck activities must do everything possible to minimize the amount of work for those engaged in bottleneck activities, even if it meant being somewhat inefficient themselves. Goldratt called this approach "critical chain"; in contrast to the traditional critical path method, it focused on identifying and removing constraints that limited throughput. Goldratt went on to author *Critical Chain* (1997), applying these practices to PM.

Goldratt's theories were embraced later by the agile community and influenced the Agile Manifesto principle of simplicity: "The art of maximizing the amount of work not done is essential." Agile practices include creating a backlog of features, a few of which are released to development for each iteration. Prioritizing feature release should not overload the team, especially those on the critical chain. In the 1990s, I spoke to a development manager who lamented his department projects were stalled. I asked him how many projects and people he had. The answer: 43 projects and 42 people. It was easy to surmise that he had high in-process "inventory" but little output. Everyone was busy (productive) building up the inventory of work in process, but there was no throughput of value.

This decade also began the transition of PM software to personal computers, including the first commercial version of Microsoft Project (DOS)[17] in 1984.

OVER THE LAST SIX decades, measures of software development success have evolved from completion to customer value. Nothing drives change like the way organizations measure success, but few things are harder to change than those measures. Return on investment (ROI) impacts organizations one way, customer value another. In IT organizations, schedule drives certain behaviors. In the early days, just completing a project was success enough; by the turn of the century, other measures ruled. I worked with one company that measured programmers by lines of code delivered and

---

17. Microsoft Disk Operating System, which dominated PCs prior to Windows.

testers by number of bugs[18] found. This rewarded programmers for coding productivity with only lip service given to quality. Testers were rewarded for finding bugs, so they didn't have any incentive to ask for better-quality code. These measures also worked against collaboration between the two groups, so the feedback loops were minimized. Luckily, most testers and programmers possessed an internal motivation to deliver quality products and often felt stymied by these poor activity-based incentive structures.

In the predictable world of old, software development measures of success borrowed from manufacturing's statistical quality control theories. In a manufacturing plant, turning metal and plastic into widgets, the process needed to be repeatable, conforming to tight tolerances time after time. Software differs from widgets, as we will see.

As performance trends evolved, activity-based measures, like productivity, that had evolved for the Industrial Age almost never worked for the Knowledge Age and were an anathema in the Innovation Age.

CASE tools

What is the solution to runaway diagrams and documentation? Automation, of course. IT was tasked with automating business processes, so why not automate their own? While there were earlier vendors of CASE tools, the market expanded rapidly when Index Technologies in Cambridge, Massachusetts, began marketing its Excelerator product for the IBM PC, as personal computers were becoming ubiquitous in businesses. Excelerator became the CASE tool market leader. It provided support for structured graphics such as DFD and entity-relationship diagrams, had a data repository for details about data stores, and provided logic details.

Other prominent CASE tools—there were nearly 100 vendors by the early 1990s—were Foundation from Andersen Consulting, Analysis/Designer toolkit from Yourdon, Automate Plus from Learmonth & Burchett Management Systems, and DesignAid from Nastec Corp. These CASE tools had similar functionality, but some leaned toward structured graphics (e.g., Excelerator and Analysis/Designer), while others leaned toward capturing documents (e.g., Foundation and Automate Plus). Everyone was jumping at

---

18. *Bug* is a term that has been used to describe a defect in code. The term was coined by Admiral Grace Hopper in 1946 to explain a hardware problem. In software development, it may have risen to prominence to deflect responsibility. A developer is responsible for a *defect*. *Bugs*, in contrast, crawl into your code all by themselves.

the chance to become a leader in an exploding market—and explode it did. Everyone in the methodology business rushed to develop their own CASE tool, and we at KOA created our version—the Design Machine (more on this later).

The allure of CASE tools was obvious, but the reality was different. They suffered from a plethora of problems. First, during this era and the next, executives and managers were looking for the proverbial "silver bullet," the one thing that would solve all their IT problems. Expectations for CASE tools were unrealistic, and so were the costs. They were expensive both to purchase and to train staff to use. Achieving an acceptable ROI was problematic.

Second, the lack of standards created challenges. Everyone seemed to have their own ideas about which diagrams to use and even which flavor of those diagrams to embrace. Compounding the problem was the rising interest in object-oriented approaches, which introduced a new set of diagrams into the mix. Later, the development of Unified Modeling Language (UML) solved this problem for the next generation of tools.

Third, the most popular tool, Excelerator, ran on IBM PCs, which for much of the period were not networked, so everyone had their own versions of data and graphics. Differences in methodologies, tools, vendors, and diagramming led to unintegrated and confusing results. IBM proposed an integrated solution to these issues with its AD/Cycle system, but the scope of its development and poor timing (took too long) scuttled the effort.

Fourth, the deployment technology transitioned so rapidly during the 1990s that CASE tool companies got whipsawed, from basic connectivity to client-server architectures (an architecture that sought to network individual devices such as PCs) and then a rapid transition to the Internet.

Fifth, the continued use of the waterfall life cycle and the belief the overall development process could be specified in detail led to the erroneous assumption that after the requirements were specified, the rest could be automated at the push of a button.

Lastly, there was the issue Dave Higgins brought up in our conversation when we discussed the rapid rise and subsequent fall of the CASE tool era. Dave said, "What I think doomed the CASE tool era was the subtle underlying assumption that programmers' jobs could be automated. We were asking programmers to build and implement systems to replace themselves! Even today low-code technology threatens the same outcome. But I think it was, is, and will be a pipe dream. We will always need developers."

The silver bullet issue reminded me of a story an educator shared about a plane trip conversation. Her seatmate asked her, "What do you think is the one thing that would solve our public education problems?"

To which she instantly replied, "People who think there is one thing that will solve our public education problems."

We fail when we attempt to use silver-bullet solutions to complex problems.

"There is no silver bullet, but sometimes there is a Lone Ranger."
—Weinberg, 1994

I like Weinberg's quote because it highlights the dichotomy between an emphasis on things (bullets) and an emphasis on people (even a fictional character like the Lone Ranger). I took Weinberg's quote another step further.

"There is no silver bullet, but there are Lone Rangers who have arsenals of bullets for different situations."
—Highsmith, 2000

For most, the hard part is understanding the different types of bullets and the situations in which each is most likely to succeed.

KEN ORR ENVISIONED our own CASE tool, called the Design Machine was partially funded by a large consulting client. The product's very name indicated the assumed prescriptive nature of software development. That and other issues led to the demise of the company—not every adventure works out. In the spirit of documenting failures as well as success, I will go into a bit of detail on this journey.

As KOA added the Design Machine product to our portfolio of training and consulting, additional investment funds were needed to fund product development, sales, and marketing. An infusion of venture capital came with conditions for reorganization. A new executive staff was brought in; Ken became the chief technology officer responsible for product development; a new company name, "Optima," established; and the general offices were moved to Chicago, leaving Ken and the Design Machine development staff in Topeka.

Trouble started immediately. The new management staff didn't get along with the development staff or the consultants in the field (who generated most of the income). The company expanded its sales and marketing staff, opening several new sales offices. Unfortunately, there weren't yet enough products to warrant such a large sales staff. In 1986, Ken approached me to come back to work at the company full-time. My official job title would be product manager; my unofficial role would be mediator between the factions. I had the respect and friendship of the consultants and developed a good working relationship with the new executives. I began commuting from Atlanta to Chicago each week. But it was a race against time.

New executives, new sales staff, and fancy new offices drained cash quickly. As with all innovative software product developments, the Design Machine schedule slipped. At some point I was in Topeka to teach a public four-day systems design workshop. Several of the developers from the Design Machine team attended the workshop. A red flag went off in my head when I realized from their questions that they didn't really understand fundamental concepts of our methodology. The Design Machine had almost no provision for feeding back changes to previous stages! It was the ultimate in automating a prescriptive serial waterfall process.

In a final effort to right the ship, the venture capitalist fired the new management staff. Ken came back as president, and I took over as vice president of consulting. But the drain on capital had gone too far and Optima was shuttered within six months. Except for a few "insider" sales, we never delivered the Design Machine to the CASE tool market. Ken resigned, and in a last-ditch effort to salvage something out of the debacle, the venture capitalist offered me the president/CEO position. I was momentarily flattered, but knew it was a lose–lose proposition, and declined.

The KOA/Optima story was my venture into the cauldron of start-up companies faced with lots of pressure from their funding sources. There were, and are, many ways to fail as a start-up and a few avenues for success. But it's hard not to reach out for the shiny golden ring. In the end, my start-up score was 0 wins, 2 losses. Fortunately, with the losses came a bit of learning.

For CASE tool vendors, the technology changes—client-server, Internet, and object orientation—required rapid escalation in investment funds. In combination with the other issues raised, the first round of CASE tools flamed out. But they also established a framework for the next round of software development tools.

After Optima, during the final couple years of the decade, I worked for McDonald Douglas Automation, teaching and consulting on its STRADIS methodology. My transition from DSSD to STRADIS was straightforward: The diagrams changed, but the underlying methodologies were similar. I taught combinations of requirements, design, STRADIS overviews, and project management. I also contracted to teach a systems thinking workshop. In the Roots of Agile era, this grounding in systems thinking was influential in shifting my mindset from Monumental Methodologies to rapid, adaptive, and eventually agile development.

Era observations

The Structured era pushed hard toward the nirvana of software *engineering*—to bring discipline and control to the development process, to be recognized as an engineering discipline. Management theory was firmly stuck in the command-control model, and managers were not happy with the lack of control over software projects. *Structured* was a good name for the times, and structured methodologies appealed widely. Of course, in practice, there was more saying than doing as people contended they were structured because they drew a couple of diagrams—much like saying, "We are now agile because we do daily stand-ups and Sprint plans."

Toward the end of this era, some emerging voices spoke to a more people-centric view of management that blossomed into the beginning of the Empathy Age. Gerald (Jerry) Weinberg had published the classic *The Psychology of Computer Programming* (1971). When a silver anniversary edition was published in 1998, I wrote to Jerry, congratulating him and saying I still had an original copy of the 1971 book. Tom DeMarco and Tim Lister published *Peopleware: Productive Projects and Teams* in 1987. *Peopleware* continued to be a top seller for decades.

Management theory pioneers included Douglas McGregor, who wrote *The Human Side of Enterprise* (1960). His book introduced Theory X and Theory Y, about what motivated individuals, into management theory. More emphasis on the people side of business and technology would emerge in the 1990s.

As always happens, the successes and failures of one era form the base for the next. CASE tools signaled the need for better tools, but also the challenges of building them. The plethora of structured diagrams underlined the need for standardization, giving rise to UML. Visions of faster, more reliable, connectivity ushered in the Internet era.

In the ongoing battle for change, both creating and selling a new product or methodology require adventurous nonconformity. It is fascinating that one of the most iconic examples of these traits was produced during this period.

Apple created the most famous television ad in history—its 1984 Super Bowl ad introducing the Macintosh computer. The ad's conceptual foundation was George Orwell's dystopian book *1984*, in which people mindlessly obey Big Brother. The black-clad crowd portrays the masses as androgynist automatons. The colorful heroine breaks through a barrier introducing both the Mac and Apple's nonconformist and empowered personality. It was also a not-so-subtle swipe at IBM. The powerful ad stuck with me for a long time.

4

The Roots of Agile

(1990–2000)

 **Roots of Agile**

IN MAY 2000, about six months after *Adaptive Software Development* (*ASD*; Highsmith, 2000) was released, I received the following email from a Midwest CEO.

I purchased your book a few months ago and have been reading and marking it since. I purchased it because the first few chapters clearly indicated Adaptive Software Development (ASD) well suited my current projects. Your narrative style makes ASD easy to understand and caused me to read it again to gain even more subtlety. I have recommended it to my peers, as ASD is what real product development is like. I have improved our results over previous projects by letting loose the employee reins while setting positive goals and necessary landscape constraints. The ASD approach allowed team members to invent solutions to the always present unexpected problems and yet deliver the product on time. Thank you for your book; it has affected the way I strategize, market, manage, develop, and deliver new products.

This email crystallized one element of my *why*—what drove me to undertake and sustain the adventures of this era? There were times when I wondered whether another Rapid Application Development (RAD) gig would ever come along. There were times when I despaired of finishing *ASD*, my first book. I can now articulate what drove me through these periods—courtesy of this email. I realized a piece of my *why* was "to promote an enlightened leadership style fitting the modern era—a style that empowers people and teams to break their bureaucratic log jams." A second *why* had something to do with delivering better software, but it would take another decade to fully articulate my version.

At age 45, I began two adventurous pivots. The first was a location change, from Atlanta to Salt Lake City, Utah. The second was an intellectual evolution from structured methods to RAD. The first led to a flurry of outdoor adventures, and the second eventually deposited me into the heart of the agile movement. There would not have been an agile revolution without the slow, but persistent adventurousness of a bunch of software iconoclasts during the 1990s. My definition of *adventurous* bears repeating: "Eager to go to new places and do exciting or dangerous things"[1] (Pearson Longman) and willing to take a calculated risk without being foolhardy. RAD was risky, but it worked out in the end.

Era overview

The Roots era was transformative in several ways. Software development methodologies began to react to the concerns with deterministic, optimizing, waterfall methodologies. The Internet ushered in exciting new possibilities. Management began to transform relationships with employees. New software development pioneers emerged. It was a busy decade, and this chapter reflects that business. I've divided the Roots era into three periods, with the divisions being related directly to the evolution of my thinking. Figure 4.1 shows these Roots periods that identify my own (not industry) transformation.

In addition to my structured to adaptive journey, the chapter profiles several client engagements that confirmed and extended my thinking, writing my first book, my foray into complex adaptive systems (CAS) theory, and taking a look at other emerging agile methodologies.

I remember the 1990s as a decade of relative peace and prosperity—the United States and Soviet Union ended the decades-long Cold War, while the rise of the Internet ushered in a pivotal new era of communications, impacting both business and personal interactions. It was the decade of Bill Clinton, hip hop music, and the seeds of ultra-partisan politics. *Jurassic Park* ousted the 1970 *Jaws* as having the scariest nature-related movie beast.

---

1. Reprinted by permission of Pearson, *Longman Dictionary of Contemporary English*, 2014. www.ldoceonline.com/dictionary/adventurous.

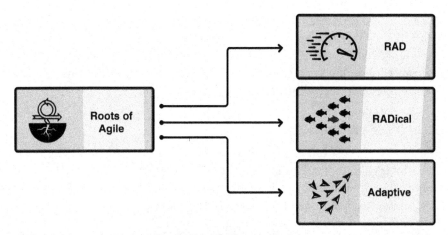

Figure 4.1 *The Roots periods.*

In 1989, my wife and I moved to Salt Lake City for her job, as manager of the flight attendant base for Delta Air Lines. I worked out of a suitcase, and my home base could be anywhere. Moreover, the thought of living out West, where climbing and skiing went from a long airplane ride to a 40-minute drive, was all the incentive I needed. When outdoor adventures were every-day events, I began to see the analogies between software development and climbing.

Technical climbing involves risks, but those risks can be mitigated by remaining flexible. Climbing plans are constantly shifting as weather and conditions dictate. It began dawning on me that climbers must adapt to the reality of a mountain, yet with software projects, we expected reality to adapt to our plans. I began the decade with my climbing and software develop-ment on separate tracks, but they soon began traveling together.

In June 1992, I wrote about this juxtaposition in an article titled "Software Ascents," for Ed Yourdon's *American Programmer* journal. In his introduction to the journal, Ed wrote, "Jim Highsmith sent us a wonderful article compar-ing software projects to mountain climbing; we think you will enjoy it." This article indicated my evolving thought process, from thinking about method-ology as a predictive process to one that was "steered," just as climbing plans changed constantly from assessing the terrain and weather conditions.

Companies were being drawn to prescriptive practices like total qual-ity management (TQM) and business process reengineering (BPR), but there was also a growing interest in teams, as evidenced by the success of *The*

Wisdom of Teams (Katzenbach, 1992), and in organizational learning (Senge, 1990). BPR advocates believed in automated, deterministic processes and considered people to be cogs in the machine. In addition, Lean principles and practices, effective in streamlining manufacturing, were translated into knowledge work, including for software development.

Structured methods to RAD

"Take too long, cost too much, do not meet our needs," executives lamented about their IT software projects, as they tried to respond to market demands. I began this decade doing independent consulting and teaching workshops in structured techniques and waterfall methodologies such as DSSD and STRADIS.[2] I ended the decade having abandoned both. In response to executive cries for help, software developers began experimenting with RAD methodologies. I led the technical team on a project to produce a RAD version of STRADIS—our ill-fated approach was to remove document and process requirements here and there. But a fundamental change was needed, as these early attempts to address the growing clamor for faster development contained neither a revision to the waterfall life cycle nor any radical change in mindset.

I began to question the conventional approach to development, in part because it wasn't the way I worked. My thoughts returned to the Wild West days and the enjoyment of having multiple roles—analyst, programmer, tester—that didn't use a prescriptive process but rather an iterative one.

An incident from the late 1980s fueled my skepticism of the waterfall life cycle and documentation. I was teaching a STRADIS requirements definition and design course in St. Louis, Missouri. This 5-day class was open to the public and conducted in a hotel meeting room. The class logistics in those days required both physical and mental strength.

First, the instructor had to check the setup. Second, you had to find the student workbooks. Often the hotel staff insisted the workbooks were not there, I insisted they were, and a search of the mail room found them. Next was checking that an overhead projector was available and working. In those days we used 8½- × 10½-inch transparencies (thin foil plastic sheets) for class information display. I had two 3-inch notebook binders crammed with "foils" I carried in a large leather bag. Including my other instructor paraphernalia,

---

2. STRADIS, for example, consisted of seven large notebooks that defined processes, document, and design diagrams in excruciating detail.

it was heavy. Portable computers replaced the heavy bag with a heavy computer, my Compaq luggable. But for a time, I had to carry both because the reliability of the luggable was suspect and you never knew if the hotel (or client) would have a compatible projector or the right hookup cables. At that point, you could start thinking about teaching the class.

In the STRADIS class, a dozen participants filled the walls with data flow diagrams, structure charts, and entity-relationship diagrams. On the last day, I queried them, "From all these diagrams you can see how to code it, correct?" The room filled with blank stares. They didn't know! On the board, as I drew connections between the diagrams and the parts of a COBOL program, the lights went on. Documentation, not even graphic documentation, was enough to convey all the information required by individuals in the next phase of work.

I knew programmers doing code maintenance always read the code for understanding because they knew documentation would be outdated. Everyone, including managers, recognized this disconnect, but continued along their classic path.

At the beginning of the decade, IT customers were not happy, and I wasn't happy. It was time for a change.

Around that time, Larry Constantine called me. He had been asked to help Amdahl (a mainframe computer manufacturer) develop a RAD method. He had declined because of a conflict (he was consulting with IBM) and asked if I was interested. This turned out to be my entrance into the RAD world and the beginning of a decades-long friendship with Sam Bayer.

Amdahl's problem was a long (sometimes 18 months) sales cycle because clients didn't understand their product. Sam was the marketing manager looking for help. Much as I had a two-pronged education in engineering and business, Sam had a double background in marketing and a PhD in chemistry (who knew chemistry was good training for marketing). We quickly became friends and colleagues. Sam was searching for a marketing strategy for a mainframe RAD software tool, named Huron.

Sam wanted to shorten the sales cycle and show potential customers how to quickly derive value from this product. Given the mainframe software's hefty price, it had not been an easy sell. Sam and I created an iterative RAD methodology, then used it to build a customer's application in four weeks. We went to a customer's location, assembled a small team that included a variety of Amdahl and customer people, delivered working software every week, and conducted "customer focus groups" every Friday to demonstrate features to customer representatives and get feedback. At the end of four weeks, we would deliver a complete application with statistics that showed multiple times better productivity and quality. But our projects often ran into trouble with entrenched organizational barriers. In one New York City bank, we delivered a working application the bank needed in four weeks, only to then be told by the IT operations department they would be able to install the application in about six months! This was a precursor of barriers to come. Sam and I conducted dozens of these projects and never had a failure.

In June 1994, Sam and I published an article in *American Programmer* magazine titled "RADical Software Development" (Bayer and Highsmith, 1994).[3] Sam later became the founder and CEO of Corevist, which used agile practices throughout the company.

I've tried to unfold this decade's software methodology evolution as it unfolded for me. It began with nearly two years working with Sam. I wish I'd kept count of the number of these RAD projects we undertook with clients, but I didn't—but I guess it was several dozen. If you work on a one-year project (not unheard of then), you get to practice specific methods one time. If you do 20 one-month projects, you get to practice each method 20 times. Whatever Sam and I learned from each project, we carried into our future work.

At the start of this decade, I read about RAD, but initially viewed it as a fad. As Sam and I worked together for several years on these short RAD projects, I began to realize the possibilities. Seeing how the methods worked, presenting running features to the customers every week, working in small collaborative teams, using one-week iterations—it all began to gel. One of my concerns was that many RAD proponents seemed to abandon proven technical practices. In the RADical article just mentioned, Sam and I wrote, "Some proponents of rapid development methods see them as a replacement for software engineering techniques. ... But abandoning what we have learned about building high-quality systems was not the answer."

Microsoft

The early 1990s also began my five-year stint teaching workshops at Microsoft in Redmond, Washington, which had about 4,000 employees at the time. Although I taught a few project management workshops, my primary

---

3. Reviewing this article for this book, I noticed the author bio included my first email address—73030.432@compuserv.com.

work was a course called Software Quality Dynamics. Jerry Weinberg had introduced this workshop to Microsoft but after a brief kerfuffle, invited Lynne Nix, who contacted me, to teach ongoing workshops. Lynne handled most of the project management and I handled the software quality courses. Jerry's quality course was based on the material in his four-volume *Software Quality Dynamics* series and was a joy to teach (Weinberg, 1994). Jerry had a unique ability to design games and simulations—House of Cards, Bead Game—that both inspired learning and were fun for workshop participants.

The House of Cards game gave participants direct practice in team dynamics, by using 80-column punch cards (they became hard to find) to build a structure. There were specs and points for height, diameter of the top and bottom, and aesthetics. Halfway through the exercise, I would take a person from one team and assign them to another. While introducing the new team member, I would casually mention this person had a great house-building reputation. What I didn't tell them was, although the dimensions had point values, each team's scoring calculation was different! One team gained points from a large dimension on the bottom and a narrow one on top, while another team's score used the opposite rubric. The new team member arriving in the middle had been working on a different scoring sheet, so, of course, they immediately tried to change the design, setting up conflict. When the game was over, I assigned an aesthetics score to each building. Yikes! There was always booing at my aesthetics scores as the participants complained about my bias, unfairness, and arbitrary scores. My reply: "Don't you think your customers are often arbitrary in their assessment of your products?"

The game was fun and got everyone up from their chairs, discussing issues loudly. The last 30 to 35 minutes of the exercise time was spent discussing a range of questions about what participants had learned. Much of the discussion centered on people and their interactions.

Having a decade of working with structured methods and waterfall life cycles, my initial thought was that Microsoft was doing everything wrong. My next thought was "But they are extremely successful." While waterfall life cycle adherents focused on the front-end requirements and design, believing programming and testing were mostly "mechanical" activities, Microsoft reversed the emphasis, believing the creative parts were programming and testing. As I learned about Microsoft's processes over the next several years, I became convinced the RAD methodology Sam Bayer and I were developing would scale.

RAD to RADical

RADical Software Development was my version of RAD, and the difference was more than a cuter name. But I don't think I understood the ramifications of the differences then. RAD was about speed. RADical was about value, quality, speed, leadership, and collaboration—you might call it "professional RAD." We didn't just need speed, we needed to be RADical in several dimensions. In our RADical article (Bayer and Highsmith, 1994), Sam and I identified five key aspects of this methodology:

- The life cycle must transform from a static, documentation-oriented process to a dynamic, evolutionary, product orientation.
- Project management needed to utilize short "timebox" techniques.
- An evolutionary[4] life cycle was needed.
- RADical required dedicated teams.
- Good engineering skills were essential.

We didn't use the word "mindset" in the article, but Ed Yourdon did in his introduction. The last sentence in this article signaled the future, though it took a decade to become reality: "If information technology is one key to reengineering corporations, it is time to think seriously about reengineering the engineers."

Portland Mortgage Software

Portland Mortgage Software, an early client, was located in Portland, Oregon. It developed mortgage processing software used in all 50 states, each of which had minor to major variations in its mortgage processing regulations. In addition, federal mortgage regulations had to be incorporated into the software. The company sold a suite of products for large financial companies, and individual products for smaller ones.

As in a typical organization, each specialty—legal, accounting, and software development—had its own organizational silos, in different sections of the building, of course. Communications between the siloed groups left much room for improvement.

---

4. During this period, I used the word evolutionary rather than iterative.

My client asked me to help improve these departments' delivery performance. In addition to engaging them in a rapid development process, I suggested they reorganize into cross-functional product groups—and sit together as teams. After the changes had been under way for a while, I asked the development manager how the new organization and process were going.

"We are getting better products out faster than before," he said.

"Any negatives?" I asked.

"Well," he replied, "the product teams complain occasionally that they don't communicate with each other enough."

This reminds me of an old systems theory saying, "Just hope your problem solution doesn't create more problems than you had in the first place." There are always consequences of change, both for good and for not so good.

Working with Portland Mortgage Software confirmed my belief that solutions come in myriad combinations—process, organization, performance measures—that differ for each organization. My thinking continued transforming from a monumental approach of "one size fits all" to "one size fits one."

This engagement furthered my understanding of, and commitment to, cross-functional, collaborative teams as the core software delivery organization. As my client was a software company, I learned about a product view of delivery.

Information technology

As my work with RAD was progressing, technology was advancing rapidly. The World Wide Web was introduced in 1990, Windows 3.0 the same year, Mosaic's browser in 1993, Amazon appeared as an online bookseller in 1994, and Google's search engine debuted in 1998. Windows had a major upgrade to version 95. Linus Torvalds introduced Linux, which set off the open-source software movement. Windows began grabbing huge chunks of the IT market because of the combination of Windows and the Microsoft Office Suite. The latter crowded out the market for individual applications—Lotus, WordPerfect, and Notes all floundered by the end of the decade.

The Internet brought unimagined connectivity to businesses and individuals' lives, enabling the success of new businesses like CompuServe and Amazon, and ushered in the person-to-person interaction era, which was poised to grow exponentially. The connectivity drove fundamental changes as computer-savvy entrepreneurs eclipsed traditional businesses struggling to make sense of the cyberworld.

The evolution of object-oriented programming (OOP) and its movement into the mainstream occurred during the 1990s, providing an alternative to the procedural languages (COBOL) of the 1980s. Alan Kay, the originator of OOP (who coined the name back in the 1960s), thought OOP provided benefits of adaptability and resilience to changes. Proponents of OOP languages such as Smalltalk, Java, and C++ battled for supremacy during this era. Three technologies—Windows and Macs with their user-friendly graphical user interface (GUI), connectivity via the Internet accessible with newly minted browsers, and OOP—created incentives to pivot software development.

During this decade, my clients were both software companies like Portland Mortgage Software and large IT organizations in companies like Nike (more on Nike later in the chapter). Obviously, I needed to keep up with the problems IT organizations were facing and how they were attempting to solve those problems. Companies were trying out a variety of solutions to their "take too long, cost too much, do not meet our needs" problem. While a few tried RAD, most stuck to traditional methodologies, but the rising interest in RAD indicated the status quo needed refreshing. As with any approach, critics of RAD abounded—and they were right on one point. RAD developers assumed applications were experiencing faster and faster obsolescence, so the emphasis was on speed rather than on quality, since system retirement was just around the corner. Unfortunately, this assumption was wrong and just increased software maintenance woes.

Adding to the problems in IT was a growing, but still feeble, understanding of technical debt. As both general and IT managers became enthralled with predictability and rigor, they forgot the fundamental difference between tangible things like widgets and intangible and malleable things like software. Once a widget emerges from a factory, it doesn't change. Software can and does. This myopia gave rise to the serious issue of technical debt, turning malleable software into a muddled, high-cost mess.

To solve all these problems within the IT realm, highly touted strategies included outsourcing and installing enterprise package software. While I was not involved with either of these areas, they certainly impacted IT organizations and continued to bias them toward prescriptive solutions. In addition, business users, tired of waiting, began to adopt end-user computing solutions.

In the 1990s, companies responded in part by following the mantra I would summarize as "Ship everything to India." One part of this trend was to offshore software maintenance and the programming phase of large development projects. The assumptions behind software outsourcing were that less skilled and less expensive programming could be accomplished with minimal communication. Much outsourcing was based on the false premises of predictability and prescriptive practices, as Indian firms rushed to promote their adherence to strict Capability Maturity Model (CMM) standards.[5]

First-generation operational business software was now clunky and outdated. As companies sought to modernize their aging legacy systems, they faced two daunting choices—build them inhouse or purchase packages. Both options were expensive and risky, but many companies opted to buy and install large enterprise resource planning (ERP) and later customer relationship management (CRM) systems. ERP and CRM implementations took several years each and were often managed by large consulting firms. Outsourcing and implementation of large, packaged software applications stripped IT teams of the expertise they would need in the coming Internet upheaval. The Internet erupted during these multiyear implementation projects, triggering the need for rework and leading to clunky ways to connect these operational systems with external customers. Smaller companies, like Sam Bayer's Corevist, thrived by offering un-clunky customer-facing add-on solutions to ERP systems.

The factors that drove RAD methods also fostered a parallel fad—end-user computing. The combination of growing user needs, PCs sprouting on everyone's desks, and the increasing sophistication of spreadsheets and RAD tools enabled end-user development that had benefits, but also significant downsides. These end-user applications could be fast and responsive. However, an analyst in the finance department developing a complex spreadsheet rarely had testing skill, so bugs crept in. One "productivity" consultant at a Southern bank developed such a spreadsheet for pricing mortgage processing services. The bank used this spreadsheet for a year until someone realized an error ensured the bank lost money on every mortgage—for the next 15 to 30 years of the mortgage's life! Backup and recovery was also a big issue since PC storage wasn't the easiest, or the most reliable,

5. The Capability Maturity Model (CMM) was a product of the Software Engineering Institute. The CMM promoted learning, which got lost in the blizzard of documentation and processes users had to implement to gain levels of "maturity." I won't get into the difference between CMM and CMMI (I = integration) in this book.

in those days. At one point in the early 1990s, my backup consisted of twenty 3¼-inch diskettes. Guess how often I backed up?

Colleagues of the spreadsheet developers would copy their spreadsheet and typically make their own modifications. Users would look up data online and manually enter the data into the spreadsheet. Now you had four or five versions of the spreadsheet floating around. The finance department manager would then approach IT with a request to consolidate all the spreadsheet versions, scale the application for multiple users, implement security measures, extract data from operational systems to populate the spreadsheet, and fix bugs. Software developers in IT typically didn't have experience with spreadsheets, and IT departments were deluged with other work, so the typical response to these requests was "You built it, you fix it." That attitude didn't do wonders for IT's reputation in business departments.

For any technology, or methodology, there is a "sweet spot" where it can be effective and beneficial. But there are also pitfalls that are not initially obvious. As an example of the past informing the present, are there parallels between the 1990s end-user computing and the early 2020s use of "low-code" or "no-code" tools?

The rapid growth of the Internet in the mid- to late 1990s had an immediate impact on communications and the rise of companies like Amazon. But it also had a lasting, significant impact on all enterprises:

> The Internet refocused software development from internal business systems to external customer-facing ones.

Today we take for granted our ability to renew driver's licenses online with state governments, pay bills from our bank's online system, buy stocks on our cell phones, or post our latest diatribe on Twitter. Previously, customers would call an order-processing person, who would then enter their order into the order entry system. Then, in the 1990s, companies scrambled to build customer-facing applications—for example, those for processing orders without a person in the process.

This shift was driven by the Internet, GUIs, and the expanding use and power of personal computers. As shown in Figure 4.2, individuals now had access to GUIs, mice, and external communications via acoustic coupler modems for their landline phones. I've never seen an estimate for the total amount of time lost by business travelers trying to hook up to the Internet using acoustic couplers from their hotel rooms, but based on my experience, it would be a substantial number.

Figure 4.2 *Roots era interactivity.*

For internal clients of IT systems, many interface designs were awful, in part because of technical constraints. During the late 1980s, when terminals were character-based, user screens might be crammed with data fields—user friendliness was seldom a design goal. If you were an order-processing clerk, speed of entry was paramount, as you were called upon to input hundreds of orders a day. However, external users needed "friendly" interfaces because they didn't process many orders. In the early days of graphical interfaces, designers mixed up these two user groups, sometimes providing internal users with friendly interfaces that drastically slowed them down! Incentives, and guidelines, for good design were still in their infancy. That soon changed. Companies were now competing for customer clicks, and interface design quickly became critical for success. GUI developers at Apple, Amazon, and Microsoft invested in interface design and identified it as a specialty role, while most IT organizations were slow in realizing the need. In the 1980s, with only character-based terminals available and transaction processing systems limited in capability, truly awful user interfaces were the norm. Poor design was less of a problem during this era because of the simple fact that internal staff had to live with these designs. But in the 1990s, that situation was turned upside down since external customers demanded better interfaces or they went elsewhere.

The new "Internet" companies eschewed Monumental Methods—they were far too slow, not conducive to innovation, and not fun. At first, these differences showed up between the Internet and traditional companies. Later, they would drive a wedge within companies, as groups developing Internet systems split from legacy system development groups. The traditional groups looked down on the Internet application developers for building "toy systems," while the Internet groups looked askance at traditional developers as dinosaurs.

With these new applications, requirements were murky. When order processing was automated in the past, an analyst would go to the order processing department and ask people how they did their work. While tasks might be complicated, there was a definite starting point. But now the technology was new, the requirements changing, and customer user-interfaces in their infancy. Waterfall life cycles were not equipped to handle this level of uncertainty.

The rise of the Internet and accompanying innovations helped upend the drive to prescriptive methods. Many of the early agilists—Kent Beck, Alistair Cockburn, Martin Fowler, Ron Jeffries, Bob Martin—were OOP gurus during the mid-1990s. In an email exchange, Martin Fowler pointed out, "I was taught to be very skeptical of waterfall from my first job, so I was already primed for agile. I also started in the object-oriented (OO) world, which always had a strong bias towards evolutionary design and had the theoretical tools and software environment (Smalltalk) to pull it off. You, on the other hand, were much closer to mainstream thinking than all of us OOers."

Making the transition from structured methods to RADical came with challenges. Just as companies had to learn about cannibalizing existing products to launch new ones, I learned about timing. I went from having sufficient structured work to scratching for RADical work. I drew crowds at conference talks, but not many who bought my services. To the ones who let me experiment on their projects, I am eternally grateful.

Nike

Another big break in my structured to RADical transition was working with Nike in Beaverton, Oregon. Nike was a hopping place, athletes everywhere, buildings named for major athletes like Michael Jordan, meeting rooms named for less well-known ones. Rather than an invitation to meet in Building

C, Room 13-002, you got an invite to Building Michael Jordan, Room Pete Maravich.

My work at Nike lasted several years and focused on three areas: implementing its first RADical project, teaching workshops on RADical development and facilitation, and managing a large enterprise data project. This work increased my confidence in RADical practices.

My friend Jerry Gordon, who had introduced me to mountaineering, had gone to work for Nike, and he brought me in to pitch RADical to a senior executive. A project in one division had run off the rails: It had taken 18 months just to produce a requirements document, and by then it was outdated. The division vice president was frustrated at the lack of progress. My biggest concern approaching this executive interview was what to wear, given the informality at Nike. Casual business dress and red Nike running shoes proved to be just the ticket—the executive noticed the shoes, and I got the job.

Using the methodology Sam and I had developed, we used one-month iterations to deliver a working application in six months. One of the techniques that caught on with the IT staff was the use of team sessions, including both IT and client staff, to rapidly identify business needs and software features. These group sessions were also used for retrospectives. I ended up teaching multiple workshops on these Joint Application Development (JAD) techniques and helped Nike build a staff of facilitators.

One kerfuffle on the Nike project highlighted a difficulty iterative development would constantly have with different functional silos. After the first iteration, I sat down with the database administrator assigned to the project, who had attended my three-day RADical workshop, and laid out the database changes needed for the second iteration.

"Oh no," he said, "You don't understand. In database land, we require the database be designed and implemented once. We need all the entities and attributes defined; then we implement it once."

I replied, "Don't you remember from the workshop that the application emerges iteration by iteration, which means the database design evolves also?"

"But," he countered, "we don't work that way in my department. I thought the iterative design was just for the developers. We can't do it your way."

"Fine," I responded. "The vice president of the product line approved this RAD-style project because of the previous failure to deliver any results.

Let's you and I go up to her office and you can explain your standard way of working to her."

After a brief pause, he said, "Maybe I can figure out a way we could do it, just for this project." And he did.

The customer focus group feature demonstration at the end of the first iteration was attended by the client vice president. After watching the working feature demonstration, she stood, thanked the group, and concluded with the comment, "This is great. I'll never say anything negative about IT again!" The IT team couldn't believe their ears.

Arguments about which parts of the life cycle could be iterative and which could not would arise repeatedly during the late Roots and early Agile eras. Not only had the serial waterfall approach impacted organizational design, but it also extended to the wider IT industry. Similar to enterprise silos, there were industry ones. Software Engineering Institute (SEI) conferences were attended by Monumental Methodologists, software conferences like the Software Development conferences were attended by traditional developers, object-oriented programming conferences by object-oriented programmers, and database management conferences by database designers. Each type of conference was attended by its own adherents. The biggest rift was between database and software development groups, as colleagues Scott Ambler and Ken Collier can attest, because they tried for years to get the database crowd to embrace agile methods.

I spent six months (traveling from Salt Lake City weekly) managing a project for Nike (I was the only non-Nike person on the project). On this project I employed collaboration and self-organizing team practices. This enterprise architecture project touched a wide number of business departments, and we needed to decide how to approach them. The team came up with an idea to concentrate on stories about the serious negative consequences of the current systems. I wasn't thrilled with the approach, thinking it was a waste of time, but the team liked it, so we proceeded. I was wrong. This analysis proved to be pivotal in explaining to the business managers the extent of the problem and led to an agreement to move forward with our recommendations.

I also witnessed various reactions to fluid, adaptive planning as opposed to traditional prescriptive task plans. One of the team leads, an important contributor, became uneasy in a staff meeting with what seemed to him a fuzzy plan. I then jotted down a series of tasks for him and discussed them with the group. After the meeting, one of the other team leads remarked, "I didn't think that was how we worked." "Agreed," I responded, "but I needed to tamp down his frustration by temporarily providing something concrete for him."

Another learning incident involved decision making. Several team members needed to travel to conduct focus group sessions. I thought through what was needed and assigned three individuals to the task—which included a coveted travel stint to offices in Europe. I thought it was a minor decision, but the team didn't agree. They informed me they didn't disagree with who was selected, but thought the team should have made the decision, not me. In building self-organizing teams, who makes what decisions can either foster self-organization or hinder it. Reflecting back on this incident, I realized that who made decisions was important, but equally so was that the team felt comfortable raising the question.

Researching project management books and the PMBoK (Project Management Body of Knowledge), I found scarce mention of decision-making practices. While *ASD* contained multiple mentions of decision making, a fuller discussion would await my *Agile Project Management* book (Highsmith, 2009).

Consultants' Camp and Jerry Weinberg

In the mid-1990s, I was invited by Lynne Nix to join Consultants' Camp, an annual, retreat-style event held at the Nordic Lodge in the mountain town of Crested Butte, Colorado (also the wildflower capital of Colorado). Jerry Weinberg was the organizer (others participated in the planning) of this event, bringing together a diverse group each summer to discuss weighty subjects and take long mountain hikes. This was my first exposure to a "roll your own" conference. This and other similar meetings were early examples of using "open space" concepts.

The first morning, the group gathered, people suggested sessions they could give, the group selected and scheduled sessions, and then people signed up. Jerry always had a few ideas to throw into the mix. It was my introduction to self-organization. Jerry would guide, and nudge, using a leadership style aligned with that emerging from my adaptive research. Reflecting on something so new, frequent camp participant Steve Smith commented in our 2022 conversation:

> I knew I didn't understand at all what we were doing. The self-organization part was really strange to me. And then the sessions, I didn't know what to expect. I didn't know what to offer from a session. Jerry was a

master influencer. He just kinda shaped stuff, he didn't force anything. Oh, occasionally he forced a decision, but maybe it was necessary. It's hard to say.

Many of the camp participants were graduates or instructors of the Problem Solving Leadership (PSL) workshop created by Jerry and Dani Weinberg. Participants raved about PSL as an outstanding and innovative social learning experience. "They really rocked your freaking world," said Steve. Somehow I never made it to PSL, although it spent a long time on my to-do list.

Long, tall Steve Smith and I enjoyed strenuous hikes laced with conversations about the day's topics, although breathing took priority over talking. Steve and I kept in touch, and he made vital contributions to my first book. I also first met David Robinson at camp; 20 years later, he co-authored *EDGE* (Highsmith, Luu, and Robinson, 2020) with me. And then there was III (pronounced Three).

III (his legal name) would roll into Consultants' Camp each summer in his psychedelic 1970s Volkswagen bus that would not have caused a stir at Woodstock or the Burning Man festival. Even in a group of nonconformists, III was a rebellious, iconoclast. He had long hair and shunned having his picture taken, part of either his spirituality or his quirkiness, we presumed. But III was also gregarious, quick to laugh, and fun to be around. Interestingly enough, his adventurous lifestyle gave way to traditional ways of working. With a Structured-era background, he had gravitated to focus on people and their interactions—specifically facilitation. He facilitated project group sessions and taught facilitation workshops. His adventurous lifestyle and cautious workstyle played well together. His classes were full of fun, informative exercises, and his demeanor encouraged participants to contribute in ways they would not have otherwise. Think of how you might open up in a fun, exercise-filled class run by an unassuming, hippie-like III versus an instructor in a button-down shirt and suit droning on about slides filled with bullet points.

III was adamant about his project kickoff process, which he called chartering—he found what worked and stuck with it. While collaborating with III in one client engagement, I remember trying hard to change a couple of things. III didn't budge. I don't remember who finally won the argument, but I bet it was III. Bringing III into several client engagements in subsequent years required careful selection, as some clients would have trouble getting past his external persona. Their loss. Once at work, clients responded positively to his style.

Intense arguments abounded at camp. One classic Steve reminded me of was over the question, "Can you measure love?" Many engineers believed anything could be measured. Tom Gilb, inventor of evolutionary development, and James Bach, a testing expert, squared off. Tom insisted "love" could be measured by galvanic skin responses. James, whose father wrote the iconic best-seller *Jonathan Livingston Seagull* (Bach, 1970),[6] was having none of it. Tom had an ego. James hated to lose. The argument ebbed and flowed for most of the afternoon, with onlookers wandering in and out of the room, sometimes chipping in a comment or two. It was a typical camp discussion question, with two smart, opinionated iconoclasts facing off, neither of whom liked to lose. Delightful insights and great entertainment!

"RENAISSANCE MAN" would be an appropriate description of Jerry Weinberg. He wrote about software development and general systems theory, but his forte was understanding people and change. He was a colleague whose ideas and friendship enhanced my career. James Bach, a fellow consultant camper, wrote a moving tribute after Jerry died in 2018: "What Jerry showed me is how to be authentic without being cruel; how to have integrity in a world of mendacity; how to live confidently with uncertainty; how to debate your teacher while learning from him; how to transition from student to colleague; how to achieve your own agency without seeking anyone's consent to do so."[7]

Steve Smith commented:

One thing I learned from Jerry was to have someone be the observer of an exercise and then report to the group what they saw during the exercise. Easy, right? Having an outsider's view of what happened during the session is critical. But what most people want to give are their interpretations. Even when I gave extremely specific instructions, people went to an interpretive mode. And I'd say your job is to record what you hear and what you see, your job is not to interpret it. You're like a court reporter. I mean, it's gotta be a standard pattern because over and over again, across years,

---

6. *Jonathan Livingston Seagull* was a phenomenal bestseller, spending two years around the top spot on the *New York Times* best-seller list. It celebrated the strength of the individual and the joy of finding one's way. No wonder James Bach took a non-measurement view of love.

7. James Bach's tribute to Jerry can be found on his website, www.satisfice.com.

that happened. Even with explicit instructions, they would still go into interpretive mode.

Jerry understood talking about communication patterns like this wasn't enough—they had to be experienced, and he was the master of experiential exercises (like the House of Cards game mentioned earlier in this chapter). This exact intrepretive problem occurred at an agilists meeting I attended years later. One participant realized the meeting "recorder" wasn't recording the "data" on the flip chart, but rather recording his interpretation. She asked to take over the recording job and focused on recording what was said rather than her interpretation of it.

Jerry was a prolific writer on a wide variety of topics. A copy of his *Psychology of Computer Programming* (Weinberg, 1971) still sits in my library. Both *Psychology* and his *An Introduction to General Systems Thinking* (Weinberg, 2001) are classics. Dorset House Publishing reissued both in "Silver Editions."

Jerry loved aphorisms. Often presented as a series of "laws," these were pithy statements of complex ideas. Here are a few examples:

- Law of Twins: "Most of the time, no matter how much effort one expends, no event of any great significance will result." (As in, how often are twins born?)
- Five-Minute Rule: "Clients always know how to solve their problems, and always tell the solution in the first five minutes."
- "If the software doesn't have to work, you can always meet any other requirement."
- "Having a high IQ is like a CPU's having a terrific computing speed. It's a great asset in problem solving—as long as the problem doesn't involve a lot of input or output."

Jerry even wrote about writing in *Weinberg on Writing* (Weinberg, 2006). This method has been the cornerstone of my writing ever since. Some authors begin at the beginning and write from front to back. I could never do that. I write like Jerry suggests: First write nuggets of narrative, and then figure out how to arrange them. Jerry reviewed my first book, *ASD*, and gave me excellent organization hints, which prompted significant restructuring and led to major improvements.

At Jerry's Consultants' Camp, I found a new group of like-minded people who contributed to my evolution. Here I was introduced to self-organizing teams and the Satir model for change that I used frequently in client engagements.

RADical to adaptive

The transition from RADical to adaptive involved the explicit identification and use of mindset. I finally latched onto a framework for a RADical mindset—complex adaptive systems (CAS) theory. This discovery caused me to relabel my approach from RADical to adaptive and propelled the collaborative, self-organizing team side of my thinking. Later I would learn other Agile Manifesto authors employed CAS theory. Three threads were woven together to create Adaptive Software Development (ASD):

- RADical Software Development methodology
- Collaboration
- CAS mindset

By the Roots era, we needed to move beyond traditional approaches to software development. The mindset that we could develop a plan and then execute it with minimal deviation, that we could prescribe algorithmic processes, that we could predict the future, that processes could drive out ugly variations, that people were cogs in the machinery of process wasn't working. Strict process engineering methods attempted to counteract uncertainty by admonishing people to be *more* certain—about as effective as telling a raging Mt. Everest storm to desist.

Since the early 1990s, a vanguard of scientists and managers had articulated a profound shift in their view about how organisms and organizations evolve, respond to change, and manage their growth. Scientists' findings about the tipping points of chemical reactions, the flocking of birds, and the swarm behavior of ants provided insights into organizational collaboration and change.

Collaboration

Waterfall life cycles resulted in functional organizational structures and an emphasis on documentation to bridge the gap between them. The earlier story about a five-day STRADIS class illustrated my concern about faulty communications, even when using diagrams rather than words. Two other engagements during the mid-1990s added to my concerns.

During a training session at an educational client in Phoenix, the systems architect on the project was determined to use UML diagrams to document his architecture. He said it would take two months. I said, "Fine, you have two weeks," after which he gave a one-hour presentation to the developers. Then came the question, "From all these diagrams you can see how to code it, correct?" Again, blank stares. Luckily this architect knew how to code. As he sat down and showed the developers how to properly code the architecture, I could see the lights going on. As an aside, this architect grumbled about having only two weeks to come up with the architecture. Four iterations into the project, he came back to me: "We had to redo a major part of the architecture. However, two months ago, I would not have considered the current architecture, no matter how much time you had given me. I finally understand an iterative approach, even with architecture."

A corporate architecture group at a financial firm on the East Coast had just delivered their architectural standards document. The development group's response: "Didn't understand them, ignored them." Talking with the architects, I asked, "What kinds of meetings have you scheduled to explain your work to developers?" "We don't have time to explain what's in the documents," they responded. "It should be obvious." Obviously, it wasn't.

Complex adaptive systems

> On the desk in my office sits EEK, an entirely self-contained, enclosed, living ecosystem. Five inches high, EEK contains algae, miniscule shrimp and snails, and multitudes of microscopic bacteria. They all live by exchanging stuff with each other or converting light to biochemical energy. Meanwhile, on the monitor beside EEK, a forest of digital beings exchange digital stuff. They live, eat each other, mate, give birth, evolve, and die—a sea of artificial life created in silicon. I used these two visions of life, the real and the artificial, as constant reminders of a new way of thinking about complex systems. (Highsmith, 1998)

In my transition from structured to agile, the critical "ah ha" moment was discovering CAS theory. Early approaches to software development were about methods. Mindsets were there, of course, but few bothered to articulate them. The Roots era changed that, as people began to understand the importance and implications of an explicit "mindset" for software development.

Indeed, my influencers during this period were more scientists than software developers.[8] My introduction to CAS theory lies in one of those memory black holes, but it was probably Brian Arthur's 1996 *Harvard Business Review* article, quickly followed by one of my all-time favorite books, George Johnson's (1996) *Fire in the Mind*. These were followed by works from authors including biologist John Holland (1995), Nobel Prize physicist Murray Gell-Mann (1995), Mitchell Waldrop (1993), and Margaret Wheatly (1992).

I began to realize communication and collaboration issues were such a critical piece of making ASD[9] a viable methodology that the subtitle of the book became *A Collaborative Approach to Managing Complex Systems*, and the first word in the title changed from *RADical* to *Adaptive*. Furthermore, the ASD life cycle emerged as "speculate–collaborate–learn" (as shown in Figure 4.3) and collaboration became a major focus of my *ASD* book. While CAS theory provided the theoretical concepts, Consultants' Camp provided practical implementations of those concepts, as did working with clients.

JUST AS QUANTUM physics changed our notions of predictability and Holland changed our perspective on evolution, CAS theory reshaped thinking. In an era of rapid change, we needed better models for sensing and responding to the world around us. Just as biologists study both ecosystems and individual species, executives and managers needed to better understand the global economic and political ecosystems in which their companies competed.

A complex adaptive system, be it biologic or economic, is an ensemble of agents who interact based on information, whose actions are based on simple rules, who evolve over time, and who often produce emergent results. An organizational *ensemble* might include team members, customers, suppliers, executives, and other participants who interact with each other. The agent's actions are driven by a set of internal rules, and a simple set of rules can generate complex behaviors and outcomes, whether in ant colonies or in project teams. Complex rules, by comparison, often become bureaucratic.

---

8. For fun I counted book references in *ASD*: pure science, 19; management and leadership, 38; technology and software development, 7.

9. The convention for abbreviations will be ASD (not italicized) for the methodology and *ASD* (italicized) for the book. Similarly for other books.

Dee Hock coined the word *chaordic* to describe adaptable organizations, those balanced on the edge between order and chaos. Hock, the former CEO of VISA, puts it succinctly:

Simple, clear purpose and principles give rise to complex, intelligent behavior. Complex rules and regulations give rise to simple, stupid behavior. (Hock, 1999)

Dipping into the science underlying CAS theory, the next question to ask, "How does it apply to software development?" The analogies that resonated with me were as follows:

- Adaptation
- Edge of chaos
- Arrival of the fittest
- Simple rules
- Emergence

Adaptation is a messy, anxiety-ridden, exciting, exuberant, bubbling, and redundant process—just this side of chaotic, but not quite there. Adaptive organizations listen to the world around them—their customers, suppliers, employees, and competitors—and respond to what they learn, not to what some process rule told them. Control-oriented managers revel in structure; collaborative managers revel in connectivity and real-world ambiguity.

Seeking the edge of chaos, lodged between randomness and structure, maximizes innovation and learning. Connectivity and information feed the hovering between the twin abysses of stability and chaos. "The underlying argument is when systems of any kind (e.g., beehives, businesses, economies) are poised on the edge between too much structure and too little structure, they 'self-organize' to produce complex adaptive behavior," write Shona Brown and Kathleen Eisenhardt (1998, p. 29). Too much structure reduces problem solving and innovation; too little creates chaos and ineffectiveness. "A little bit less than just enough" is my guideline for implementing rigor.

John Holland, a biologist, was the author of *Hidden Order: How Adaptation Builds Complexity* (1995). His premise was that Darwin's survival-of-the-fittest theory was insufficient to explain the complexity of life. Holland compared it to the chance of a tornado sweeping through a junkyard and assembling a Boeing 747. He postulated another concept was at work—namely, *arrival-of-the-fittest*, wherein agents (cells, animals, people) collaborate to form the next highest-level agent. Thinking about communications failures and the arrival-of-the-fittest concept led me to focus on collaboration as a key part of adaptive development.

Emergence is a property of complex adaptive systems that creates some greater property of the whole (system behavior) from the interaction of the parts (self-organizing agent behavior). Emergent results cannot be predicted in the normal sense of cause-and-effect relationships, but they can be anticipated by creating patterns that have previously produced similar results. Creativity and innovation are the emergent results of well-functioning agile teams.

Adaptive software development book

Authoring a book had been on my bucket list and I now had enough background and experience to consider such a project. Working with Sam, Nike, and others gave me experience with real projects. I was working on bolstering my writing skills, in part by attending two science writers' workshops in Santa Fe, New Mexico, taught by George Johnson, a *New York Times* writer. George had close ties with the Santa Fe Institute, and the workshops furthered my understanding of both CAS and writing. Publishing numerous articles had strengthened my writing capabilities, although I was to learn writing a bunch of articles was way different than writing a book.

I started working on the *RADical Software Development* book in the mid-1990s. As I worked, I kept having this niggling feeling something was missing and labeled it "Chapter 3." CAS theory turned out to be just what I was looking for.

"Only at the edge of chaos can complex systems flourish."
—Michael Crichton, *The Lost World*, 1995

The ASD methodology consists of four pillars: knowledge, experimentation, mindset, and analogy. Knowledge of software methods and methodologies enabled me to experiment with new methods and learn from them. Knowledge mitigated the risk of experimenting. Mountain climbing provided a physical, visceral analogy that helped people understand the new methods. CAS concepts provided an analogy for making the appropriate mindset change. Figure 4.3 shows the adaptive life cycle from ASD, its three main components (speculate, collaborate, and learn), and the primary processes within those components.

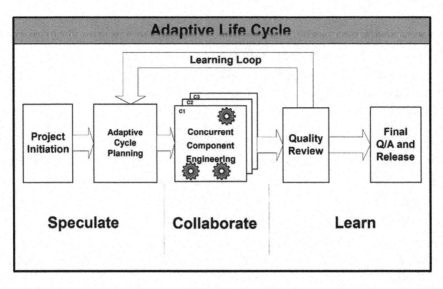

Figure 4.3 *The adaptive life cycle.*

The *ASD* book did not evolve easily. At first, Chapter 3 included all the background CAS theory. Luckily, Jerry Weinberg suggested putting all the theory in one chapter might bog readers down. Agreeing with him, I reorganized and spread the theoretical discussion throughout the book. That was a major reorganization, but there were also many smaller ones, enough I despaired of ever finishing, or getting the book published. Finally, I realized I had to finish it for me, regardless of whether it got published.

I submitted a draft of the book to Dorset House Publishing in New York. Dorset was a small, boutique publisher of software engineering books several industry notables I admired had worked with. Wendy Eakin, the president of Dorset House, gave me a green light—she wanted to publish it. In July 1997, I submitted the first manuscript. Just before Christmas 1999, the FedEx truck delivered the best gift I (and my wife) received that year (Figure 4.4).

If I could, I would give a copy of Jim Highsmith's book to everyone involved in developing large systems—end users, managers, IT professionals, and most especially IT project managers! Jim's message is simple but vitally important: Large information systems don't have to take so long, they don't have to cost so much, and they don't have to fail. Unfortunately,

Figure 4.4 *Adaptive Software Development: book and Jolt Award.*

as simple as Jim's message is, making it happen is an enormously difficult undertaking in most large organizations. (Ken Orr, from the foreword to *ASD*)

It was beyond thrilling that *ASD* won the 2000 Jolt product excellence award for the best software engineering book of the year. At past Software Development conferences, I had watched Jolt winners receive their awards; it was a great affirmation to be similarly recognized.

I'VE ALWAYS STRIVED to write narratives that were both informative and enjoyable to read. I've used client stories, dialogue, analogies, informality, and interviews. *ASD* used the analogies of complex systems and climbing— both of which require an adventurous spirit.

In the 1980s, I trekked to the North Cascades for mountaineering trips. In the 1990s, living in Salt Lake City, where every canyon contained climbing crags, I opted for rock climbing. Why climb mountains? The climber's cliché is "Because it's there." For me, it's a handful of things:

- Exhilarating
- Fun
- Being out in the natural world (and away from my desk)
- Intensely focusing
- Encourages adaptation

Why use mountain climbing as an analogy to developing software? Primarily, I enjoyed both. But there are three key reasons: skills, risk, and mindset. Climbing requires a variety of skills. In climbing you need rock and ice techniques—placing protection devices, rope handling, weather forecasting, route planning, and more. You also need risk assessment and mitigation skills—knowing when to push on, knowing when to back off, recognizing when a climb is within your skill level and when it's not. You only learn this with experience, getting a feel for the mountain, the terrain, the weather, your energy level. No amount of reading or planning substitutes for experience. Finally, you need an adaptive mindset. You have a clear goal, but the path may change. You have constraints—time and conditions. You must constantly adjust at both a micro level (your immediate surroundings) and macro level (overall assessment of whether to back off). Tackling a big mountain with a prescriptive mindset is a sure path to injury, or worse.

These same factors of skill, risk, and mindset apply to software developers and to organizational culture. I'm not suggesting you rush out and climb a mountain, but I do recommend you find an activity that tweaks your adventurous spirit.

IN 1999, AS my *ASD* book was nearing publication, I was looking for interesting conferences to attend and found Cutter Consortium's annual Summit Conference. There were speakers and topics that appealed to me, and the roster of speakers included individuals I admired—Ed Yourdon, Tom DeMarco, Tim Lister, and Ken Orr. I had authored several articles published by Cutter, so I emailed Ed Yourdon, and explained why I should speak at the conference. Ed emailed me back and said the speaker slots were full but offered me a spot on one of the discussion panels. Thus began another of the inflection points in my career.

The evening prior to the conference start, all the speakers, organizers, and panel members gathered for dinner, usually at Cutter CEO Karen Coburn's home. In this informal setting, with dinners scattered throughout the house, I ended up sitting beside Anne Mullaney, Cutter's vice president of marketing. As we talked about aspects of the IT industry, I mentioned I had a book near publication, and I enjoyed writing. It was one of those infrequent star alignments that appear to be incidents of complexity's strange attractors concept. Ed Yourdon had been writing a monthly software development research report for Cutter and wanted to move on. Anne asked if I might be interested in authoring the report.

I said yes and ended up with my first writing job that had a fixed monthly deadline. This 16-page report on some aspect of development required that I decide on a topic each month, research it, draft the report, and work with the editors to refine it, so Cutter could get it into snail mail each month. The report started out with the title "Application Development Strategies" and then shifted to "e-Business Application Development." It was fun, a great learning experience, anxiety producing, and daunting all at the same time. In two years (1998–2000), I wrote on topics as varied as outsourcing, managing distributed teams, application servers, and knowledge management. I attended conferences as part of the press, giving me access to people with whom I would not have interacted otherwise. I went on to work with Cutter for 10 years.

Additional agile roots[10]

By the middle of the 1990s, I realized I wasn't alone. I found an early Scrum paper, "Scrum Development Process," written by Ken Schwaber and Jeff Sutherland in 1995. In turn, Jeff and Ken's work was based on a 1986 article, "New New Product Development Game" (the double "new" is correct) by Hirotaka Takeuchi and Ikujiro Nonaka in the *Harvard Business Review.*

In the early 1990s, there was an "agile manufacturing" consortium. I didn't delve into it, except to note the software community wasn't the first to use the word "agile."

Jeff DeLuca developed feature-driven development (FDD) in part based on his work on a 15-month, 50-person software development project at a large Singapore bank in 1997. Jeff, an Australian, had been using a

---

10. Additional information on agile methodologies can be found in *Agile Software Development Ecosystems*, my overview of Agile book (Highsmith, 2002).

streamlined, lightweight process framework for many years. Peter Coad, who was brought in to develop the object model for the project, had been advocating a granular, feature-oriented development framework but hadn't embedded it in any particular process model. These two threads—one from Jeff and the other from Peter—came together on this project to fashion FDD. I talked with Jeff several times about FDD and the Singapore project.

In the fall of 1999, I exchanged manuscripts with Kent Beck—my *ASD* manuscript for his *eXtreme Programming Explained* (2000) manuscript. We instantly recognized our common ground, which led to Kent's invitation to attend an XP meeting in Rogue River, Oregon, a precursor to the Agile Manifesto meeting. It was an auspicious beginning to the next decade, which both produced new friends and launched the agile movement.

The Dynamic Systems Development Method (DSDM) was a formalization of RAD practices that arose in the early to mid-1990s. DSDM was another "professional" RAD methodology. It originated in England and became popular in Europe, but was less extensively adopted in the United States. DSDM has proven to be a viable methodology for many companies.

As DSDM evolved, the meaning of the DSDM words changed, until finally the DSDM Consortium decided to just use DSDM, without explanation of what the letters stood for. In the beginning, according to my exchange with Dane Falkner[11] the first "D" was for "dynamic," reflecting the ability to adapt to on-the-fly changes, and the "S" reflected a focus on business "solutions." At the time the Agile Manifesto was written, Arie van Bennekum, DSDM Consortium board member, represented DSDM.

I wasn't aware of Alistair Cockburn's Crystal methods until later, but the genesis of his ideas was in the Roots decade, as were those of Lean development. Other individuals and teams were working in a lightweight (the early designation for agile) fashion, but as yet had drawn little attention.

At the Software Development conference (organized by *Software Development* magazine) in 1997, I met Martyn Jones, CEO of Software Education in Wellington, New Zealand. Martyn invited me to give a keynote address at his software conference in the fall of 1997. He and his staff were a joy to work with, and this visit began a decade of travels to New Zealand and Australia working with SoftEd clients and speaking at conferences. Martyn was an early promoter of agile methods "down under," and he remains a colleague and friend to this day. At the 1997 conference, I also met Martin Fowler (I have to be careful with Martyn and Martin to keep them straight), another

---

11. Dane Falkner was then the chair of the North American DSDM Consortium (in 2001) and president of Surgeworks, a U.S. company that provided DSDM training and consulting services.

one of those serendipitous meetings that had unforeseen agile movement consequences. Martin, Martyn, Steve McConnell, and I got together at the SoftEd conference in 2002 (Figure 4.5).

Figure 4.5 *Software Education's 2002 conference brochure. (Courtesy of Skills Consulting Group Limited.)*

Era observations

In the 1990s, the methods and methodology of software development continued to be deterministic and formal, but slivers of RAD and iterative development began to creep in, especially for rapidly expanding Internet applications. Serial, waterfall structures dominated business and IT, but exciting new team structures were being experimented with. The mindset of people as cogs in a machine was being replaced by one of organic, self-organizing teams. The seeds of the agile movement were solidly in the sprouting stage.

An example of the mindset that gave rise to Monumental Methodologies—that is, the view of people as being cogs in the machinery of process—was published in a *Computerworld* article (Anthes, 2001; no longer available online) about Ashutosh Gupta, CEO of Deutsche Software India, a subsidiary of Deutsche Bank AG. Although the following passage was published in 2001, it exemplifies the culture agilists were complaining about in the 1990s.

> "There is this myth that software development is a creative effort that relies heavily on individual effort," says Gupta from his air-conditioned office high above the din of traffic-clogged Mahatma Gandhi Road. "It is not. It is just very labor-intensive, mechanical work once the initial project definition and specification stage is past." (Anthes, 2001)

One phrase that arose during this Roots of Agile era was building a "software factory." It epitomized the traditional approach to software development the Agile era sought to change: deterministic, people as cogs in the machine, and hierarchical—not the baggage to carry into the dynamic, uncertain, rapidly moving, technological-boom early years of the twenty-first century.

Whenever you propose something radically new, you need a foil, a windmill to tilt against. For early agilists, that foil was waterfall life cycles and monumental methodologies, which were railed against in articles and books. I remember getting rebuked at a conference for saying negative things about the CMM. You might conclude from agilists' rhetoric that structured and monumental approaches never delivered anything useful—and you would be wrong. Having worked on and with teams of developers during this era, I know we delivered tremendous value. Systems may not have been delivered fast enough or proved useful enough or as easy to maintain as envisioned, but practitioners certainly built a base for the next two eras.

Selling new ideas requires touting the advantages of the new and pointing out the deficiencies of the old. Structured methodologists railed against the deficiencies of no structure. Agilists railed against too much structure. Kanban proponents railed against agile sprints.

Agile pioneers needed an adventurous spirit—they pursued new experiences and thoughts and were willing to learn from experimentation. Adventurous undertakings led to innovations that occurred when plans went awry, and one ventures into the unknown. Kent Beck energized a generation of programmers venturing into the unknowns of Extreme Programming. He took risks and faced criticism but persisted. Jeff Sutherland and Ken Schwaber dared upend their own Monumental Methodology business to champion a nonprescriptive, empirically based approach with the odd-sounding name "Scrum."[12] These and other agilists were dissatisfied with the status quo and sought to focus on customers both inside and outside organizational walls. It really isn't a surprise agilists latched onto the concepts of complex adaptive systems, a scientific outlier, as a conceptual foundation that helped explain their outlandish approach to software development.

"There is no certainty; there is only adventure."
—Roberto Assagioli, Italian psychiatrist,
pioneer in the fields of humanistic
and transpersonal psychology

Looking back, the 1990s were pivotal years, for both technology and software development. As computer and network technology advanced repeatedly, developers had to respond in major ways. Eric Ries, author of the ground-breaking book *The Lean Startup* (2011), defines a pivot as "a change in strategy without a change in vision." Pivoting is an adaptive strategy required when things go wrong—not just a little wrong, but big-time wrong. It is a difficult behavior because the "go wrong" events damage one's pocketbook and ego. But good entrepreneurs and adventurers learn to pivot and move on, and many pivoters were needed in the 1990s.

I couldn't leave the Roots era without again acknowledging and thanking Tom DeMarco, Ken Orr, Larry Constantine, Jerry Weinberg, and Ed Yourdon. These software engineering and structured methods pioneers and luminaries, whom you might expect to resist the new methods, methodologies, and mindsets that would bring forth the agile revolution, did not.

---

12. Except to rugby aficionados.

They supported and encouraged me in a number of ways. Ken was initially skeptical of agile development, noting the problems with RAD, but we engaged in valuable back-and-forth conversations. He wrote a wonderful foreword to my *ASD* book. Tom responded positively to the agile movement and wrote the foreword to my second book, *Agile Software Development Ecosystems*. Larry contacted me about a gig that started my RAD work. Ed and Larry accepted multiple articles of mine for Ed's *American Programmer* magazine and Larry's management forum in *Software Development* magazine. Ed encouraged my participation in Cutter's annual conferences and wrote a favorable article about Extreme Programming in the then influential newspaper *Computerworld* in July 2001 (Yourdon, 2001). And lastly, Jerry introduced me to collaborative, self-organizing teams and helped in the development of *ASD*, for which I am most grateful.

The seeds of agility germinated in the early 1990s, sprouted in the late 1990s, and flowered after February 2001 with the writing of the Agile Manifesto. But without the germinating and sprouting, there would not have been any flowering.

5

The Agile Era

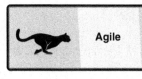

A FAD BLASTS into existence and delivers a quick rush of joy, but seldom lasts. A trend indicates a direction, solves a problem, and gains strength over time. A trend may eventually fade but it has longevity.

"A trend satisfies a different human need. A trend gains power over time, because it's not merely part of a moment, it's a tool, a connector that will become more valuable as other people commit to engaging in it."
—Seth Godin, Sethsblog/2015, August 21, 2015

Agile methods, methodologies, and mindset, after more than 20 years of gaining acceptance and use worldwide, appear to be a solid trend, not a fad. As the clock ticked over to a new century, teams were already using agile-like methods to add tremendous business value, as I found at Trimble Navigation.

Never do anything that is a waste of time and be prepared to wage long, tedious wars over this principle—that was the sentiment of Michael O'Connor, project manager of the Survey Controller team at Trimble Navigation in Christchurch, New Zealand. Michael proved once again that simplicity wasn't simple, but it was a cornerstone of his rather irreverent approach to software development.

Michael was prophetic in his internal battle to keep the company's methodology effective and simple. Corporate norms kept trying to increase order where it was unneeded. This chapter first describes the challenges companies faced as the twenty-first century got under way, then expands on the Trimble Navigation story illustrating how the agile movement sought to meet those challenges. My conversation with Martin Fowler about the unfolding impetus behind agile development (when the reference was to lightweight methodologies) then precedes the story of the Agile Manifesto's creation. Quickly thereafter, new organizations and conferences rose to support the movement. A brief overview of three agile methodologies is provided before identifying three distinct periods within the Agile era.

New challenges

As the new century began, change kept accelerating. The world was shaken by the World Trade Center and Pentagon terrorist attacks, which led to the Iraq War and two decades of troop deployments to Afghanistan. In the United States, Republican George W. Bush replaced Democrat Bill Clinton as president, who was then replaced by Democrat Barack Obama. The Enron scandal shook the financial world, taking down the Arthur Andersen accounting firm, and led to the passage of the Sarbanes-Oxley Act. Beginning before Obama took office and continuing into his first administration was the worldwide Great Recession. Rising pop music stars included Gwen Stefani and Beyonce. Continuing through the second decade of the twenty-first century and the beginning of the third, the COVID-19 pandemic and the Russia–Ukraine war left individuals, organizations, and countries worried about the economic and social impacts of these events.

The first two decades of the century would move the predictability level from chaotic to near disorder in the Cynefin framework. The transformations driven by the Internet would continue in high gear, technology would ramp up yet again, the pandemic would upset economies and individuals in ways yet undetermined, and the acceleration of climate change would overshadow the world.

Two decades into the twenty-first century, the old metaphor of "the light at the end of the tunnel being an onrushing train" isn't daunting enough. Today we see lights of various intensities, some of which are invisible, approaching on multiple tracks.

In 2003, Nicholas Carr wrote a controversial, and hugely mistimed, article in the *Harvard Business Review* titled "IT Doesn't Matter." In it, Carr argued that IT had become a commodity and, therefore, could not contribute to sustainable competitive advantage. Notably, this article emphasized the focus on cost reduction as the path to success for a commodity product.

Ten years later, Rita McGrath (2013), a professor at Columbia Business School, wrote that in today's fast-paced, uncertain world, sustainable competitive advantage itself was no more, and had been replaced by transient competitive advantage in which learning and adapting quickly were the tickets to success. In Carr's world, IT should be governed by cost considerations. In McGrath's world, responsiveness and customer value should drive IT. No wonder IT executives were perplexed. Here were two well-known management professors providing diametrically opposite views on the future of information technology.

AWASH IN THE TURMOIL of the business world, IT organizations faced five daunting challenges.

First, customer demand exploded. The opportunities dangled by the Internet and the fear of getting left behind redoubled the pressure on firms to churn out innovative customer-facing applications quickly. Acquiring and retaining technical talent proved difficult.

Second, as applications transitioned from automating internal business processes to satisfying external customer needs, companies had to innovate and expand their technical and product design capabilities. New specialties like user interface designer, product owner, data scientist, and experience designer required new investment. Some of these capabilities had already been adopted by Internet software companies, but for IT organizations, most were new.

Third, in the mid-to-late 1990s, organizations had to invest substantial resources in software maintenance to thwart the feared Y2K (Year 2000) "technical debt" problem. Because many legacy systems used a two-digit date field, a fear arose that when December 31, 1999, rolled over to January 1, 2000, chaos would ensue. Older companies spent hundreds of millions of dollars fixing these legacy systems problems while newer Internet companies had no such expensive baggage.

Fourth, technical debt (covered in Chapter 7), which had been growing rapidly, was still almost invisible to business executives, with the exception of the Y2K problem. IT staff struggled to convince business leaders to approve the investments required to reduce technical debt, thereby enabling continuous value delivery.

Fifth, IT organizations faced pressure from the high costs of IT. The challenges of the 1990s, the "ship everything to India" strategy, and their Y2K investments left many companies without the money or the talent pool to respond to the pressures of the 2000s. Not only was Y2K expensive, but those investments were also devoted to people with old skills (COBOL, Assembler, Fortran), not the new skills needed in the Internet era.

Adding to these trends was the cost-centric approach described by Nicolas Carr (2003). Just as businesses were trying to respond to these five challenges, an article in the *Harvard Business Review*—a publication highly respected by many CEOs—declared IT didn't matter. How many CIOs struggled to explain their investment budget requests to their CEOs and CFOs in the aftermath of this article? Monumental Methodologies were no longer up to the task of solving these problems, so agile methods took up the gauntlet.

Martin Fowler

In the summer of 2022, I talked with Martin Fowler to get his thoughts on what sparked the agile movement. Martin and I first met in New Zealand in 1997, and our paths continued to intersect over the next two decades, including our time together at Thoughtworks.

What do you remember from our first meeting in New Zealand?

Well, I went to this older guy's talk, expecting to hear about structured methods and traditional development. What you presented caused me to sit up and think, this guy understands an iterative, collaborative approach and has a handle on how complexity theory provides a conceptual basis for his methodology.

Why do you think agile concepts caught on?

I think a big factor was Ward's wiki.[1] That led to a lot of sharing of the details of Extreme Programming (XP). XP discussions sort of took over the wiki, which Ward had intended to be about patterns. It was a real trigger point talking about XP.

I started writing about these concepts for *Distributed Computing* magazine in the 1997–1998 time frame. The articles included "Keeping Software Soft" and "The Almighty Thud" (about documentation).[2]

---

1. Ward Cunningham invented Wiki and was one of the three early promoters of XP, along with Kent Beck and Ron Jeffries.
2. Both articles are available on Martin's website (martinfowler.com).

The XP story was developing from what happened at Chrysler, and that became a real trigger point for talking. I certainly wrote about stuff along those lines myself.

Another thing I did that may not be so obvious but may have had some impact was my *UML Distilled* book (Fowler, 1999; first edition, 1997) was extremely popular because UML was a thing at that time. I deliberately wrote Chapter 2 to basically subvert the movement towards heavy methodologies and talk about things like XP. I don't know if I mentioned XP by name. I certainly pushed in that direction because I wanted to push people away from the Monumental Methodologies.

It's interesting that structured diagrams from the 1980s were combined into Monumental Methodologies, and what you were trying to do, if I understand you, was to head that off with UML.

Yeah, I pointed people towards a way of thinking and towards early methodology books that talked about iterative styles. Kenny Rubin's book, for instance, or Grady Booch's (1995) *Object Solutions*. And I mentioned that Kent Beck was working on a book on project manager patterns and that it should be an excellent resource.

What else was being written at that time?

One of the things to bear in mind is these books, while pushing towards this more iterative style, weren't anywhere near as aggressive about it as XP was. The sense from them was you want to iterate every few months; maybe a six-month iteration seemed radical at the time. And then Kent goes to a month, or even two weeks. I think the other thing Kent really contributed was a notion that design can evolve, providing you've got good tests and a good way of evolving the design, which was refactoring.

What impact did Smalltalk have?

You could develop rapidly with Smalltalk in a decently modular, structured way that allowed you to evolve. Because you could build well with Smalltalk quickly, it opened a whole set of possibilities that were just otherwise unavailable to people at that time. Much of the focus on short iterations came out of people's experience with Smalltalk.

The seeds of agility came from a number of places and people, as Martin's comments suggest. Software developers came from different perspectives that were more, or less, amenable to the agile message. Todd Little, whose tireless promotion of agile development is described later in this chapter, added his perspective on this issue:

> I particularly enjoyed the pre-agile days as I lived a similar path, starting my career a bit later in 1979 at Exxon Production Research in Houston. While there were a lot of similarities, working on engineering software was a bit different than working on business systems. We were all chemical and petroleum engineers and never had the chasm between business and IT. We still had our Wild West period, but as I look back over my career, I avoided the mega methodologies even though I knew they were around. CMM was intriguing, but it just didn't jive with my engineering background or with how I had been developing software. I think what I experienced instead was more of a steadier evolutionary path from the Wild West to agility.

My work with Trimble further points out the upside, and the downside, of using nontraditional approaches to software development.[3]

Trimble Navigation[4]

I consulted and conducted a workshop on adaptive development for Trimble Navigation during one of my trips to New Zealand in August 2000. Trimble uses global positioning system (GPS) technology in a wide variety of products, including equipment for the land survey and construction markets. Its hand-held Survey Controller unit ran on a proprietary operating system and was a core piece of several products.

This Trimble engagement took place just prior to the Agile Manifesto meeting in 2001. I was still testing my approach, and I'm sure I learned as much from the Trimble staff as they learned from me. What they were already doing was another confirmation that the methods I was advocating

---

3. At a morning coffee session with Glen Alleman, who has significant experience with large, mission-critical aerospace systems, he reminded me there was a rich history of iterative, incremental development within aerospace systems development. I haven't delved into the roots of these systems since I don't have personal experience with them. I hope someone else writes about this segment of history.
4. The Trimble Navigation story presented here is an edited version from Highsmith (2002).

worked in practice. The sessions were also confirmation for them that they were not alone, that others were pursuing similar methods.

I was fascinated by their approach to teams. "We don't organize a new team around each project," said Michael, "we build up teams and then throw work at them." What a concept—keeping well-working teams together rather than continuously reorganizing them. The word *team* itself lost meaning in this setting.

The Survey Controller product team didn't use a particular named methodology approach. "We started with 'code-and-fix' with a lot of input from users and slowly adapted according to various ideas of good engineering, but with a severe eye to 'what actually works,'" said Michael. "We would basically invent a process for the current situation and apply it." Trimble's process included feature-driven, time-boxed delivery in which the dominant customer value was delivery schedule. Features were traded off as needed, and costs were of less importance.

Michael defined the team's process as "extremely" lightweight. Lightweight meant no written design documentation. "We tend to have written requirements and specifications, but we are currently looking to reduce the level of written material. Lightweight means accepting we cannot identify and control every little task. Lightweight means we don't submit much in the way of status reports. We tend to just try things rather than analyze them to death. Lightweight means we spend little time on estimates."

According to Michael, "We find we expend time to fend off other people's ideas about good practices." The team's improvement process was of continuous small changes, mostly simplifications.

This team developed a set of principles and values that defined their software "culture." Using a fascinating process, they constructed these definitions and wrote them down. In addition to the "Never do anything that wastes time" principle cited earlier, their cultural guides included:

- The orthodox is almost always wrong—and when it's right, it must be refitted for local conditions.

- Think hard about the code. There is nothing other than the code (except, maybe, the test cases). The most important attribute of the code is readability.

- The processes must be ordered around the people, not vice versa.

- Plan continuously but don't write plans down. (Actually, the teams do use whiteboards a lot.)

- Simple is good. It takes great skill to keep things simple.

"Projects have been very successful, as they are pretty much on time with the required functionality," said Michael. "The product is relatively bug free, and the product owner is very pleased with us."

However, Michael's lightweight process didn't excite other Trimble development groups. "We are too radical for other groups," Michael lamented. Other groups viewed the Survey Controller team as having a total lack of methods, rather than a set of lightweight methods focused on the essentials. This was a typical situation at that time as lightweight methods were labeled "ad hoc" by opponents.

The Agile Manifesto

Agility drives the future, touts the current literature (2018–2022)—in the *Harvard Business Review*, *Forbes*, *MIT Sloan Management Review*, and *McKinsey Insights*—with a growing landslide of articles advocating the necessity of IT and enterprise agility. But it wasn't this way in 2001. The rush to agility started with a trickle, from a few leaders in the management community, and from the agile software pioneers with the publication of the Agile Manifesto. By the year 2000, the roots of agile development were robust enough to support growth. As those of us engaged in these practices learned about other "light" methodologists and methodologies, the energy to get together and collaborate on what we were each doing separately accelerated. The first meeting was organized by Kent Beck in Oregon. It was followed by the now famous meeting at Snowbird, Utah, which announced the movement to the world.

Ultimately, this agile software movement propelled the transformation of software development. The initial agile trickle became a stream, then a river, and finally a flood that couldn't be stopped.

On February 11–13, 2001, at the Lodge at Snowbird Resort located near the top of Little Cottonwood Canyon in the Wasatch mountains of Utah, 17 people[5,6] met to talk, ski, relax, and try to find common ground.[7] What emerged was the Agile Manifesto. Representatives from Extreme

---

5. Seventeen people, all men. We have been criticized, and rightfully so, for the lack of diversity in the group.

6. Kent Beck, Mike Beedle, Arie van Bennekum, Alistair Cockburn, Ward Cunningham, Martin Fowler, James Grenning, Jim Highsmith, Andrew Hunt, Ron Jeffries, Jon Kern, Brian Marick, Robert C. Martin, Steve Mellor, Ken Schwaber, Jeff Sutherland, Dave Thomas.

7. This section contains an edited version of the manifesto history that I wrote and is posted on the Agile Manifesto website.

Programming, Scrum, DSDM, Adaptive Software Development, Crystal, feature-driven development, and pragmatic programming, and others sympathetic to the need for an alternative to documentation-driven, monumental software development processes, convened. Little Cottonwood Canyon hosts great recreational rock climbing and "champagne" powder skiing. The Snowbird Cliff Lodge itself has a 115-foot climbing wall on which some of the world's best climbers have competed.

The meeting at Snowbird was incubated at an earlier get-together of XP proponents, and a few "outsiders"[8] like me, organized by Kent Beck at the Rogue River Lodge in Oregon in the spring of 2000. At the Rogue River meeting, attendees voiced support for a variety of "light" methodologies, but nothing formal occurred. This meeting was my introduction to the movers and shakers of XP. During 2000, articles were written referencing the category of "light" or "lightweight" processes such as XP, Adaptive Software Development, Crystal, and Scrum. In conversations, no one really liked the moniker "light," but it seemed to stick for the time being.

In September 2000, "Uncle" Bob Martin initiated the next step with an email: "I'd like to convene a small (two day) conference in the January to February 2001 time frame here in Chicago. The purpose of this conference is to get all the lightweight method leaders in one room. All of you are invited; and I'd be interested to know who else I should approach." Bob set up a Wiki site and the discussions raged.

Early on, Alistair Cockburn weighed in with an epistle identifying the general disgruntlement with the word *light*:

> I don't mind the methodology being called light in weight, but I'm not sure I want to be referred to as a lightweight attending a lightweight methodologists meeting. It somehow sounds like a bunch of skinny, feeble-minded, lightweight people trying to remember what day it is. We hope our work together as the Agile Alliance helps others in our profession to think about software development, methodologies, and organizations, in new ways. If so, we've accomplished our goals.

A bigger gathering of adventurers and nonconformists would be hard to find, and what emerged from the 2001 meeting was symbolic—The

---

8. When I first wrote this section, it contained the phrase "others like Alistair and me." I was sure he was at that meeting—but during our discussion in mid-2022 he said it wasn't him. Memory is funny that way.

Manifesto for Agile Software Development—signed by all participants. We called ourselves the Agile Alliance.

Alistair Cockburn's initial concerns reflected the thoughts of many participants: "I personally didn't expect this particular group of agilists to ever agree on anything substantive." But his post-meeting feelings were also shared: "Speaking for myself, I am delighted by the final phrasing [of the Manifesto]. So, we did agree on something substantive."

The Agile Manifesto consists of four primary value statements and 12 principles, such as "Simplicity—the art of maximizing the amount of work not done—is essential."[9] The principles were hashed out over the next several months via Ward's wiki and email. We agreed on four values, and their wording, in two days. Getting 17 people to decide on and wordsmith the 12 wordier principles, however, went slowly—several months.

The Agile Manifesto

We are uncovering better ways of developing software by doing it and helping others do it.

Through this work we have come to value:

Individuals and interactions over processes and tools

Working software over comprehensive documentation

Customer collaboration over contract negotiation

Responding to change over following a plan

That is, while there is value in the items on the right, we value the items on the left more.

© 2001, the above authors this declaration may be freely copied in any form, but only in its entirety through this notice.[10]

---

9. All 12 principles can be found at http://agilemanifesto.org/principles.html.

10. I've included the notice because people miss it due to the small print on the Agile Manifesto webpage. The authors wanted to clearly state that the Agile Manifesto was for anyone to use—adopting an open-source model. In a brilliant move, Ward Cunningham added the signature page where individuals could comment—and tens of thousands did.

At the close of the two-day meeting, Bob Martin joked that he was about to make a "mushy" statement. But while his words were tinged with humor, few disagreed with Bob's sentiments—that we all felt privileged to work with a group who held a set of compatible values, a set of values based on trust and respect. We wanted to promote people-centered management. At the core, I believe agilists are about "mushy" stuff—about delivering great products to customers by building an environment where people matter— where mindset comes first, and methods and methodology follow.

> The Agile movement is not anti-methodology; in fact many of us want to restore credibility to the word *methodology*. We want to restore a balance. We embrace modeling, but not to file some diagram in a dusty corporate repository. We embrace documentation, but not hundreds of pages of never maintained and rarely used tomes. We plan but recognize the limits of planning in a turbulent environment. Those who would brand proponents of XP or Scrum or any of the other Agile Methodologies as "hackers" are ignorant of both the methodologies and the original definition of the term *hacker*. (Highsmith, 2001)

In his book *The Code Breakers*, Walter Isaacson (2021) tells the story of Jennifer Doudna and the discovery of CRISPR, the biotechnology that enabled Pfizer and Moderna to develop their vaccines for COVID-19 so rapidly. In the race to advance CRISPR's gene editing technology, Doudna and other scientists collaborated endlessly, sharing what they had learned about genes, DNA, and RNA to be of service to the medical community and patients. Of course, there was equally intense competition among the same players, especially in the races to publish first and to obtain patents. The scientists' collaboration was heightened a few years later as the community worked together to develop a COVID-19 vaccine. Collaboration of like-minded competitors, whether scientists or software developers, may offer the best solutions to the challenges of the early twenty-first century.

During the meeting at Snowbird, the attendees shared philosophies and details about each of their approaches. We discovered differences, but amazing similarities as well. There was no doubt that this collaboration produced a result that would have a profound and lasting impact on the world. There was also no doubt that we would leave the meeting and compete, just as the CRISPR scientists did. Several of us raced to publish new books on agile topics.

In an email, Alistair Cockburn reminded me about an incident that helps explain the collegiality and collaboration of the Snowbird meeting:

> At some point we were talking, wondering why Bob Martin had invited Steve Mellor because he didn't appear to be a light methodologist. Steve introduces himself, "Hi, I'm Steve Mellor and I'm a spy," and all of our eyes got big. Like, oh my gosh, you said it.
>
> Then there was this one particular moment with Ron [Jeffries] and me talking to Steve, and we frankly don't like his stuff. Right. Because he's got lots of drawings. The magical thing was we didn't attack, but began to ask questions, like, "What do you do after? Why do you do this?" And he said, "Well, my goal is from the pictures you push a button, and the code comes out." Ron says, "Yeah, but then you have to maintain the code and the pictures are all out of sync." And he goes, "No, no, no, you maintain the pictures. You should never touch the code again." Ron says, "So you mean that the pictures are the source language." He goes, "Yeah." And Ron and I both go: "We don't care what the source code language is. It could be pictures for all I care as long as I don't have to maintain it in two places." And Steve goes, "That's what I'm saying." I go, "Well, yeah, we're all onboard with that. Like, we don't think you can do it, but if that's your intention, we don't have any problems with the intention."
>
> And suddenly we're all on the same side of the table; suddenly we're in agreement. We don't agree his current techniques get there, but his intention is the same as our intention. Suddenly, we had a big agreement where we'd had a big disagreement before. So that kind of magic, you know, what happened, was what I called a very generous form of listening, listening with generosity, you don't see in most meetings.

Exchanges like this were responsible for all 17 attendees agreeing to the final Agile Manifesto value statements.

It's somewhat ironic that an iconoclastic bunch of techies launched a movement based on a fundamental belief that "individuals and their interactions" was paramount to success.

The Agile Manifesto meeting mirrored that belief, as it emerged not from a formal agenda with stated, desired outcomes, but rather from a collaborative, self-organizing environment that fostered innovation and surprise. This may be a missing link in many organizations between "doing" agile and "being" agile, especially at mid-management and executive levels. Agile teams work hard at collaboration (daily stand-ups, retrospectives, inceptions), which isn't an easy feat with cross-functional team members. How many management and executive meetings follow this example? Two client stories in Chapter 7 will examine how management's commitment to adopting agile practices makes a difference in the success of an organization's transition to agility.

DURING THE LATE 1990s, Unified Modeling Language (UML) became popular as it brought a variety of diagramming practices together. But, like the emergence of Monumental Methodologies in the 1980s, UML became subsumed into the newest Monumental Methodology—namely, the Rational Unified Process (RUP).

In addition to incorporating UML diagrams, RUP included process guides, a life cycle that could be interpreted as iterative, and an online knowledge base. As agile approaches became popular, RUP proponents argued their life cycle was indeed iterative and you could simplify the process for smaller projects. Unfortunately for them, neither of these assumptions proved viable to the agile community. Large IT organizations continued to use the RUP life cycle as a waterfall approach, and it was too easy to keep "stuff" rather than take a chance with simplification. Agile practitioners continued to exclude RUP as an agile, or even iterative, methodology.

In an XP discussion group about vendors promoting their methodologies as tailored to smaller projects, Larry Constantine chimed in:

> However, doing XP by way of RUP strikes me as a little like buying an expensive 18-wheel moving van, then throwing away the trailer, chopping down the cab, swapping the diesel for an economical 4-banger, and adding extra seats to have a sprightly little runabout for getting quickly around town with the kids and the groceries. If you must pay the price, perhaps this approach is better than nothing, but it seems that doing XP simply by doing XP would be cheaper and more efficient.

Agile organizations

Once the Agile Manifesto was released, momentum grew rapidly, driven by the Manifesto authors launching the Agile Alliance, new books, continuing Extreme Programming conferences, and a growing blizzard of papers.

Just prior to the Manifesto meeting, I wrote the cover article, "Retiring Lifecycle Dinosaurs," in *Software Testing & Quality Engineering* (Highsmith, 2000).

In the fall of 2001, Martin Fowler and I wrote the cover article in *Software Development* magazine, "The Agile Manifesto" (Fowler and Highsmith, 2001), pictured in Figure 5.1. Looking at this magazine recently, I was struck by the subtitle, which included the phrase "17 *anarchists* agree on... ." That same fall, Alistair Cockburn and I wrote "Agile Software Development," in *IEEE Computer* (Highsmith and Cockburn, 2001). Meanwhile, others were writing about Scrum, XP, and DSDM[11] agile practices. Alistair and I became co-editors of Addison-Wesley's Agile Series, which featured a dozen books by 2010.

Figure 5.1 *The first major article on the Agile Manifesto.*

---

11. DSDM originally stood for "Dynamic Systems Development Methodology." However, the Agile Business Consortium now uses just DSDM as the name.

In the years after the release of the Agile Manifesto, several organizations formed to promote agile methods, methodologies, and mindset: The Agile Alliance, Agile Conferences, the Agile Project Leadership Network (APLN), the Scrum Alliance, and Scrum.org.

THE AGILE ALLIANCE, officially chartered in late 2001 with fewer than 50 members and a huge budget of $7,350, has certainly grown since its founding. As of 2021, the Alliance had more than 8,500 members, a newsletter audience of 70,000-plus, and an operating budget of more than $4 million. Since 2001, the Agile Alliance has been informing and inspiring people and organizations as they explore, apply, and expand the values, principles, and practices outlined in the Agile Manifesto.

While writing the Agile Manifesto, the attendees began referring to ourselves as the Agile Alliance, but there was no formal organization. During 2001, organizational issues were churning that resulted in the founding board meeting on November 19, 2001, in Chicago. Some Manifesto authors wanted to participate in the formal Alliance, others didn't. The attendees at this meeting included Mike Beedle, Ron Crocker, Jim Highsmith, Bob Martin, Ken Schwaber, Mary Poppendieck, Grady Booch, Steven Fraser, Chet Hendrickson, Jacqui Horwitz, Jon Kern, Linda Rising, Dave Thomas, and Martin Fowler.[12] Our objective was to grow the movement, but few had any idea about how widespread it would become.

Today, the multinational Agile Alliance provides educational materials (books, research, blogs, meetups), support for local events and groups, and its cornerstone—large conferences. In addition to a diverse volunteer board (in 2022) of 10 members representing 7 countries, it now has a director and other paid staff. The Agile Alliance has had a managing director for more than 15 years. Phil Brock served for 13 years before he resigned in 2020.

---

12. In researching for this book, I found copies of the original board minutes, budgets, and constitution for the Agile Alliance in my archived files. I forwarded these to the current Alliance staff.

Agile Alliance Today[13]

Agile Alliance is a global non-profit membership organization founded on the Manifesto for Agile Software Development. We support people and organizations who explore, apply, and expand Agile values, principles, and practices.

Our membership consists of a thriving and diverse community of more than 72,000 people who share those interests.

Our membership and staff enable the Alliance to provide a global set of resources, events, and communities to help people reach their full potential and deliver innovative solutions like never before.

Agile Alliance undertakes a variety of activities to build an inclusive global community, advance the breadth and depth of Agile, and provide value to members. Those activities include:

Conferences that bring the Agile community together face to face

A website full of information about Agile and the Agile Community Membership that provides access to valuable resources created by community members

Initiatives that address specific areas of interest in the Agile Community and provide support for Local Community Groups

While there had been an XP conference for several years, as of early 2002 no Agile conference was on the horizon. In the summer of 2002, Alistair Cockburn and I had one of those "back of the napkin" meetings to outline what an Agile conference would look like. Ken Schwaber then joined in the planning, and we decided on June 25–28, 2003, in Salt Lake City, as the inaugural dates and secured a venue. I moved from Salt Lake City to Flagstaff, Arizona, leaving Alistair with much of the planning (he's never let me forget my bailing out on him). Todd Little stepped in and became an early and regular organizer for the conferences.

Todd was instrumental in promoting agile, as an implementer in his companies and in organizing industry events. While Alistair and I initiated the conference, Todd knew how to actually organize one. I met Todd during a 1998 Software Development conference in San Francisco, and he

---

13. From Agile Alliance website: www.agilealliance.org/the-alliance/.

invited me to speak at his internal Landmark Graphics (part of Halliburton) conference in 1999. During the early fall of 2002, Alistair, Todd, and I attended the Cutter Consortium's Summit conference in Boston, where we recruited Todd (it wasn't hard) to help organize the first Agile conference. Todd went on to chair many Agile conferences, was an Agile Alliance board member, and served as a co-founder and board member of the Agile Project Leadership Network (APLN). The Manifesto launched the agile movement, but the hard work and dedication of individuals like Todd ensured that the launch vehicle achieved orbit.

From notes and memory, Todd emailed additional details about the meeting in Boston.

> One evening a group of us went to the MIT museum as part of an outing organized by the Cutter Conference. It was there I first met Alistair. We hit it off quite well from the get-go, and as our group was walking back to the hotel we ended up stopping at the Miracle of Science Bar & Grill. After a couple of drinks Alistair pulled out a couple of pieces of paper with some drawings on them. He passed them around and asked the group which we preferred as a logo for an Agile conference he was planning. Of course, this piqued my interest as I had quite a bit of experience organizing Landmark Graphics Worldwide Developer conferences over the past few years.
>
> After a quick assessment of the logo options, the conversation quickly moved towards some of the things we had done at our internal conferences that might be of interest. I started by explaining what we had done to build our community and to bring people together. We had a saying in our company about "How can you build integrated software solutions unless you integrate the people?" Of course, this was music to Alistair's ears as he had long been an advocate for the human side of software development.
>
> The next evening, we had a great chat along with barely sufficient documentation on the back of a napkin (Figure 5.2). We agreed on a general vision and kicked off a great friendship with Alistair. While the napkin was just enough to get things rolling, Alistair did later create a charter document for the conference which was quite helpful to anchor our efforts.

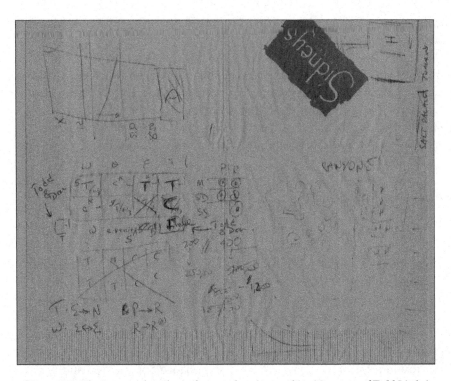

Figure 5.2 *The inaugural Agile conference planning napkin. (Courtesy of Todd Little.)*

The first Agile Development Conference was designed to foster and grow an agile community during and after the conference (Figure 5.3 shows the conference invitation cover). The design included traditional speaker presentations, but also guided informal sessions on key topics. Agile was new, generating a buzz of excitement in the air. This first conference was a success—programs and discussions received good reviews. About 250 people attended, and it made a little profit. The last point was particularly relevant for Alistair, Ken Schwaber, and me, as we had guaranteed to cover any shortfall. Todd chaired the next several conferences as attendance grew to 300 over the next couple of years, and then to 700 as the XP and Agile conferences were merged, and then ramped up to 1,100. In the years before the pandemic, conference attendance was capped at 2,500 (see Figure 5.4). As with any fast-growing movement led by opinionated individuals, there were a few bruised egos and feelings during the growth period. However, the results were spectacular, and bruises healed. There were no broken bones that I know of.

Figure 5.3 *Agile Development Conference invitation, 2003. (Courtesy of Todd Little.)*

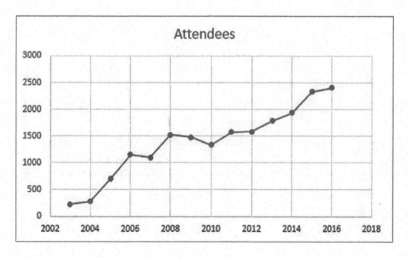

Figure 5.4 *Growth in Agile conference attendance. (Courtesy of Todd Little.)*

Two years after the first Agile conference, the XP conference was blended into the Agile conference (after intense negotiation) under the auspices of the Agile Alliance. However, the Alliance continued to sponsor separate XP conferences, and a growing number of others.

THE AGILE PROJECT Leadership Network (later named the Agile Leadership Network) was launched over the course of three meetings. The first was an impromptu meeting that I initiated at the 2004 Agile Development Conference in Salt Lake City to gauge the interest in a project management group separate from the Agile Alliance. This was followed by a second meeting in Chicago in October 2004. In late January 2005, we convened the third meeting at the Microsoft campus in Redmond, Washington. At these meetings, as well as in ongoing discussions on a Yahoo group, we discussed the role of project managers and project management in agile development and then formed the APLN.[14]

Attendees in Redmond were Sanjiv Augustine, Bob Wysocki, Preston Smith, Christopher Avery, Todd Little, Donna Fitzgerald, David Andersen, Ole Jepson, Alistair Cockburn, Doug DeCarlo, and Jim Highsmith. These attendees had a range of backgrounds in software development and project

---

The Declaration of Interdependence

We increase return on investment by making continuous flow of value our focus.

We deliver reliable results by engaging customers in frequent interactions and shared ownership.

We expect uncertainty and manage for it through iterations, anticipation, and adaptation.

We unleash creativity and innovation by recognizing that individuals are the ultimate source of value and creating an environment where they can make a difference.

We boost performance through group accountability for results and shared responsibility for team effectiveness.

We improve effectiveness and reliability through situationally specific strategies, processes, and practices.

---

14. Todd Little added to my memory and old email exchanges about these founding meetings, but any errors are mine alone.

management. For example, Preston Smith was an author (Smith and Rein-ertsen, 1997) and consultant on manufactured products. The results of that meeting were the finalization of the Declaration of Interdependence and preliminary organization of the APLN. Others contributing to the organizational process after that meeting included Mike Cohn, Pollyanna Pixton, Lowell Lindstrom, and Kent MacDonald.

The Redmond meeting was modeled after the Agile Manifesto conclave (Figure 5.5). At the time, there was sentiment in the agile community that "We don't need any darn project managers." The Redmond group didn't agree: We thought project management was essential, but project managers should have an agile mindset. We needed project managers who were adept at managing people first, rather than tasks. Part of this debate was terminology, part was redefining roles for project managers. Did the "project manager" name need to change to drive home the point something was new? The XP contingent debated the need for any project management, while others opted for a name change to accompany the role change. Strangely enough, I never heard a similar debate about changing the programmer/software developer name, even though XP redefined that role.

In the first two to three years, APLN meetings discussed program goals and action initiatives for our members. Our biggest success story was establishing local chapters. Several board members wrote a "cookbook" to assist local groups, and the national APLN provided a legal foundation. Several local groups that were established in the late 2000s continue still—in the San Francisco Bay area and Houston.

An ongoing debate—it lasted for two years—was whether to create an Agile Project Management certification program. At that point, the Project Management Institute (PMI) ran a traditional certification program that did not include agile. The Scrum organization had certification programs for the Scrum roles. But the non-Scrum agile community continued to debate the efficacy of certification. The APLN board was divided into three contingents: (1) those who supported certification and were quite comfortable with existing certification models, (2) those who generally opposed certification on the basis that agility was not inherently certifiable, and (2) the group in the middle, who were willing to consider certification but were not comfortable with what they called "certification 1.0." The concern was that traditional certification models were based on validation of learning against a relatively static body of knowledge, yet that was at odds with the nature of agility. The board sanctioned a group to investigate a certification program, but in the end voted to abandon further efforts.

Figure 5.5 *Alistair Cockburn and Jim Highsmith at the Redmond APLN meeting.*

The certification discussions, within the APLN and the wider agile community, boiled down to a debate between conformity and customer pressure. Given that the Agile Manifesto was created by 17 nonconformists, certifications were considered the ultimate conformity by many, as well as ineffective. But, argued the certification supporters, agile methods focus on customers, and a great many companies and individuals want some measure of capability certification. Do you give customers what *they* ask for, or what *you* think they *should* want? While much of the surface debate centered on the issue of certification's effectiveness or ineffectiveness, the larger issue was often missed. This quandary exemplifies a paradox on which the answer to the certification question depended: If we only give customers what they ask for, do those asks become the sole source of new product ideas? Do we give customers what they ask for, even if we think it's wrong? One of the leadership skills required in our fast-moving world is the "riding paradox"—separating problems, for which there are solutions, from paradoxes, for which there are only resolutions that will change with time. Certification seems to be one of these paradoxes.

The APLN continued for several more years, but never gained traction in the wider project management community. PMI began offering an Agile Project Management certification in 2011. The APLN was now competing with the Agile Alliance, PMI, and the various Scrum organizations. The APLN sponsored several local conferences, but negotiations with the Agile

Alliance to host the project management part of the Agile conference were unsuccessful. Without the funding mechanism of either a certification program or a major conference, the national APLN (by then the Agile Leadership Network) didn't survive.

Agile ecosystems

Over the years, there had been confusion over the umbrella term *agile* and specific methodologies such as Scrum and XP. To head off the confusion, prior to the Agile Manifesto gathering, I began thinking about a survey book on agile methods. During the Manifesto meeting, I interviewed participants for this second book, which was ultimately titled *Agile Software Development Ecosystems* (*ASDE*; Highsmith, 2002).

The *ASDE* book surveyed the methodologies represented in the Manifesto meeting. It included interviews with agile luminaries: Kent Beck, Ken Schwaber, Martin Fowler, Ward Cunningham, and Alistair Cockburn. Tom DeMarco wrote a wonderful foreword that included these words:

> The nineties were the Decade of Process for IT. We prostrated ourselves before the CMM and ISO. We sought not just perfection in the way we built software, but total predictability. We concluded that it wasn't enough just to do things right, we also had to "call our shot": to say in advance exactly what we intended to do, and then do exactly that. Nothing more and nothing less. We were determined (in CMM terms) to "plan the work and work the plan."
>
> Today the era of fat process is over. As Jim Highsmith has said, "Thin is in." To optimize speed and responsiveness, we need to put process on a diet. We need to shed paperwork and bureaucratic burden, eliminate endless code inspections, and invest in our people so they can steer themselves sensibly through the chaotic maze that is a modern-day IT project. This is the genesis of the Agile approaches to software development. (Highsmith, 2002, pp. xv–xvi)

For each methodology, I interviewed key players—for example, Kent Beck and Ward Cunningham for XP, Ken Schwaber for Scrum. Transcribing, editing, and getting feedback on these interviews was the single hardest part of writing this book, but also proved to be of high value to readers.

I used the term *ecosystem* to describe a holistic mindset that included three interwoven components—a chaordic[15] perspective, collaborative

---

15. The word *chaordic* was coined by Dee Hock.

values and principles, and a barely sufficient methodology—and the term *agilists* to identify those who are proponents of agile methodologies.

One telling quip came from Ken Schwaber, who in the 1990s was CEO of Advanced Development Methods. His company's product MATE (Methods and Tools Expert) automated its structured methodology. Ken related a conversation he had with Jeff Sutherland (co-creator of Scrum):

> At some point Jeff asked me, with all these methodologies—Coopers', IBM's, our own, etc.—which one did we use for building our MATE product? "None," I said. "If we used any of them, we'd be out of business!" So, we sat down with our own developers and asked them what they actually did, how they worked. And the answers were quick turnaround, evolving object diagrams, adaptive requirements evolved, and that everything kept getting better and better.

Agile methodologies

These next narratives reflect the state of three specific agile methodologies in 2002 when I conducted these interviews for *ASDE*. They focus on the philosophies and the contributions of each since the methods and methodologies have evolved considerably since then. So, when you read the overview of Scrum and it mentions Scrum has been in use for nearly 10 years, that period reflects that this piece was written in 2002. These edited sketches provide a benchmark showing how much these methodologies have changed—and haven't changed—over the last 20 years.[16]

SCRUM, NAMED FOR the scrum in rugby, was initially developed by Ken Schwaber and Jeff Sutherland, with later collaborations with Mike Beedle and others. Scrum provides a management framework that organizes development into 30-day Sprint cycles[17] in which a specified set of backlog features is delivered. A core practice in Scrum is the use of daily stand-up team meetings for coordination and integration. Scrum has been in use for nearly 10 years and has been used to successfully deliver a wide range of products.

---

16. These sketches are edited versions from *ASDE*.
17. Cycles are shorter or even continuous these days.

In 1996, Ken Schwaber wrote an article for *Cutter IT Journal* titled "Controlled Chaos: Living on the Edge." Even at this early date, Ken brought an understanding of complexity theory to software development and project management.

Ken, an expert in rigorous, process-centric methodologies, began to realize the increasingly detailed and specific methodologies—overburdened with phases, steps, tasks, and activities—had a fundamental flaw. "The core of the Scrum approach is the belief that most systems development has the wrong philosophical basis," Ken says. He asserts software development is not a "defined process," as rigorous methodologies assume, but an "empirical process."

In his investigation of industrial process control, Ken discovered the differences between defined and empirical processes were not only profound, but also required a completely different management style. A defined process draws heavily on fundamental physical and chemical laws that "define" the transformation of inputs to outputs. Defined processes can be repeated time after time with little variation. An empirical process doesn't conform to scientific laws, so it cannot be consistently "repeated"; hence, it requires constant monitoring and adaptation. "Developers and project managers are forced to live a lie—they have to pretend they can plan, predict, and deliver," says Ken. You can, however, bound the empirical process with explicit monitoring criteria and manage the process itself with constant feedback mechanisms.

Traditional project management practices assume projects are predictable and variations from the "plan" are caused by poor execution. Scrum (and other agile software development ecosystems) views work as unpredictable and trusts people are doing their best under the circumstances. Therefore, project management should emphasize communication, collaboration, coordination, and knowledge sharing.

Defined processes depend on repeatability, an impossibility for processes besieged by constant changes and a lack of formulaic transformation. Empirical processes can spin out of control quickly, so the key to success is constant monitoring via the daily Scrum meeting and Sprint Backlog Graph, while at the same time facilitating the creativity required to solve complex problems.

Scrum says, "Do these few things well, and projects will succeed." Furthermore, "If you don't do these few things well, it doesn't matter how many other hundreds of things you do well, you won't succeed."

EXTREME PROGRAMMING (XP) exploded onto the software development scene and hit a nerve that vaulted the entire agile category into the spotlight. Several reasons explain its success. First, its audience was developers, and there were legions of them in the world tired of "methodologies" getting in their way. Second, with the advent of the Internet, there was a perceived need for a development approach geared to speed, flexibility, and quality. Third, Kent Beck was an effective promoter. Fourth, Kent picked a great name— Extreme Programming—that targeted the developer audience and told the world there was something new, something "extreme" inside.

XP, as developed by Kent with later assists from Ward Cunningham and Ron Jeffries, promotes the values of community, simplicity, feedback, respect, and courage. Important contributions of XP were its view of the cost of change and its emphasis on technical excellence.

Although Kent didn't claim practices like pair programming and iterative planning originated with XP, this approach did include important new concepts. Kent had ideas about how to manage change—which explains the subtitle of his 2000 *eXtreme Programming Explained* book, *Embrace Change*. XP was derived from good practices that had been around for a long time. As Kent says, "None of the ideas in XP are new. Most are as old as programming." I might differ with Kent in one respect: While the practices XP includes weren't new, the explicit values and selecting practices that worked together were.

In the early days, XP offered specific practices for a well-defined problem domain—small, co-located teams. Kent wrapped the conceptual ideas of embracing change, collaborative teamwork, altering the often-dysfunctional relationships between customers and developers, and simple, generative rules into a set of 12 practices guided by a set of well-articulated principles.

ALISTAIR COCKBURN CREATED the Crystal family of people-centered methods.[18] Alistair is a "methodology archaeologist" who interviewed dozens of project teams worldwide trying to separate what worked from what people said *should* work. Alistair focused on the people aspects of development collaboration, good citizenship, and cooperation. He used project size, criticality, and objectives to configure practices for each member of the Crys-

---

18. Reminder: This is Alistair's work in 2002. He, and other agilists, have contributed much
    more since then.

tal family of methodologies. Software development is "a cooperative game of invention and communication," says Alistair.

Alistair proposed a "set" of methodologies from which teams could select a starting point and then tailor it to their needs. The name *Crystal* refers to the various facets of a gemstone—each a different face on an underlying core. The underlying *core* represents values and principles, while each *facet* represents a specific set of elements: techniques, roles, tools, and standards. There were only two absolute rules in Crystal: (1) Incremental cycles cannot exceed four months and (2) reflection workshops are used to ensure the methodology is self-adapting.

All too often, arguments over practices take on the proverbial "apples" versus "oranges" characteristics, because one side is talking about a 500-person aerospace project and the other side is talking about an 8-person web content project. Crystal's domain definitions help focus discussions, and methodologies, on appropriate problem domains.

Agile periods

While the Agile era spans more than 20-plus years, it encompasses several distinct periods and time frames, as shown in Figure 5.6. The Rogue Team period (2001–2004) began with the Agile Manifesto's release and extended for the next few years as the agile movement kicked into high gear. The movement took off much faster than the Agile Manifesto authors had expected— although the truth is we didn't really know what to expect. Its evolution moved along two tracks. The first was focused on industry promotion—writing papers, speaking at conferences, organizing conferences. The second was putting these ideas into practice in organizations. In this first period, agile methodologies were adopted overwhelmingly by individual teams. They wanted to be in the forefront but first had to convince their management to let them try it.

The Courageous Executive period (2005–2010) followed as enterprise leaders grew curious about the agile stuff. The Rogue Team period, by contrast, had been driven from the bottom up. Evangelists (there was plenty of evangelizing in the early years) who had worked on successful teams tried to convince upper management to make an enterprise switch—and mostly failed.

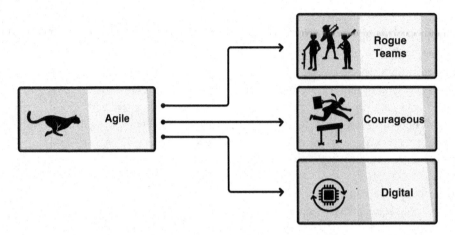

Figure 5.6 *Agile periods.*

But, while progress was often slow, the critical influencers continued to push forward, then back, then forward again. As the agile movement gathered momentum, as measures of success changed, and as the business environment demanded even more performance, agilists began to have conversations with senior leaders who wanted their organizations to "go agile." They often didn't really understand what they were asking for, nor were they realistic about what it would take to make the transition, but they forged ahead anyway.

Courageous executives saw the value proposition and began to think about comprehensive implementations. For example, Salesforce, one of the earliest companies to fully embrace agile development, used its ability to speed delivery and adapt to scale rapidly, winning the top spot in *Forbes* magazine's top 100 innovators list several years in a row.

The Digital Transformation period (2011–2021) addressed agility at the enterprise level. As the agile movement entered its second decade, the momentum shifted from courageous IT executives to enterprise executives— from CIOs to CEOs. In 2010, IBM interviewed more than 1,500 CEOs and published its findings in *Capitalizing on Complexity*:

> Our interviews revealed that CEOs are now confronted with a "complexity gap" that poses a bigger challenge than any factor we've measured in eight years of CEO research. Eight in 10 CEOs expect their environment to

grow significantly more complex, and fewer than half believe they know how to deal with it successfully. (IBM Corporation, 2010)

Technology was creating vast opportunities for organizations but capitalizing on them created vast challenges at the same time.

Era observations

Many software engineers, who had spent the previous decade bringing structure and discipline to software development, were concerned about the nascent agile movement. They viewed agile development as a retreat to ad hoc practices of the past. However, anyone watching a skilled XP team practicing test-driven development, refactoring, pair programming, and story planning, while documenting their work using whiteboards, story cards, and flip charts, could tell team members were highly disciplined, but worked somewhat informally. Agile (XP in this case) shifted the emphasis from documentation to collaboration, replacing traditional formality.

Another off-putting issue with agile development was agilists' "extreme" positions. Detractors missed the point. Agilists were testing how far to push practices. The XP community focused on critical technical practices and pushed them to the limits—to the extreme—which did the industry a great service. At one conference I heard Ron Jeffries question limits: "If agile development says reduce documentation, what if we don't do any?" That didn't mean Ron thought no documentation was universally good (although I'm not sure about that), but rather that it was okay for a small, co-located team. Additional formalization would be necessary for larger, distributed teams or life-critical applications such as medical pacemakers. Ron went on: "If a little upfront planning is better than months of planning, what about continuous incremental planning? If frequent testing is good, what about test-first?" By pushing the limits, new possibilities were uncovered.

Exploring the limits identified edge cases. Understanding those edge cases gave us a better understanding of the range of options available. Before XP came to the fore, people thought in much narrower ranges about what was "acceptable (iteration length, for example)." This exploration of the edges was critical in the early stages of the agile movement—we had to take extreme positions to get people's attention. Would anyone have listened if Kent Beck had developed "moderate programming?"

Detractors also missed a core agile mindset—learning and adapting. From end-of-iteration team reflections to end-of-project retrospectives, true agilists are always adjusting their practices to the reality of what worked and what didn't.

Another misconception voiced was that agilists didn't invent anything new. Biologist John Holland (1989), writing about complex adaptive system theory, says creativity comes not only from some new scientific theory, but also from people who put scientific building blocks together in a new way—in essence, creating something new. While there are early roots for every agile method, agile methodologies are a combination of (1) "selected" methods (old and new) from the realm of technical, project management, and collaboration practices; (2) a well-stated mindset of fundamental values and principles; and (3) an integration of these ideas into a methodology. Kent Beck didn't "invent" most of the 12 XP practices, but he did assemble 12 that were complementary, consistent, and effective together. He energized these practices with specific values. While each individual piece of XP may not be Kent's innovation, the combination certainly was.

As a final observation, I want to repeat something I wrote about in the preface—that braiding the evolution of software development with my personal stories gave me a basis for limiting the scope of this book. Every Agile Manifesto author, and others, have a set of similar stories to mine. Thus, my history of the agile movement is distinctly my viewpoint—with luck, a lens rather than a bias. Maybe *Wild West to Agile* will inspire someone else to write a comprehensive agile or Scrum history.

6

Rogue Teams

(2001–2004)

IN MID-2002, Alias Systems (now part of Autodesk) in Toronto, Canada, started developing Sketchbook Pro, a software package to be announced concurrently with the launch of Microsoft's Tablet PC operating system that fall. I worked with Kevin Tate, their chief architect, to introduce them to Adaptive Software Development to assist the company in responding to a new market initiative.[1] The product management and software development team didn't begin with a lengthy product planning effort. The team's marketing and product strategy evolved over several months, but development effort began early, and in parallel with the strategy process. The team had a vision—an easy-to-use, consumer-focused sketching product worthy of a professional graphics artist—and a deadline, the November Microsoft launch date. Alias's principal product was a professional graphics and animation package for movie studios. Walls in their offices were plastered with movie pictures.

With Sketchbook Pro, the team literally didn't know past the next iteration which features would be included in subsequent development as the product evolved in two-week iterations. For each iteration, a short planning session identified features to be developed. Then, within the constraints of the Tablet architecture and a fixed delivery date, the product evolved iteration by iteration. Team members did have a clear product vision and a

---

1. The Alias Systems story is an edited version of the tale first published in *Agile Project Management* (Highsmith, 2009).

business plan. They did have a general idea about which features were needed in the product. They did have active involvement from product management. They did have an absolute time deadline and resource expenditure constraints. Within the boundaries set by this vision, business objectives and constraints, and overall product roadmap, they delivered tested features every two weeks and then adapted their plans to the reality of product reviews. The team's process was one of envisioning and adapting, not planning and doing.

In the end, the product was delivered on time, met high-quality standards, and continues to be successful in the marketplace. The product wasn't planned and built, but rather was envisioned and evolved. Alias didn't start with architecture models, plans, and detailed specifications—it began with a vision, followed shortly by the first iteration of the product. The product, the architecture, the plans, and the specifications evolved as the team adapted to the ever-unfolding reality of the market and the technology.

Sketchbook Pro epitomized the need for an envision–explore rather than a plan–do approach to development. First, this was an "exploration" project—a new venture into a retail market and a new mobile device. A plan–do approach might have taken half of the six months simply to complete the plan and requirements, leaving a nearly impossibly small development period.

With any project, when push comes to shove (and it always does), something must give. With traditional projects, the "give" was usually quality. Agile practices use time as a constraint, not an objective, meaning something else must give when things change. In this case, it meant features needed to be trimmed or deferred. At the end of each iteration, the team responded to the same question: "Do we still think a viable, valuable product can be delivered on time?"

However, as the product launch date approached, the team opted to give a little on quality in the rush to finish. And then they did something unusual: They convinced management to give them time to refactor and further test to eliminate the tech debt accumulated. While managers grumbled about the cost, it was quickly forgotten when, a few months later, marketing came to the dev team with a new opportunity that they were able to implement quickly. Several of the managers then retracted their grumbles.

Alias approached Sketchbook Pro as a product requiring not a one-time delivery, but rather continuous delivery of value, iteration by iteration, release by release. It was a good call. Sketchbook Pro is still on the market in 2023, more than 20 years later!

This was a typical rogue project for these times, as Kevin Tate[2] brought in agile practices for this project but had a harder time convincing Alias's commercial product teams that agile development would work for them. The company's commercial product had more than 30 million lines of C++ code and extensive testing time was required, particularly for the overwhelming number of user options.

The Sketchbook team included about a half-dozen people, so this project was yet another confirmation that the agile approach worked for small co-located teams on projects that required innovation and speed. It also confirmed that the agile movement didn't yet have a viable message for legacy systems organizations.

THE PHRASE "ROGUE TEAM" personified the first Agile-era period from 2001 to 2004. Individual teams received dispensation to try this "agile" stuff, and occasionally organizations completed several successful agile projects. Then, organizational antibodies attacked, limiting further extension of agile practices. In this period, teams focused on iterations, stories, daily stand-ups, backlogs, iteration planning, and co-locating teams—but the core technical practices (automated testing, pair programming, continuous integration, test-driven development) were often bypassed. Teams, except those practicing Extreme Programming (XP), tended to focus more on iteration management practices than on technical practices. This unfortunate trend was countered by people like Mike Cohn, who integrated Scrum and XP in his teaching and consulting, and Kent Beck, Ron Jeffries, Josh Kerievsky, and others who continued to champion XP's technical practices.

In a conversation with Mike Cohn, he recounted a client interaction early in the Rogue Teams period. The vice president told Mike that the company had three agile teams and explained where to find them. Checking back at the end of the day, Mike told him about meeting with *four* agile teams. The vice president insisted there were only three. It turned out the fourth team was doing agile development surreptitiously. Their burndown charts and Kanban board were in their team area, but were well hidden from random traffic on the floor. Rogue, indeed!

Rogue teams were often siloed rather than cross-functional. While developers dramatically increased their unit testing and started automating

---

2. Kevin would go on to write his own agile book, *Sustainable Software Development: An Agile Perspective* (Tate, 2005).

testing, testing groups were often reluctant to join agile teams. Similarly, on the front end, getting near full-time participation from product management or internal users (called Product Owners in Scrum) proved difficult. Agile projects' success was often downplayed by others: "It was just a small project," "It was a green-field (new) project," "The project got the best talent," "They didn't have to follow our standards [as if the other teams did anyway]." Agile teams were informal, filling walls and whiteboards with story cards, flip chart designs, notes, diagrams, and more. Josh Kerievsky tells the tale of one successful rogue team who arrived at work one Monday morning to find their walls denuded. Another team, jealous of their success, had come in over the weekend and removed all their informal documentation!

Cutter and travels

As the agile trend got under way, my work with the Cutter Consortium increased; it is woven throughout this chapter, as are several client stories. In addition, the chapter contains an important technology update for the pivotal year, 2007, and a look at agile project management topics relevant to this era. During both the Rogue Teams and Courageous Executives eras, I worked with clients and promoted agile approaches by speaking at conferences, writing books and articles, and working with the Agile Alliance and Agile Leadership Network to promote, educate, and raise awareness of agile methods. Most of my promotional work was covered earlier in Chapter 5. This chapter focuses on client work, after a brief foray into my work for the Cutter Consortium and my various travels.

Early in this period I became the director of Cutter Consortium's agile project management consulting and research practice. As the Internet continued to adversely impact printed materials of all types, from magazines to books, we discontinued the e-business research report I had been writing, and I focused on client work and writing books. My consulting work in these early Agile-era years was with both software companies and internal IT departments.

During this time with the Cutter Consortium, I was also a fellow on the Cutter Business Technology Council, whose members at that time included Tom DeMarco, Ken Orr, Rob Austin, Karen Coburn, Tim Lister, Lou Mazzucchelli, Lynne Ellyn, Christine Davis, Peter O'Farrell, and Ed Yourdon. Several times a year, we published opinions on newsworthy IT topics. We used a process proposed by Tom DeMarco, who was a student of the U.S. Supreme Court.

The Cutter Business Technology Council approaches the identification of important new trends using a process adapted from the United States Supreme Court. While other analyst firms prognosticate without explaining how they reached their conclusions, making the whole process seem like guesswork, the Council's strongly worded opinions and concurring and dissenting opinions display the thinking behind the predictions, including and explaining any contrary views.[3]

Discussions were lively and enlightening. The process added remarkable depth to our conversations by having, and presenting, both pro and con opinions. It was yet another model for collaboration.

During the early years of the Agile era, I also spoke at a number of conferences, including the 2002 XP Conference in Sardinia, Italy. At some point, Martin Fowler casually invited me to a planning meeting for the next year's conference. Not knowing he had a hidden agenda, I ended up chairing the 2003 XP Conference in Genova, Italy. In this first period of the Agile era, I traveled extensively speaking at conferences, conducting workshops, and consulting in far-flung locations including India, Italy, China, Denmark, Australia, Germany, Poland, and New Zealand.

My client engagements during this period ran the gamut from single workshops to year-long engagements. The larger or noteworthy endeavors are described in their own sections later in this chapter, but a couple of the interesting shorter ones include trips to Poland and Australia.

In 2003, I conducted a workshop in Australia for Fujitsu Consulting. Karen Chivers, the company's senior consulting director and project management practice manager, had this to say in an email about their subsequent foray into agile development: "In the last 12–18 months, Fujitsu Consulting has seen the potential benefits of adopting 'Agile' approaches to the way we deliver and manage some of our projects and has encouraged our clients to embrace an 'Adaptive' project culture."

Government organizations were generally slow to investigate agile methods—but not Centerlink, the Australian social security service organization. In 2003, I gave the keynote address at its internal IT conference and had fruitful conversations with Centerlink's CIO and other senior managers.

Borys Stokalski, president of InfoVide, an IT consulting firm, invited me to Poland in 2004 to give a talk at his company's annual get-together, then

---

3. www.cutter.com

teach an Agile Project Management workshop. After this three-day workshop in Warsaw, Borys began offering adaptive/agile methods to their clients.

While teaching workshops in India in the early 2000s, I spoke at a meeting of the Computer Society of India in Mumbai. At that time, Indian companies were touting the Capability Maturity Model (CMM) as their competitive advantage. After my presentation, one individual spoke up: "Your approach is actually how we work; we just can't admit it." This was a whirlwind trip teaching Agile Project Management workshops in Chennai, Hyderabad, and Mumbai. Indian software organizations were still in the throes of the CMM, but seemed open to thinking about agile methods.

The Australia, Poland, and India travels just described represent typical engagements of mine during the Rogue Teams period. Enterprises were both curious and hesitant about agile approaches. Nevertheless, except for smaller firms, few were thinking about enterprise-wide implementations. The impetus for adopting agile methods came from developers, whereas Monumental Methodologies had been touted as best practices by management. Thinking back, structured methods followed a path of practitioner excitement first, management involvement later. There is a danger that agile development will follow the same path, turning it into Monumental Agile Development (MAD).

In 2005, I received the International Stevens Award, a software engineering lecture award given by the Reengineering Forum to recognize outstanding contributions to the literature or practice of methods for software and systems development. The award was given out from 1995 until 2005, and included contributors Larry Constantine, Grady Booch, Gerald Weinberg, and Tom DeMarco. It was another indication that the agile movement was being recognized in the wider software engineering and development communities.

My stories convey examples of the expanding interest in agile development. But all of the Agile Manifesto co-authors, and many others, have similar stories. Scrum, through its certification courses and the formation of the Scrum Alliance, extended the agile movement's reach further than any other agile approach did. While XP had the early lead in market share, Scrum quickly sucked up the rest of the oxygen in the market. Whether certification was truly effective was the subject of much debate. That certification made money was not debatable—it did.

As a consultant and director of the Cutter Consortium's Agile Project Management group, I spent considerable time with clients from a wide variety of industries, company sizes, countries, and stages of agility. The following engagements are explored here to illustrate a variety of agile implementations, challenges, and successes.

The Mustang Team at Cellular, Inc.[4]

Jeremy and his product team at Cellular, Inc., in Vancouver, British Columbia, epitomize the headaches, heartaches, and tensions of working in highly uncertain business environments. The product team—code-named "Mustang"—faced major business, organizational, and technical hurdles in its quest to make up a competitive deficit. The project's goal was to deliver software for next-generation cellular telephone chips. In late 1999, it became apparent that their outside software contractor was far from meeting expectations, so management decided to bring the product development back into the company. With nearly 300,000 lines of embedded C code already developed, their first job was to figure out just what the vendor had accomplished.

Once repatriated, the team realized what truly foul shape the code was in—300,000 lines of code in which the requirements were poorly implemented. Interestingly, the design documents were reasonable, but the translation from design to code was atrocious and very buggy. The team's first job was to stabilize the code by developing an adequate testing environment. As testing proceeded, the team was constantly finding specified features, which had supposedly been implemented, were just not there.

Product requirements were in a constant state of flux. The team's initial goal was to deliver software that met a consortium's set of standards. These large customers (major cellular phone suppliers) had established an interoperability lab to which suppliers submitted their products for certification. Unfortunately, the consortium's "requirements document" left many questions, and Cellular's product marketing group seemed unwilling—or unable (I heard only one side of the story)—to help clear up requirements ambiguities. Sometimes the requirements from prospects were virtually "make it do what *this* phone does." When the team finally submitted its product to the interoperability lab, the staff there were very willing to answer questions and eventually the team met its interoperability goal.

During this engagement, I conducted an Adaptive Software Development (ASD) workshop and consulted with the development staff and managers. I interviewed three key people: Jeremy was the development

---

4. This story is a briefer version of that presented in Highsmith (2002).

manager, Luke was the software process manager, and John was a key developer. Their perspectives had similarities and, naturally, some differences. Each of the three considered the project to be a success—at least from the perspective of meeting the interoperability goal. Luke, however, was not entirely convinced that this goal should be considered a true success, considering the actual product release was still several months away.

Constantly changing requirements frustrated the teams to the point they came up with a solution—freeze the requirements. While that solution might have eased frustration, it meant their customers wouldn't be happy. In a volatile industry, they needed to figure out ways to adapt to the market needs.

The team employed iterative planning and time-boxed release processes. I helped them tweak their process with components of ASD. They planned goals by quarter through year's end. These quarterly goals contained major functionality, but the team members had some latitude with features. They called this process "scrolling planning window with telescoping granularity." Thus, they always had a one-month plan with one-week granularity, a three-month plan with one-month granularity, and a one-year plan with one-quarter granularity. They referred to this methodology as time-boxing, because the release dates were all fixed and the only variable was the features assigned to each release.

Several team members, including John, were uncomfortable with this "adaptive" planning, as Jeremy referred to it. John felt that too much time was wasted getting ready for the monthly releases. Also, at times both he and Luke thought the time pressures of the short iterations forced the team into concentrating too much on getting features done rather than on trying to deliver better quality. Although the team members attempted to do some redesign (refactoring) work, they were in a different position than a team starting with a clean slate—they were constantly battling with the existing real-time code, and even their expensive testing equipment contained unruly bugs.

"Your Adaptive Software Development workshop helped reduce the level of anxiety in the group," Jeremy said, "by giving everyone an outsider's view that the turbulence and tension on this type of project are normal." I also heard from several supervisors and team leads. When people are unaware of the normalcy of life at the edge of chaos (and even sometimes when they are), they tend to react negatively. Unfortunately, some of the team leaders magnified the problem. To a team member's lament that "Everything is screwed up and getting worse daily," some of the leads would respond, "It sure is" (or words to that effect), which only amplified individuals' anxiety.

One of the jobs of people in leadership positions is to absorb uncertainty and ambiguity, not reflect it back and thereby worsen the situation. Just having someone admit things are somewhat chaotic, that situation is normal, and they realize some inefficiencies will occur can help relieve tension. The worst approach is attempting to deny the anxiety, as in "You shouldn't be anxious." Being agile means responding to changes requiring rework and revisiting priorities. Both process and attitude can contribute to easing the tension.

The experience of the Mustang team was typical of this period: They were attempting a form of agile development because of the high-change, high-risk nature of their product development. The team had concerns about their traditional methodology working for this effort, so they convinced management to allow them to go rogue for this effort. But again, their successful approach didn't catch on within the wider organization.

Technology (1995–2007)

This technology chronology differs from that of the eras identified elsewhere in this book because of two key inflection points. The first was the rapid rise of the Internet, which began in the early 1990s and accelerated in the latter part of the decade and into the early 2000s. The second involved the tremendous technology innovations that arose in 2007.

The year 2007 was an epic inflection point, causing turmoil in both the economy and specific enterprises. In his book *Thank You for Being Late* (2016), Thomas Friedman, a three-time Pulitzer Prize winner, bestselling author, and columnist for *The New York Times*, anointed 2007 as the year when multiple technologies came to fruition and kicked digital acceleration into high gear. Apple introduced the iPhone, Hadoop ushered in the Big Data era, GitHub multiplied software development capabilities, Facebook and Twitter expanded the reach and influence of social media, Airbnb showed what small companies could do with these new technologies, the Kindle changed book reading and the publishing business, and Google launched the Android operating system for smartphones. The confluence of all these technologies enabled new platform companies, such as Airbnb, which managed more beds than all of the major hotel chains combined. Thus, 2007 accelerated the march toward digital enterprises and placed new demands on software developers.

Two major architectural pivots occurred: from mainframe architectures early in the period to client-server architectures, and then to Internet architecture at the end. Of course, these architectural changes overlapped considerably from organization to organization. The answers to four basic questions characterize each transition:

- Were the physical computer system components (computer, database, user-interface devices) local or remote?
- Was application data stored locally or remotely?
- Was computational logic local or remote?
- Was presentation layer logic local or remote?

Let's label this the "allocation-to-layer" issue. During the mainframe period, all three layers were local. Computers were owned by the enterprise. Data storage devices were owned and located in a computer center. Computational and presentation logic was local. "Dumb terminals," containing little logic capability, were attached to the computer by physical wires, using an Ethernet protocol.

Then, it all began to change: from the mainframe period, when everything was local; to the client-server period, when the distribution of data and logic and devices migrated outward; to the Internet period, when the network absorbed everything. Client-server architecture required decisions about where logic and data would reside—on a mainframe or client terminals or network servers. Some broke the computational layer into several parts—business logic layer and presentation layer logic. The client side often contained the presentation layer and maybe some local data. These allocations could become very messy. Companies, especially software companies, struggled with this allocation-to-layer issue and spent large amounts of money adjusting to the changes.

Two technological advances then altered the allocation-to-layer issue once again—the Internet and cloud computing. Cloud computing enabled on-demand use of data storage and computer processing over the Internet. Mainframe computers gave way to vast server farms, but many companies retained their own servers. Cloud computing enabled companies to outsource their owned farms to a services provider like Google or Microsoft. Advantages of the cloud approach included easy, smooth, and rapid scaling, as well as variable (rather than large, fixed) cost increases. Disadvantages were loss of control, data security, and potential downtime performance.

Cloud computing encouraged new software development practices such as microservices. Microservices and domain-driven design began around 2004 as a way to decompose monolithic software architectures. Cloud computing facilitated microservices development and management. In the era of "serverless architectures" (an outgrowth of cloud computing), developers were no longer responsible for capacity planning, configuration, fault tolerance, or scaling. Enterprises once again faced difficult choices, including whether it was worth the cost to convert applications to cloud services. During this period, end-user devices tended to be personal computers—though that would soon change.

As described in earlier chapters, the technology of person–computer interfaces had evolved from punch cards to the wide variety of personal electronic devices. Today, this evolution continues unabated:

> Interfaces continue to evolve across gesture, voice, and touch—engaging all the senses. Devices that work with us in our everyday lives are commonplace and a richer pairing of software and hardware. Devices themselves are becoming more ergonomic, designed to slot into everyday interactions with minimal disruption. We now see more intelligent devices, with local and cloud-based AI [artificial intelligence] solutions supporting day to day decision-making.
>
> Autonomous driving is not the only example of evolving interactions but provides powerful examples of this lens in action. We've moved very quickly from real-time, traffic-based mapping services to self-driving cars that are constantly simulating all the possible future actions of the vehicles on the road to realize lower risk outcomes. (Thoughtworks.com, n.d.)

As the Internet and cloud computing altered the landscape, Software as a Service (SaaS) became the architecture of choice, especially for software companies. Remember the real old days (the early 1990s), when programs were loaded via 3¼-inch diskettes that were no longer floppy? Then came programs on compact disks (CDs), much faster and with fewer disks. Today, nearly all programs are downloaded off the Internet. SaaS model also uses the capabilities of the Internet and cloud to provide application services with minimum logic on the client systems. This provides quick access to new features without major installation costs.

The SaaS approach completed the transition from applications on a mainframe with attached terminals (the model for IT in organizations until the early 1990s) to fully Internet-based applications by the mid-2000s. Client-server systems, in which business application logic was split between the client and the server, were a transitional technology for many, but were also modernized and still useful.

These transitions were not trivial, from either a technological or a managerial perspective. The technology transition was expensive because it involved two major architectural shifts within a span of about 10 years. IT managers went from showing guests their massive mainframe computer center to showing them a laptop computer. Now, even the hardware was intangible—it was in the "clouds" somewhere! At first, objections to SaaS included safety of data, service downtime, and control. All too soon, though, the "as a service" architecture concept spread widely to areas such as Infrastructure as a Service (IaaS), Platform as a Service (PaaS), and Everything as a Service (EaaS).

THE OTHER MAJOR TECHNICAL advance in the mid-2000s was Big Data—and it was, indeed, huge. In 1999, 1 gigabyte (GB) of data was considered "big." I remember a time when 1 terabyte (TB; 1 TB = 1,024 GB) seemed far, far off; in 2022, you could purchase 2 TB of storage from Amazon for $62. In 2022, Big Data was measured in petabytes (PB; 1 PB = 1,024 TB) or exabytes (EB; 1 EB = 1,024 PB). eBay is reported to have two data warehouses with capacities of 7.5 PB and 40 PB, and another Hadoop cluster of 40 PB. Remember when PCs used floppy disks? It would take 728,177 floppy disks to store 1 TB of data. In 1970, a brand-new IBM 2314 disk drive with 146 MB (0.15 GB) of storage cost $175,000. At that rate, 1 GB of 2314 storage would cost $1.2 million in 1970, $10,000 in 1990, and $0.10 in 2012.[5] These plunging costs were a significant enabler for Big Data's evolution, as was the introduction of Hadoop to manage these massive databases.

These huge numbers sound like cosmologists talking about the number of stars in a galaxy or the universe. But with Big Data came big problems. Specialty roles like data scientist were created that added complexity and cost, new terms like *data mesh* flourished, and the decades-old schism between software developers and database designers needed fixing. I first experienced this schism with my Chicago Stock Exchange work in the 1980s (described in Chapter 3), and again in the 1990s at Nike (described in Chapter 4). It had persisted for a long time.

---

5. Any number of sites provide their version of these numbers. Pick one.

Ken Collier is the technical director of data and AI for North America for Thoughtworks and author of *Agile Analytics: A Value-Driven Approach to Business Intelligence and Data Warehousing* (Collier, 2012). He and I were introduced by a mutual friend when I moved to Flagstaff, Arizona, in 2002. When we both were in town, we met for coffee and conversation on a regular basis. I worked with Ken on Cutter Consortium projects and later at Thoughtworks.

Ken and I are both amateur adventurers—climbing, hiking, river running, biking—although I was more amateurish at these activities than Ken. My most memorable outing with him started in Cameron, Arizona, on the Navajo Reservation, cycling to the Desert View Watchtower just inside the east entrance of the Grand Canyon National Park. We were pooped after this 62-mile, 4,100-foot-elevation-gain ride. On the way up, we met a Japanese bike tourer who had been on the road for three months, biking all over the western United States. He was the only other cyclist we saw that day.

What I wanted to talk about is your experience of the schism between data and the development organizations going back a long way. I remember having arguments with data people in the mid-1980s. What are your thoughts about the schism and how did you, Scott Ambler, and others try to bridge that gap?

Part of this has to do with how databases evolved and especially data warehousing in the nineties. In the early days of hierarchical databases in the seventies and eighties, software developers wrote code. There were few data tools. Then relational database management systems emerged such as IBM's DB2, then Oracle. In the early days, databases supported finance, supply chain management, and other operational applications.

In the nineties, business intelligence (BI) and data warehousing systems delivered management information. Quickly thereafter, vendors created tools that reduced or eliminated the need for programming. People became data practitioners instead of software engineers. Businesspeople started focusing their resumes on tools—for example, an Informatica extract-transform-load (ETL) developer who rarely wrote code. Various roles, such as SQL programmers, data modelers, and database administrators, created additional IT functional silos.

That's when the schism occurred. I saw people coming out of computer science programs who were software engineers, and out of

CIS [computer information systems] programs in schools who didn't write code or have any concepts of writing test plans or tests.

When I met you in the early 2000s, I had a project that was going badly. The requirements took a year to collect; then they hired me as the tech lead to run the implementation project. Given the requirements, their fixed schedule was unrealistic. When I was doing agile enablement projects with you, I worked with data teams talking about test automation, build automation, and creating testing frameworks. The minute I would show a line of Java code for adding some tests around whatever tool they were working with, the class would riot—"No code, no code."

During this period, Scott Ambler, a few others, and I tried to get the data practitioners to think about agile methods, but they considered them unsuitable for the complexities of data management and analytics.

The situation changed again when Hadoop, a set of technologies for handling massive amounts of data, emerged in 2006. The complexities of managing massive data sets required writing code again. This began a reconvergence of data engineers and software engineers.

In the 1990s, people built careers around being a specialist in a particular tool. Now data engineers are software engineers with additional knowledge about "How do we scale? How do we deal with volume? What are best practices for managing your data and evaluating the data quality?"

Do firms have more architectural choices in the cloud?

They do. But what I'm starting to see is a repeat of the 1990s. Each of the three major cloud vendors—Google, Amazon, and Microsoft—is producing a bunch of managed services, which are effectively commercial tooling they're trying to get their customers to adopt. If you're a Microsoft Azure customer and you bought into the collection of tooling that's on Azure, they have you locked in because it's hard to migrate from Azure to AWS [Amazon Web Services] if all your code is in proprietary tools.

This data schism was emblematic of the spread of role-based silos that were impediments to agile implementation. The braid of constantly evolving technology helps us understand the environment in which companies and software development organizations had to work, as the next three customer stories indicate.

Three agile stories

I consulted with an Irish software company in Dublin in 2003. Managers were concerned with schedules and productivity and were interested in agile methods to improve performance—in essence, they wanted me to advise them on "fixing" their development efforts, particularly schedule delays. After interviewing developers, testers, supervisors, and managers, I concluded development was not the cause of the scheduling delays. Decision making was! Their home office was in the Silicon Valley, and it seemed that even minor decisions—about product features, primarily—required headquarters (HQ) approval. Being halfway around the world, the Irish group's priorities were often overlooked, and even minor decisions took time to make and implement.

While I thought they should think about agile methods, the first order of business was fixing their decision-making breakdown. First, they needed a product manager on the Dublin team who could work with the team to make 80% to 90% of the product decisions locally. They also needed to empower the dev team to make many of the technical decisions. This meant scaling back the decisions needing HQ approval to a small number. Second, HQ staff needed to shorten their response time, and suggested that the Dublin office keep a log of request and response times until the situation improved. Pushing decision making to the team level creates empowered teams, which in this case sped delivery considerably.

Sometimes, project management fixes are key to improved performance. After this engagement, I did some research and was amazed at how little attention was being paid to decision making in project management books and even in the Project Management Institute's Body of Knowledge. I was motivated to correct that omission in the project management book I was working on.

THE INTERNET HASTENED the demise of print media. Publishing Company, Inc. (PCI), a publisher of scientific and research journals, faced the challenge of coping with this trend away from print publishing. Its U.S. division had a daunting task in adapting to this change, as its IT systems were geared toward internal applications that supported printing and distribution of journals, papers, and books.

During this decade, many organizations faced a similar paper-to-online transition. Companies like Amazon provided models of where others might go with customer-facing applications, but behind the scenes their software development methods and prowess were less visible. Publishing companies ranging from magazines to newspapers to books faced major upheavals—not only in their products, but also in how they developed their products. Publishing was one of those industries the Internet remade. For many of these enterprises, their successful agile implementations encouraged method and mindset changes in their business units.

A Cutter Consortium team worked with PCI on its agile implementation. The team included Mike Cohn, Josh Kerievsky, Ken Collier, and me. What follows is a highly edited version of Ken's assessment of PCI's progress:

> I (Ken) spent the last two days at PCI alongside Jonathan doing our final coaching and assessment. Crystal is a bit concerned about "taking the training wheels off," but I assured her we could come back.
>
> The team has had good success in adopting the agile technical and agile project management practices to date. While they have room for growth in test-driven development (TDD) and continuous integration, both Josh and I agreed they are above average for a new agile team with only eight iterations under their belt. One weakness was estimation and tracking. I ran a one-hour session on estimation yesterday, teaching them Mike Cohn's methods of coarse-grained estimating in story points. I felt good about the outcome.
>
> I was concerned that the internal agile coach, in his enthusiasm, came across as an agile zealot. Rather than being a facilitator, he tended to have a command-control style. I had a one-on-one meeting with him and while he was defensive, I hope my recommendations motivated him to tone it down a bit.

I (Jim) had a call with the PCI leadership steering team to review our agile practice scorecard and our assessment of the interpersonal issues. PCI went on to establish an agile methodology in other development teams.

IN 2003, I CONDUCTED AN Agile Project Management workshop for Mountain Region Health. They had a new CIO who was an XP proponent. The CIO decided that henceforth all projects would utilize XP, including a just-under-way 100-person effort. The group organized into 12 XP teams and launched into 2-week iterations. For several iterations, velocity (as explained later, velocity isn't a good performance metric) steadily increased. And then the velocity reversed course. Each team had operated independently, and interteam dependencies began to slow progress—dramatically over time.

The company thought my Agile Project Management workshop might help right the ship. I recommended using agile project management practices and making a couple of organizational changes, including forming part-time interteam coordination groups who worked on fundamental issues like a common continuous integration pipeline. With the hiring of an architect and utilization of the concepts in my workshop, the company was able to regain the momentum that using XP alone had started.

This client had run into a problem that the agile community was only just beginning to address—scaling. Some detractors used "failures" like this to prove agile development didn't work. Mountain Region Health had ignored Kent Beck's caution—that XP was designed for small teams, not 12 interdependent teams. Additional structure would be needed for larger efforts.

Agile project management

By 2002–2003, I was thinking about project management (PM) issues and began pivoting to consulting and teaching PM and drafting an agile PM book. Analyzing the lessons learned from client engagements gave me plenty to think about:

- Agile had successfully delivered results (Alias Systems, Cellular, and PCI).

- Agile really shined in projects that were exploratory (Alias Systems and Cellular).

- Moving from small, co-located team projects to larger ones required additional PM, but not the traditional kind (Mountain Region Health).

- As was true in previous eras, organizational structure, personal interactions, collaborative teams, and decision making were still critical to success (Irish software company and Mountain Region Health).

- Culture, personality, and team issues blocked faster implementation.

- It was hard for people, teams, and leaders to adopt an agile mindset.

- Early agilists were technical and/or PM experts, not psychologists or change management experts. We needed help.

These revelations are not unique to the client stories presented in this chapter, but rather were indicative of issues that all agile practitioners were encountering. Most of these topics will be covered in this chapter's overview of agile PM. Two of them—value management and organizational change—are covered in Chapter 7.

My book *Agile Project Management: Creating Innovative Products* (*APM*) was published in 2004 (and a second edition in 2009; Highsmith, 2009). I wanted to present methods, methodology, and mindset for managing projects and products. The endorsement from Roy Singham, founder and former CEO of Thoughtworks, captured my rationale for writing it: "Finally a book that reconciles the passion of the Agile software movement with the needed disciplines of project management. Jim's book has provided a service to all of us."

The agile movement arose from a need to develop software differently—to be iterative instead of serial, to create teams that self-organized, and to eschew tradition. The general comment from agilists was "We don't need any project management," with the generalized form of that being "We don't need any management." New names were coined—iteration manager, product owner, and others—to indicate a move away from traditional roles.

I remember talking with a project manager in the 1990s who was using SuperCalc (an early competitor to Excel) as his PM tool. I asked him how often he walked around and talked with his team members or had short team meetings. "Not often," he replied. "Keeping the task information up-to-date in SuperCalc takes up all my time." This management of tasks rather than people was what agilists were complaining about. What was needed was a different style of PM—one that emphasized people and their interactions (mindset) rather than process and tools (methods); envisioning and exploring (experimentation) rather than planning and doing; and customer experience (mindset) rather than documented requirements (methods).

Under the influence of waterfall life cycles, organizations had placed project managers in a separate organizational box—sometimes within the IT department, sometimes not. Project management offices (PMOs) became, to the IT teams, the project police, enforcing Monumental Methodology standards and phase reviews, rather than acting as PM consultants to the teams.

My intent in writing *Agile Project Management* (*APM*; Highsmith, 2009) was to help bridge the gap between traditional and agile approaches to project management. To point out what was valuable in each. To show the agile community a bit of structure was needed, particularly as projects got bigger, to keep from falling into chaos. Chaos isn't any better than rigidity. Figure 6.1 shows the envision–explore processes as two integrated cycles.

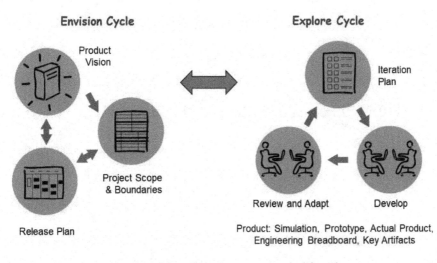

Figure 6.1 *The agile project management life cycle.*

WHILE THE CYNEFIN model had been useful in categorizing the pace of change and high-level coping strategies, I thought additional categorization was needed at the project or product level. To meet this need, I introduced the exploration factor (EF) in my workshops and then in the *APM* book.

An EF acts as a barometer of the uncertainty and risk of a product or project. Big projects are different from small projects; high-risk projects are different from low-risk ones. It is important to identify the various problem domain factors, but it is even more important to tailor processes and practices to the problem and to adjust expectations accordingly.

The EF, shown in Figure 6.2, is derived from a combination of the volatility of a product's requirements (ends) and the newness—and thus uncertainty—of its technology platform (means). It is determined by four categories of requirements volatility (erratic, fluctuating, routine, and stable) and technical categories (bleeding edge, leading edge, familiar, and well known).[6] Ratings are determined using a four-by-four table with EF values of 1–10, with the latter being the highest level of exploration.

---

6. Ken Delcol, formerly of Sciex, commented: "This guides the PM in both how the project and individual requirements should be managed. For example, erratic requirements need a more iterative approach and should be planned that way up front regardless of the overall state of the remaining requirements. Not all requirements fall into the same bucket. The trick is to realize which requirements are key to overall product success—there is no point rushing forward to specify the stable requirements when critical, high-risk requirements are erratic or fluctuating!"

	Product Technology Dimension			
Product Requirements Dimension	Bleeding Edge	Leading Edge	Familiar	Well Known
Erratic	10	8	7	7
Fluctuating	8	7	6	5
Routine	7	6	4	3
Stable	7	5	3	1

Figure 6.2 *Project exploration factor.*

By determining the EF, teams could now discuss how to proceed given the overall uncertainty and risk of the problem space. Matching team capability to project EF should be as thoughtful as matching a mountaineering team's ability to climb a particular peak.

TRADITIONAL PM, AND organizational management in general, is often based on fear—fear a manager won't appear resolute, all-knowing, and strong. "*My* project won't fail because of the indomitable will of my own personality" may be the assumption lying just underneath the surface. Admitting uncertainty, the possibility of being wrong, or making a mistake keeps managers and project teams from learning about the most critical aspects of projects. Without a change in mindset, iterative life cycles are often no better than linear ones.

Iterative life cycles have allowed us to explore design and requirements—revising designs and prototyping for new requirements—but they rarely extend to seriously examining overall PM issues such as scope, schedule, executive sponsorship, and customer participation. An example was a project I managed years ago for an IT organization in a large consumer goods company. In laying out the project plan to the executive steering committee—multiple cycles with review points, deliverables, and so on—I made the point that our objective during the early cycles was to make mistakes! Lucky for me there wasn't an immediate mutiny. I went on to explain there was no way to accomplish a project like this without mistakes, and we wanted to make mistakes early so we had time to correct them and end up with the right product.

Sure enough, at the end of the first development cycle, we made a major blunder—right in front of the executive steering committee. The project team's confusion over the product scope was reflected in a disorganized presentation and a few steering committee members left disgruntled. To this organization's credit, the team was allowed to regroup, think through the issues, and explore alternatives with the executive sponsor of the project. The team (which included a significant user contingent) then spent an agonizing couple of weeks reexamining the project scope and deliverables. The "solution" also included a complete restructuring of the steering committee itself. The steering committee had been put together based on a previous project's failure, not the current project's needs.

These were difficult lessons. A project team doesn't go through an assessment like this without experiencing some painful emotions. However, as this review was based on delivered components, not documents, the team couldn't escape critical scrutiny. The review occurred 5 weeks after the project started, not 6 or 9 or 12 months later, and the team had time to regroup and recover. Having to face problems early contributed to later success. Finally, although some of the managers weren't too happy about the initial results, as a group they allowed the team to stumble and then recover.

As the agile movement transitioned from the Rogue Teams era to the Courageous Executives era, both project and product management would increase in importance.

Period observations

Some individuals refused to engage in pair programming. Some thought agile teams had too many meetings. Project managers rebelled because they no longer managed tasks; instead, their teams did. Scrum leaders struggled with defining their roles, even though it seemed to be spelled out in the Scrum literature and workshops. Facilitation skills needed to improve. Who made which decisions? What was going on here?

In some ways, implementing agile technical practices was easy. It was difficult intellectually, for sure—but not socially (an exception would be pair programming). Agile collaboration practices—co-located teams without physical barriers, working closely with other people (every day!), confusion over roles and responsibilities, adding testers and product owners to dev teams, tenuousness about accepting team accountability, middle managers unsure about their role—incorporating the social and interpersonal challenges were the greatest impediments to agile adoption.

This first period of the Agile era led to mixed results. Many managers were pleased with project performance, better return on investment, faster results, higher quality, and improved customer relationships. Those organizations utilizing both team management *and* technical practices had a better record of improving both quality and overall results.

IN CHAPTER 4, I mentioned wrestling with a purpose statement about delivering better software. At that time, I had not yet come up with a statement I liked. Now it was time to try again.

Jerry Weinberg's book series, *Software Quality Management*, volumes I–IV, runs some 1,538 pages. Anyone can say they are in favor of "excellent" or "high" quality, but those adjectives are so overworked they are essentially meaningless. Is quality intrinsic, in the eye of the beholder, equivalent to running/tested code, or something else? Do you think the testing for the latest Facebook features should be as intense as that for the James Webb Space Telescope software?

After 1,500 pages, which need to be read to fully understand the nuances, Jerry's definition of quality was deceptively simple: "Quality is value to some person."[7] Now, all we must do is articulate what is meant by "value" and "some person."

Jerry's definition of quality assisted me in extending my personal purpose statement for better software delivery: *"To enable the continuous delivery of customer value by creating advanced software and management methods, methodologies, and mindsets."*

I know it's a little wordy, but this statement contains elements important to me. First, it conforms to Jerry's definition by incorporating the notions of *value* and *person* in the form of a customer. Second, it says I've devoted a career to "creating advanced software and project management, methods, methodologies, and mindsets." Continuous delivery (CD) requires technical excellence. I'm not speaking about CD in the sense of an automated testing and deployment pipeline, although that might be a key piece. Instead, I'm addressing another level of CD, building the capability of releasing versions of software supporting customers as easily with the tenth version as with the first.

---

7. Weinberg, 1992, p. 7.

In Chapter 8, this narrative on quality will be combined with two other components, value and constraints, to build an enterprise performance management model consistent with agile methodologies.

Why did Monumental Methodologies fade, and agile methodologies ascend? Examine closely any of the Monumental Methodologies—STRADIS, DSSD, Method/1, or RUP. They tasked us to "do" something—diagrams, documents, processes, approvals, etc. But they were short on value statements that provided a basis for making decisions. Individuals had a difficult time deciding how to adapt these approaches because they didn't have comparative value statements. The Agile Manifesto value—*Individuals and interactions over processes and tools*—expresses what agilists believe, that a mindset provides a criterion for decision making. None of the Monumental Methodologies declared, explicitly, what they valued. People, therefore, made assumptions, like "I guess they value documentation given that there is so much of it."

My observation of the state of the agile movement at the end of the Rogue Teams period is summed up in the last chapter of my *Agile Software Development Ecosystems* book:

> In some ways, we Agilists are like Don Quixote and his sidekick, Sancho Panza, riding around the software development landscape, tilting at the windmills of traditionalism. We've made dents here and there, but the bulk of large corporate and governmental development remains skeptical. Even in organizations in which teams have successfully implemented Agile projects, their peers often remain unconvinced. This is always the case with something new that challenges the status quo. (Highsmith, 2002, p. 381)

7

Courageous Executives

(2005–2010)

 **WHO QUALIFIES AS** a courageous executive? For nearly two years I worked with three of them—Ken Delcol, Paul Young, and Gary Walker at Sciex in Canada. They initiated, supported, and drove Sciex's excursion into agile software development. Paul was the CIO, Ken was the director of product management, and Gary was manager of software development. These three "courageous" executives led the way. They were ahead of the curve in the agile transition from the Rogue Teams to the Courageous Executives period. Leadership pioneers like these three executives took "prudent" risks in committing their organizations to change.

What is a courageous executive? Someone who thrives on adventure, the corporate kind, and has the ability to sort through a myriad of opportunities, engage others with their enthusiasm, and demonstrate results though action.

> They are boundless in their thinking, bold in their actions, and passionate about technology. This is why we believe Courageous Executives are the next major disruptive force in business, creating a powerful competitive advantage through their leadership style. (Guo, 2017)

As always, important events punctuated the years 2005–2010, which were bracketed by the devastating hurricane losses in the U.S. Gulf of Mexico region and the Great Recession. In 2006, scientists declared Pluto was not a planet, which frustrated astronomers at the Lowell Observatory, where Pluto had been discovered in 1930. The iPhone was launched by Apple, Barack Obama replaced George W. Bush as U.S. president, *Avatar* became the highest-grossing movie ever, and the Large Hadron Collider went online to the delight of physicists.

By the mid-2000s, the Internet era was creating both fantastic opportunities and dire threats. Companies were concerned about getting disrupted: "Will we be the next Kodak? Or will we be the next Salesforce?" Salesforce, a sales application software services company, was ranked the number 1 innovator by *Forbes* magazine in 2011 and 2012. Its 5-year average sales growth was 39.5%, and its 5-year average net income growth was 78.7%. Part of this company's success came from its implementation of agile methodologies across the organization beginning around 2005. According to Steve Green, former vice president of development, "Agile is the foundation of our innovation!" Kodak, once the world leader in film processing, saw its run end in bankruptcy proceedings. Salesforce succeeded, but others have failed in larger transformations.

As the Courageous Executives period unspooled, agile approaches moved from rogue teams to larger initiatives as CIOs and vice presidents of engineering decided to transform their entire development organizations. The Internet was busy wreaking havoc on companies' business and IT plans. Agile project management (APM) became increasingly important, as did an emphasis on technical practices like continuous integration (CI).

In this chapter, five client stories are cited to identify conditions for success, and those that can lead to failure. First we visit Sciex; then we look at two mid-size agile implementations (one successful and another not so much), followed by a huge agile implementation effort in China; and finally we consider a *business* agility story at Athleta. Woven into these stories are the impacts of major technology innovations, organizational change management, and scaling practices required for larger companies and projects.

Sciex

MDS Sciex develops mass spectrometers (and other instruments) for life sciences, pharmaceutical, and forensic analysis customers. From 2004 through 2006, I worked in Toronto, Canada, with this company to implement an agile "combo" methodology consisting of Extreme Programming (XP) and APM. Along with Josh Kerievsky and other Cutter Consortium consultants, we initially worked with software teams and then extended selected agile practices into other engineering groups.

In an email exchange in 2022, Gary Walker (then manager of software development) conveyed the situation that then existed at Sciex and the results of its agile implementation.

In determining whether we needed to "transform our development organization," we quickly realized we really didn't have a choice! Our instrument software was a couple of million lines of code riddled with years of technical debt. Every new fix or feature just created unexpected new problems, and each new release was more unstable than the last.[1] Unstable software was a huge problem for our "Big Pharma" drug discovery and development customers; when our software crashed, they often lost an experimental drug sample that took weeks to create. Even competitors referred to our software in their marketing materials with slogans like "Our software won't crash."

This had an immense impact on our development teams. They were very nervous to add new functionality to this huge unstable code base; hence, they would usually "take the safest possible development route," adding even more technical debt to the code base. There was no pride in the product and the developers would take customers' feedback personally.

As I recall, we began to see a change in the team mindset and behavior approximately 18 months after we initiated the Agile transformation. Hard data from the Cutter team showed the development teams were now delivering higher-quality product releases faster and at lower cost. Feedback from our customers was starting to be more positive. This had a huge impact on the team members' mindset and the overall environment for the development community. Developers were once again feeling confident in their skills and pride in the product they were delivering to our customers.

Also, the Agile principles, values, and practices provided the framework to foster an environment of "psychological safety" (Edmondson, 2002). Team members regularly challenged each other, pushing the team to generate more creative and higher-quality product features. Once again, it had become fun to come to work!

Sciex was an ISO-certified organization. Like many companies, this was a business requirement—our customers expected it. This was especially critical because we were developing high-end instruments for

---

1. Josh Kerievsky, as a visual demonstration of tech debt, printed out a method from one of their objects. Laying the pages end-to-end on the floor, the method was more than 10 feet long!

international pharmaceutical companies in the drug discovery and development industry.

We had to grapple with the question: How do we reconcile the iterative adaptive practices of Agile to the requirements of ISO? Those requirements were based very much on the Big Up-Front Design (BUFD) principles of waterfall delivery, and relied on rigorous documentation of processes, plans, and recorded results.

Working with Jim and Josh,[2] we developed the concept of distinguishing "governance" from "execution." Governance focused on "time and money" (i.e., schedule and budget). We applied the planning and execution documentation at the governance level to meet the needs for continued ISO certification.

And we applied the Agile principles and practices at the "execution" level, thereby leveraging the benefits of Agile execution in our context of extreme uncertainty (business, scientific and technical). This allowed us to "have our cake and eat it, too." We leveraged the benefits of Agile for execution and addressed the needs of ISO certification.

We started the Sciex agile implementation with a software project. Staff were then sitting in individual offices, so Josh and I convinced them to create a team workspace. Sometimes the most innocuous impediments get in the way—like getting hardware ordered and delivered on time, or in this case getting the building maintenance crew to build out the new workspace. With the space partially completed, the building crew left for the weekend. The dev team surreptitiously completed the space over a weekend so work could start Monday morning, much to the chagrin of the maintenance manager.

Josh and other consultants worked with the teams to institute technical practices from XP. I worked on organizational, project management, and management practices and issues. While we conducted several workshops, Josh and I confirmed, again, that working day-to-day with teams was really critical to success.

With several successful projects under our belts, Ken Delcol (director of product management) made the call to use agile development for their next-generation mass spectrometer instrument product—a hugely courageous step, as using agile methods in a combination hardware/software project was a big stretch. Our off-site project visioning and kick-off meeting

---

2. Josh and I later used this approach in our Telecom China engagement described later in this chapter.

included software developers; mechanical, electrical, and systems engineers; several scientists; product managers; and a purchasing analyst. In laying out the total project timeline, the purchasing analyst was invaluable since he knew the lead time for many of the components.[3]

At the end of an exhausting but productive week, Ken returned to review progress. He had kicked off the first day, establishing an executive perspective for the new product. Everyone was eager to get back to their offices and get to work, but Ken had one more surprise.

"One last thing," Ken said in wrapping up the day. "You will not be going back to your individual offices. During your week here off-campus, we have restructured your entire work area to enhance collaboration, a continuation of what you have done this week. You are now a cross-functional product team responsible for delivering this product to market." Eventually Ken reconfigured the entire product development department from individual offices to team areas in three sizes—small, medium, and large.

The gnarliest problem with big systems has always been integrating the various pieces, which historically occurred near the end when the clock was ticking. From software to automobiles to industrial control systems, the lesson learned had been the same: The less frequent the integration, the more difficult and expensive it was to find and fix integration problems. Agile practices enabled teams to integrate early and often, substantially reducing this endgame problem.

Ken Delcol used this approach at MDS Sciex.

We have just gone through this process. Our firmware group delivered firmware to the hardware group in iterations based on its testing schedule. Once sufficient functionality was confirmed, the software group was brought in to add applications. With this approach we didn't need a fully populated digital board to begin firmware and hardware integration testing. We achieved several things (the best we have ever achieved): Integration testing started sooner, hence issues were resolved more quickly (better schedule and cost); integration was continuous once minimal hardware was in place, hence no peak in resources; and communication was improved because all groups participated in the integration.

---

3. You don't always know ahead of time who will supply critical pieces of information.

Ken, Paul, and Gary created a vision for their agile future, supported the effort with appropriate resources, encouraged their staff during periods of anxiety, and were truly knowledgeable about agile approaches themselves. Josh and I conducted workshops for the managers and executives and worked with them on developing agile mindsets and understanding agile methods. This agile transition effort impacted both software and hardware development—advancing the state of the art.

A new generation of pioneers

During this Courageous Executives period, I met new people, worked with clients on CIO-level agile implementations, wrote the second edition of *Agile Project Management* (Highsmith, 2009), and founded the Agile Project Leadership Network (covered in Chapter 5).

Early on, I met Pat Reed, of the GAP, who had previously held positions at Disney and other companies. Pat invited me to the GAP to talk about value and the Agile Triangle. She was then director of Internet delivery management services (portfolio, project and release management, IT finance and strategy, audits and quality). As you will see, she is a whirlwind, full of ideas, an incessant reader who possesses boundless energy. She had instituted agile development in her department and became a pioneer in agile management and adaptive leadership. The GAP's corporate IT group had experimented with an agile pilot project with success, but struggled to scale agile practices and were unconvinced agile methods could be used in their legacy systems work. Many legacy IT organizations were in a similar situation, burdened by overwhelming technical debt from their legacy systems, with only a fuzzy roadmap for implementing agile practices in these groups at that time.

Pat and I started a discussion about adding an Executive Forum to the annual Agile Development Conference to meet the growing demand by senior executives to learn about the latest strategies and best practices for adopting and scaling agile development. The Executive Forum debuted at the Agile Development Conference in 2011, in Salt Lake City. The main conference was celebrating the 10th anniversary of the Agile Manifesto, so Pat and I settled on the executive theme, "Now is the time for enterprise agility," and the following conference vision statement: "To create an extraordinary and valuable experience for executives where they can connect and engage to explore the business opportunities and challenges of the next decade by blending Agile delivery, Agile leadership, and advanced technologies."

This first Executive Forum, which was designed exclusively for senior executives, attracted 7 international, 13 C-level, and 23 vice president–level executives. Launching the forum as part of the Agile Alliance annual conference enabled executives to attend conference keynotes and other non-executive sessions throughout the week-long event.

In 2010, Pat fielded an inquiry from Rob Oliver, manager of Playa Info at the Burning Man Project, which led to a lunch in downtown San Francisco with the CEO, CIO, and other staff from the Burning Man Project. I didn't know much about Burning Man at the time, and after an enlightening lunch, decided I liked their adventurous spirit. This seemed like just the organization to embrace agility, as they had compatible principles and a mission inspired by wisdom from Hopi elders. (Burning Man principles include radical inclusion, gifting, decommodification, radical self-reliance, radical self-expression, communal effort, civic responsibility, leaving no trace, participation, and immediacy.)

Pat was, and is, a fountain of new ideas. She envisioned an agile management curriculum and convinced Berkeley University extension program executives in San Francisco to experiment with a class. Pat and I formed the advisory council and put together the workshop, and I traveled to San Francisco to co-teach the first class. It was a fun experience, with attendees including IT managers as well as a surprising number of non-IT managers. I enjoyed teaching this class with Pat, but the travel back and forth from Flagstaff, Arizona, to the Bay Area negated my meager compensation as an adjunct professor. Pat has continued expanding the curriculum beyond the initial offerings to include agile management fundamentals, principles, and practices; APM; agile management mastery; agile product ownership; delivery management; and value innovation.

In the Sciex story earlier in this chapter, and in the next client stories presented here—Integrated Financial Software, Southern Financial Software, and Telecom China—my partner was yet another agile pioneer and outdoor adventurer, Josh Kerievsky. Josh founded a company focused on XP and advancing the state of the art—usually experimenting with the methods with his own development staff first. His company, Industrial Logic, Inc., has grown to more than 50 staff and consultants. Josh was one of the first to experiment by turning XP's two-week iterations into continuous delivery. He has also experimented on the human side of development, such as formulating ideas about personal safety on projects. Josh is the author of *Refactoring to Patterns* (Kerievsky, 2005) and the *Joy of Agility* (Kerievsky, 2023). He initiated our Piha Canyon trip, once again demonstrating the adventurous trait of pioneers.

Adventuring in Piha Canyon with Josh Kerievsky

Josh and I had an exhilarating adventure during a trip in 2008 to speak at a New Zealand Software Education conference. I arrived at the Auckland airport early in the morning after an overnight flight (more than 12 hours in the air), checked into our downtown hotel, changed clothes, and hopped into a van with Josh for a New Zealand–style canyoneering trip down the Piha Canyon river.

In this steep, nearly inaccessible, volcanic rock valley, a series of wonderful waterfalls cascade their way down the valley toward the ocean. Suiting up in wet suits and old sneakers, provided by the guide service, we walked and swam down the river, rappelled over the majestic Kitekite Falls, then descended a narrow slot canyon. Along the way were a cave, jumps down small waterfalls, and natural rock pools to swim in. Being among the first to descend the 130-foot-high Kitekite Falls, I stretched out in a small pool. Some frantic waving by the others at the top of the falls alerted me that I was sharing the pool with a 4-foot-long freshwater eel! This canyoneering adventure was far better than trying to sleep off jet lag.

In May 2010, I presented a keynote address for the Carnegie Mellon Software Engineering Institute's (SEI) Architecture Technology User Network Conference (SATURN 2010), in Minneapolis, Minnesota. Linda Northrop, director of SEI's Research, Technology, and System Solutions Program, said, "What Jim brings to the table is the ability to describe the importance of teamwork, planning, and adaptation to ever-changing environments." Invitations such as this one showed that the agile movement was continuing to advance into the mainstream of software development.

Integrated Financial Software

In 2005, while I was director of APM at Cutter Consortium, we undertook a large-scale agile implementation at Integrated Financial Software (IFS). I've included aspects from several other engagements in this story and will go into considerable detail, as our findings and solutions were typical of those encountered during the Courageous Executives period (and are still being encountered today).

Our engagement began with a comprehensive assessment of the Software Products Division. The core Cutter team included Josh Kerievsky, several consultants, and me as the engagement manager.

As many successful companies like IFS were finding, they needed to improve their performance because competitors were gaining traction and customers were demanding ever more features. IFS had a large customer base and aging legacy software that had moderate technical debt. New competitors, less burdened by legacy software, offered faster feature improvements. IFS had also been whipsawed by the rapid expansion of client-server systems in the 1990s. Just as the company had converted its products to client-server architectures, the explosion of the Internet required a further technology transition.

Our findings confirmed management's concerns that while the overall performance and delivery capability of the organization were within industry norms, they were not world-class. Many of their performance measures were trending in the wrong direction: Productivity was declining; the organization was straining to handle growth and product complexity; quality and product adaptability were declining; and the ability to deliver to plans was troubled by deficiencies in overall delivery capabilities and an erosion of technical skills and domain knowledge. All these trends were impacted by growth.

In an early presentation to his staff about the transition to agile methods, Dan, the CIO, posed the question, "Why introduce agile? We didn't have to change. We weren't 'broken.' Products are getting shipped. The company is growing." However, he went on to explain the growing "costs of scale"—what worked well for 75 engineers delivering 5 products might not be best for 400 engineers delivering 12 products.

Warning signs of these issues abounded: quality—problem reports felt high; features—increasing time spent on debugging, decreasing time spent creating new features; predictability—the last three "annual" releases each had extended several additional months; and no fun—people were getting worn down by the growing challenges.

Dan had three key objectives for the engagement:

1. Assess performance.

2. Adopt an agile methodology.

3. Act on improvement recommendations.

Our assessment consisted of a series of interviews with managers and directors as well as staff from quality assurance (QA), development, product management, architecture, and human resources.

The results of the assessment fell into several categories:

- Lack of cross-functional teams
- Issues with quality
- Wish-based planning
- Waterfall life cycle
- Technical skills

Not everyone agreed on the types of changes needed, but they were supportive of the need for change and appeared willing to try new methods. Successful projects and releases had been the result of commitment and hard work, but sometimes people didn't feel recognized for their efforts. People wanted to improve performance: "We've done project postmortems before, but nothing seems to change."

When under pressures related to size and complexity, team dynamics and relationships often suffer—and this happened at IFS. There is always tension if different parts of the organization are not aligned on the same goals. IFS was typical in that development, QA, and product management were in different organizational units, and the interactions between them had become static and bureaucratic rather than fluid and collaborative.

There was an undercurrent, both vertically and horizontally within the organization, of decreasing respect and trust. Comments such as "The organization is more fractured than it used to be, with more finger pointing" and "Trust is mixed; I don't think people tell me what they are thinking" were heard all too frequently. There was an attitude that "The 'other' groups are underperforming." It was an "I'm OK but you're not" attitude.

We heard comments such as the following:

"Development groups are not productive enough."

"There has been a bad relationship between QA and development at a high level."

"There is a distrust of product management in development, and vice versa."

"The architecture team just throws stuff over the wall to us."

The development–QA–product management organizations were functional silos—again, typical of organizations using a waterfall life cycle. Staff at the individual contributor level in these three areas often didn't work together well, and decisions tended to be escalated to managers in the hierarchies rather than be solved at the working level.

At IFS, responsibility, accountability, and ownership resided in the functional departments, not the teams. The teams had little decision-making power. "We had one issue that came up which took several meetings of 6 to 12 people—nearly 30 hours of work—to make the decision on a 15-minute fix. Very inefficient, to say the least," said one developer.

We heard from management that schedule *and* quality were important. But we heard something different from the engineering staff: "Schedule is king around here." People felt lip service was paid to quality. There was little consistent qualitative or quantitative measurement of quality other than bug counts. Performance measurements emphasized schedule.

The software marketplace places brutal pressure on software companies to respond to customer feature requests and meet tight schedules. These market pressures drive product management to beef up product plans to include as many new features as possible, putting development into the awkward position of always rejecting those plans. The focus on schedule and features drives out any emphasis on quality, raising the product's technical debt, which in turn makes it more difficult to implement features in a timely manner in the future. As release dates approach and reality sets in, features hurriedly added without sufficient testing are jettisoned, resulting in lost work and lost enthusiasm.

IFS's culture led people to commit to a plan that exceeded their capacity and then bail out toward the end. A "can-do" attitude led to infeasible feature commits. One outcome of schedule pressure (perceived or actual) was people who focused on their own priorities and didn't help other teams. There were comments such as "Minor changes to support us have no priority. The attitude is, if it doesn't affect my area, then I can't help you."

A waterfall life cycle exacerbated the weak team orientation because it encouraged a "throw it over the wall to the next department" syndrome. Several teams tried a form of iterative development, but lack of training and no familiarity with iterative development resulted in a negative experience.

Josh and I presented our assessment evaluation and a preliminary action plan to the senior management group. They accepted the assessment findings and wanted an aggressive action plan.

Typically, companies used a project-at-a-time implementation strategy, which implemented agile practices for a project team (or a couple of teams) and then seeded new teams with experienced practitioners from the initial teams. This strategy was generally slower, but less risky.

However, in IFS's case, an organization-wide strategy was adopted for two main reasons. First, the entire suite of products was integrated and released together. Having some teams doing iterative development and others doing traditional waterfall development would have been difficult to coordinate. Second, IFS leaders wanted the entire organization to feel a part of the improvement initiative. A project-by-project strategy would leave out some teams.

To succeed, an organization-wide strategy requires visible and continuous support from top management. While a project-by-project strategy can succeed with limited top management support (which does help), an organization-wide strategy cannot.

The IFS action plan had two objectives: (1) strengthen teams and individuals and (2) improve technical practices. Strengthening teams and individuals dealt with team structure: revising the structure to be cross-functional, improving the trust climate between groups, and involving the entire staff in the process improvement initiatives.

Improving technical practices centered on what we labeled "agile lite" practices, in which "lite" indicated not all practices would be implemented initially. The implementation team, consisting of IFS staff and Cutter consultants, recommended a set of project management, collaboration, and technical practices deemed critical to IFS. Josh and I combined my APM methods with XP technical practices into this "agile lite" methodology.[4] Although we had concerns about delaying some practices, we thought it was necessary given the large audience and condensed time frame for implementation.[5] IFS's goal was to always stay as close to shippable quality code as possible— a daunting objective given the size of the existing code base.

During this engagement, I devised a simple metric to gauge progress, called "shortening the tail." In a waterfall project, there was frequently a time called *code-freeze*, which meant no more new features. After the code-freeze

---

4. We used this approach in several engagements.

5. This process of adapting an agile approach to a specific situation is essential to ongoing success. That said, adaptations also need someone, like Josh, who understands both the individual methods and the interactions among those methods to assist in the adaptations. Understanding the interactions is particularly critical.

would come bug fixes, integration testing, documentation, and operational readiness for deployment. On a one-year project, the time from code-freeze to ship might be months, several months, and sometimes many, many months. The goal of an agile team is to shorten that tail to near zero.

At IFS, as "tail-time" decreased, benefits became evident: Quality improved, morale improved, and collaboration increased. One measure of the company's success occurred about four months into the transition, when a marketing manager came to the engineering vice president with an urgent enhancement request. The product team split off a temporary small team to respond and the new feature was deployed quickly. This type of response had been rare before agile development was adopted, and the marketing manager applauded the response.

THE AGILE IMPLEMENTATIONS at Sciex and IFS were quite different. One change approach was project-by-project, whereas the other was organization-wide. Was one right and the other wrong? Was one better than the other? The answer is murky: Success depends—on leadership, organization, trust, technical skills, collaboration, risk, and uncertainty, and much more. We must be more attuned to a both/and perspective rather than an either/or mindset. That said, I would rate our success at Sciex a little higher than our achievements at IFS—not because of the overall strategy, but because of the entirety of these other factors. When the goal is organization-wide implementation of agile principles, the deciding success factor isn't which of these two tactics is used, but rather executive and management leadership.

Between the IFS engagement and the other client experiences described in this chapter, Josh and I learned a lot. First, while we knew that organization-level transitions were different from team-level ones, we learned *how* they were different. Leadership was much more important: In addition to *involvement*, both leaders and teams needed to *understand* the methodology and mindset. We had to learn how to train and coach at all organizational levels for a reasonable cost. We had to get better at setting and managing expectations, as executives wanted demonstrated value in a reasonable (or unreasonable) time frame. We learned the difference between impediments and barriers (see the Telecom China story). We learned that changing measures of success was both necessary and challenging. As we learned from one engagement, we applied those learnings to the next.

Southern Systems Software

Like the IFS story, Barry's story at Southern Systems Software (SSS) includes elements from several engagements reflecting common situations encountered during this period. I met Barry in 2008, when he was the director of software development for a mid-sized software company located in the southeastern United States. From the first time we met, I could sense his intensity. As we talked about his business, his organization, and his concerns, two main themes emerged: He was concerned about lagging responsiveness to customers, and he was concerned about the quality of the company's software.

As was the case with many software companies of the day, SSS's product was on a one-year release cycle. To handle critical client requests, it maintained a separate enhancement and maintenance group that could implement new features outside the normal release cycle—but this fragmented operation contributed to multiple code streams that increased the quality problems.

"I feel like I'm on a treadmill going round and round in circles," said Barry. "We are always hurrying towards the end of a release and testing never has enough time. In the last month or so before code-freeze, developers are rushing to get new features into the code base, they are less and less concerned with quality. We now take up nearly half of our release cycle in various types of testing and integration. Nothing new gets added in the last four months of the release unless it's an emergency—and, of course, with that much time, product managers are always coming up with emergencies."

Developers were constantly stressed and couldn't see the way out of the morass. They wanted to produce quality code; they just felt the time pressure was too great. "We don't know much about agile except for the name" was a comment from Nancy, a developer. Her thoughts mirrored those of several other employees: "Anything is better than what we have now, so I'm willing to give it a go!"

This seemed the perfect scenario for a successful agile transformation—but it wasn't. The delivery teams struggled but managed to make a partial transition over the next year. They implemented agile practices, worked in two-week iterations, began developer unit testing, practiced daily stand-ups, and brought product managers into iteration planning meetings. The implementation seemed to go well—for a time.

But management missed the boat. For example, as the agile champion, the person who would oversee the transformation, executives appointed a manager known for his command-control tendencies. The managers, including the director, never made the transition to an adaptive management style. They continued to measure progress in traditional ways, continued their wish-based planning and their micromanaging. In other words, while management supported the transition, they never embraced agility themselves.

As Josh and I worked with larger agile transformations, it became clear *our* organizational change skill set needed improvement.

Agile project management

As agile implementations were expanded into enterprises by courageous executives, project management increased in importance. With our clients, Josh Kerievsky and I used an XP/APM combination methodology. We addressed the *type* of project management question that was circling around in this period. The Agile Project Leadership Network pondered this question as well, and the Project Management Institute (PMI) began taking notice of agile project management. The first edition of my *Agile Project Management* book, released in 2004, addressed the *type* question, but in 2009 it was time for an updated version.

The next sections cover key project management topics (value determination, constraints, the Agile Triangle) and one dangerous agile trend (the unfortunate demise of release planning). One key question I wanted to pursue was "If change, adaptation, and flexibility are the trademarks of agile projects, and conforming to plan is the trademark of traditional projects, then why do we still measure success on agile projects using traditional measurements?" Performance measures—at the team, product/project, and organizational levels—are critical to changing mindsets and methodologies. While other APM topics are covered in this chapter, performance measurement is a primary focus.

DURING A 2006 conference, Paul Young (Sciex) presented a story about an application internal developers built for their marketing department. Based on prior experience with IT, the marketing department generated a list of 100 features that they wanted.

"Fine," said Paul. "What are your top three?"

"All 100 are really needed" was the marketing manager's reply.

"We understand, you will get all of the features, but we will deliver the three highest-value features in early iterations and then work down your list."

At the end of the first delivery, Paul asked the question again: "What are your next top three?"

It seemed the process hadn't been fully understood by the marketing manager. He again asked for all of the remaining 97 features.

"As we promised, we will do them all. We just need the next three now," said Paul.

This process proceeded iteration by iteration until about 20 features had been implemented. Paul asked the "next top three" question again.

"Well," the marketing manager offered, "the features you have delivered to date are valuable and we are already using them. So, for now, we would like to hold up the project and learn to fully use what we have. The other 80 features would be somewhat nice to have, but we may not get to them."

As Paul related to the audience, if the team had used a traditional waterfall approach, all 100 features would have been documented and delivered. "We might as well have taken the money and lit a bonfire. A big benefit from going agile is all the stuff you don't do!"

Paul's story stimulated my thinking about the relationship between value and cost. In looking at value capture, agile managers need to examine cumulative value delivered versus cumulative cost incurred on a project. Then questions can be posed, such as "Do we want 100% of the planned value for 100% of the planned cost, or would we prefer stopping at 90% of the value for 70% of the cost?" Because agile development delivers the highest-value features early, this type of management trade-off becomes reasonable, even imperative. This view of value also changed how we think about portfolio management. Developing the last 10% to 20% of marginal functionality on one project may delay capturing the higher value on the next project. Clearly, managers must evaluate not just development cost, but also opportunity cost.

After showing a 90% value for 70% cost chart during a CIO forum presentation, one participant commented, "Do we reward our project managers for deleting low-value functionality and early completion? I think not, but maybe we should."

In 2010, I visited the Thoughtworks office in London to consult with a client and meet with a team engaged with another client. After learning about their project, I asked, "So, from your perspective, this appears to be a successful engagement. What is the client's view?"

"The client appears to be pleased with our progress so far" was the reply.
"What seems to be the client's greatest concern?" was my next question.
"Velocity" was the instant response from the team.
"And what other metrics do you report?" I queried.
"None really, just velocity."

Velocity[6] isn't a measure of success. It can help a team with capacity planning, but it is a poor performance metric that can be counterproductive. Looking at the team's story cards on the wall, I suggested that, in addition to the estimated story points, they work with their customer's product leader to assign value points (just a relative 1–5 evaluation). At the end of each iteration, they could then report they had delivered 35 value points and expended 25 story points. When I followed up a few months later, they reported the customer liked the idea of value points and rarely complained about velocity anymore. Sometimes a simple change in performance measures can have a profound effect.

On traditional projects, serious time was spent calculating project costs and benefits—beginning with portfolio management groups for prioritizing projects. These calculation binges were often based on shaky assumptions about the certainty of the future. One benefit of planning based on story points is that they are relative, not absolute. If the future is uncertain, why bother with rapidly obsolete but time-consuming calculations? Wouldn't the same question apply to benefit, or value, determination? As with the London teams' use of value points, they can be incredibly useful, more so than absolute numbers in most cases, and consume minimal effort.

Chapter 6 delved into the quality quagmire, and this chapter has done the same for value. It's now time to address "constraints" as the final corner of the Agile Triangle.

CONSTRAINTS ARE GUARDRAILS, guideposts that keep the range of adaptive actions from exceeding predetermined limits. They provide dev teams with limits to their decision making. Furthermore, constraints trigger innovation.

Once on vacation, I visited the Mingei International Museum in San Diego. During a tour by the museum director, we were looking at a mid-1930s

---

6. Velocity measures story points per time period. Story points represent the relative size (effort) of a piece of work.

Santo Domingo Pueblo (New Mexico) necklace. "Interesting about this necklace," the director said, "are the 'nots'—not coral, not obsidian, but old melted phonograph records for the black element. During the Depression, the Native American artists were constrained by the lack of materials. Everyone thinks creativity and innovation are driven by freedom. In the art world, they are often driven, instead, by constraints."

Project management constraints are scope, schedule, and cost—the components of the Iron Triangle of traditional project management. Of these, schedule has been abused the most. Like quality, time is more complex than it seems at first.

Time deadlines have been a pervasive theme in software development projects. But which time? What defines "late"? Is time the most important control metric? I can think of several time topics: planned versus actual, elapsed time, benchmark performance, and cycle time. Lastly, how should we use time—as an objective or a constraint?

Project managers emphasize planned versus actual time. Making the plan is good; not making the plan is bad. Between the problems with fuzzy requirements (all requirements are fuzzy), inconsistent estimating, future uncertainty, politics, and a myriad of other factors, it's clear planned versus actual time is a complex topic. Unfortunately, plans are often more about politics than estimates—I call them wish-based plans. Missed delivery dates are probably the greatest cause of dissatisfaction and loss of credibility between management and software development.

A second perspective on time is elapsed time—time from the beginning to the end of a project. When managers complain, "The project is late," they may mean the project is taking too long, irrespective of the planned date. Complaints increase over time, regardless. For example, even though a project is planned for two years and is on schedule, the perception is often negative because of the overall length of time it is taking. By comparison, a project that delivers results in 3 to 6 months may be considered successful, regardless of plans. Reducing project delivery time can, by itself, improve the perception of success.

Benchmarking provides another perspective on time, as in "How do we compare?" I've seen projects be considered failures from a plan-versus-actual perspective even though they had above-average schedule performance when compared to industry norms. If a product team receives an unreasonable schedule based on industry or internal norms, who should be accountable for dates?

Continuous delivery (CD) technology causes us to ask whether schedule time or cycle time is more important. But which cycle time? Deployment frequency (days, weeks, x times per day), feature cycle time (release from backlog to delivery), or project cycle time (beginning to end)—all of these have a place.

In my early work I often said, "Time-boxing is not about time; it is about making hard decisions." With short iterations and short projects, hard decisions come early and often.

When time functions as a constraint, it forces hard decisions. Waterfall methodologies tended to kick the can down the road, where it eventually landed by the dumpster load on the poor souls at the bottom of the waterfall—the testers. Staff earlier in the waterfall stayed "on schedule" because they declared documents done. So, near the "end" of the schedule, time allocated to testing shrank from six months to three weeks. You can fake the completion of a requirements document, but you can't fake tested, running code.

ONE OF MY PRIMARY goals when writing the second edition of *Agile Project Management* was to discuss performance measurement issues and introduce the Agile Triangle (see Figure 7.1) as a replacement for the Iron Triangle used in traditional project management. I heard agile teams complain, "Management wants us to be agile and adaptive, but we also must conform to the project's planned scope, schedule, and cost objectives." Management, it seemed, wanted agility, but with traditional performance measures. If adaptation and flexibility are the trademarks of agile projects and conforming to the plan is the trademark of traditional projects, then why do we still measure success on agile projects using the same traditional framework? If an agile leader focuses on *adapting successfully to inevitable changes* rather than *following the plan with minimal changes*, then measuring success by strictly adhering to a scope, schedule, and cost plan would be dysfunctional. So, I created the Agile Triangle, shown in Figure 7.1. Its dimensions are as follows:

- Value goal: deliver a product of value to the customer
- Quality goal: build a reliable, adaptable product
- Constraint goal: achieve value and quality within acceptable constraints

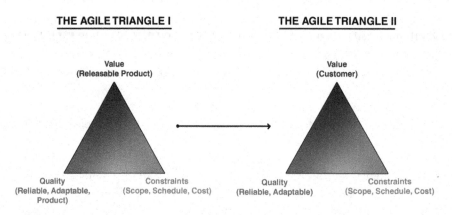

Figure 7.1 *From Agile Triangle I to Agile Triangle II.*

Since *Agile Project Management* was published in 2009, I've worked on enterprise digital transformations and made a couple of modifications to the Agile Triangle. First, I replaced the descriptive phrase "releasable product" with "customer," and second, I removed "product" from the phrase "reliable, adaptable product." I think these minor changes extend its applicability to organizational units, as well as products, services, and projects. Initiatives of any kind (in Chapter 8, "initiatives" will be used at the action level of a Lean Value Tree) can be evaluated by their impact on customer value and quality (sustainability), while remaining within the established boundaries (constraints).

Measuring success is tricky. Motorola's 1990s ill-fated, multibillion-dollar, satellite-based Iridium project was a spectacular failure in the market. Meanwhile, the movie *Titanic*, which was severely over budget and schedule—and viewed by early pundits as a $200 million flop—was the first movie to generate more than $1 billion in worldwide revenue. By Iron Triangle project management measures of success—scope, cost, and schedule—*Titanic* was a failure. Within some circles, Iridium was considered a success because it fulfilled the original specifications within the cost and schedule plans. Using the Agile Triangle, the *Titanic* project would be considered a success— it delivered value even though it exceeded its constraints. Iridium would have been considered a failure because it failed to deliver value, even though according to traditional project measurements, it succeeded.

In the Iridium project, the Iron Triangle enabled tangled accountability. The engineers could say, "We built what you told us to build," while product managers complained, "But it isn't what we need today. You provided what we thought we needed two years ago." Nothing highlights this problem more than the following quote from colleague Helen Pukszta at the Cutter Consortium. The quote always stunned me, but unfortunately was normal practice in traditional IT organizations.

> I recently asked a colleague CIO whether he would prefer to deliver a project somewhat late and over budget but rich with business benefits, or one that is on time and under budget but of scant value to the business. He thought it was a tough call, and then went for the on-time scenario. Delivering on time and within budget is part of his IT department's performance metrics. Chasing after the elusive business value, over which he thought he had little control anyway, is not.

A person who greatly influenced my thinking about measures of success is my friend and colleague Rob Austin, who provided a quite different view of measurement. *Most measurement systems are doomed to failure* describes the essence of Rob's book *Measuring and Managing Performance in Organizations* (Austin, 1996). Rob is a professor at the Richard Ivey School of Business at the University of Western Ontario, located in London, Ontario, and formerly an associate professor at Harvard Business School.

You have to change measures of success to succeed with agile development.

Rob's organizational performance model predicts why so many measurement programs fail. Based on economic theory, he builds a convincing model of the difficulties in motivating through measuring, particularly in knowledge work. He defines measurement dysfunction as measuring something to get a particular result in which the measurement causes exactly the opposite response. As Rob shows, reliance on simple measurements in complex situations nearly always leads to dysfunction.

Constraints are still vital project measures, but they are not the project's goal. Value is the goal, and constraints may need to be adjusted as the project moves forward to increase customer value. Schedule might still be a fixed constraint, but then value is adjusted to deliver within the schedule constraints. If we want adaptability, we must reward it. Adjusting constraints to meet value or quality goals helps organizations meet this need.

One organization I worked with used delivery date and document completeness to measure product managers' performance. Furthermore, because of the yearly product release cycle, once the product managers completed requirements for Release 2, they had to immediately move on to Release 3—leaving no time to collaborate with the development staff. These, and other performance metrics, had to change before any agile implementation could be successful.

In the mid-2000s, PMI represented a traditional approach to project management. As APM was becoming more popular, I spoke at local PMI chapters around the United States. I had a standard set of questions related to the Iron Triangle. The Iron Triangle was intended to illustrate the trade-offs among three components, but even the name "Iron" contradicts that interpretation and leads managers to view all three as fixed.

"Do you have projects with different profiles?" I asked. "For example, one might be an office move project for which you need a sequenced set of tasks that are easily definable, and another might be, say, an artificial intelligence project for which innovation is paramount?"

"Of course," they would answer.

I would ask the next question: "Are they very different kinds of projects?"

"Of course."

"And do you use the same measures of success—scope, schedule, cost?"

And you could see the lights coming on. The answers were still "Yes"—but a much more hesitant "Yes." They could see the conundrum I'd led them into. Scope is a constraint, not an objective.

During a recent visit to a new doctor, I spent lots of time talking to the top of his head as he banged away on his laptop. Remember (not too long ago) when doctors felt entering data on a keyboard was beneath them? Think of the poor software developers trying to build the first doctor/patient applications and interactions. Do you think scope, schedule, and cost should have been the key performance objectives?

During this second Agile-era period, there was considerable discussion about agile project management, whether project managers were necessary, and other topics. Maturing agile organizations realized project management was still a critical aspect of effective teams, and knew they should focus on an agile *style* of project management. They realized good project managers could be effective catalysts of large-scale transformations because they could be a bridge between agile teams and management in areas such as governance, organization, performance measures, and process.

Pat Reed and I worked, with others, on the launch of PMI's Agile Community of Practice to equip PMI members with agile knowledge and skills.

Thoughtworks hosted the launch party during the 2009 Agile Alliance conference in Chicago. PMI drew on this Community of Practice to develop its Agile Project Management certification program (2011). In 2012, PMI launched this certification program, which had nearly 3,000 certificate holders in the first year. Today PMI offers four Agile Project Management certifications and the seventh release of the PMBoK in 2021 included significant agile content.

The introduction of the Agile Triangle to replace the traditional Iron Triangle of project management was significant as we approached larger agile transformations such as those at Integrated Financial Software and Telecom China (which we will visit shortly).

ONE OF MY CONCERNS about agile methodologies, from the beginning, was an overreaction to the problems with traditional planning. While traditionalists got bogged down in their overly detailed, deterministic plans, many agilists forgot about planning completely.

Agile has become mired in the micro short term.

At the time I wrote *Agile Project Management* (*APM*) in 2004, I was concerned agile teams were so focused on delivering stories every one to two weeks that longer-term product and technical goals were getting swept aside. *APM* devoted an entire chapter to release planning—laying out goals, constraints, and guidelines for the project or product. I asked Mike Cohn[7] recently how many of the teams/organizations he was working with (in 2022) did release planning. His answer, "Virtually none." He agreed this laser focus on weekly, daily, hourly feature delivery was a damaging trend.

You might argue traditional management over-planning ushered in the agile reaction of under-planning. The very words "planning" and "project management" became anathemas to agilists. But rather than redefine those terms, many preferred to abandon them. Agile planning should be outcome oriented—value and goals. Remember the story I shared about Alias Systems? We adapted the release planning and iteration planning outcomes based on real-time feedback. The team delivered in two-week iterations, but always had their product vision, feature priority, and time constraints in mind. They held onto their short-term and long-term goals concurrently, balancing the two.

---

7. Mike Cohn is another post–Manifesto Agile pioneer who made extraordinary contributions to the field.

Too often individuals and teams concentrate so hard on shorter iterations that they forget the big picture. They have become so averse to the word "planning" they abandon the future, the overall value proposition for the project or product. This is the reason I like the terms "speculate" and "envision"—they convey a sense of purpose to a team, a direction rather than a prescriptive plan.

The practices of DevOps—continuous integration and continuous deployment—have contributed considerable benefits and value to businesses, but the downside is their contribution to micro-focusing. When developers *can* deliver new features 10 times a day, the next question is *should* they?

Teams without release plans often oscillate in iteration planning because they lack the overall theme and context such a plan provides. Separating oscillation from iteration isn't always easy, but it's a skill good product owners, project managers, iterations managers, and teams need to cultivate.

Organizational change

As the Rogue Teams period drifted into the Courageous Executives one, agilists needed to acquire or refine another set of skills—those of organizational change management. The practices necessary to get a small team to use agile development and those necessary to get an entire IT organization (much less an entire enterprise) to embrace agility are vastly more complicated. Do we implement from top to bottom, or from bottom to top? Do we start with a few teams and use their experience to seed others, or do we "sheep dip"[8] everyone? What is our strategy for moving agility up (the organizational hierarchy) and sideways (other departments, other divisions)? How do we instill both *being* agile and *doing* agile? Whose change model and approach do we use?

For most early agilists, change management was midway down on our skills list, and such was the case for me. My colleagues and I were not experts in the change management field, so we read what others had to say, worked from our prior experience, and managed to muddle through. I used a combination of two approaches to change management with clients.

---

8. "Sheep dip" was a term that originated in the 1980s and was applied to "dipping" everyone in a workshop or two and then declaring that they were now "structured"—akin to the Agile era's two-day "dip" to become a Scrum proficient.

JERRY WEINBERG WAS an early thinker about change management. During Consultants' Camp workshops in the mid-1990s, he introduced the group to Virginia Satir's Change Model, shown in Figure 7.2 (Smith, 2000). I liked this model because it emphasized some key points:

- Things get worse before they get better (this is a difficult realization for management, particularly if the change was sold as a quick cure-all).
- People may give up on a change if it gets too uncomfortable.
- The ride from current performance to better performance is bumpy.
- Successful transitions require investments in both time and money.
- Trust and understanding are needed to overcome fear and resistance.

At one client's office, Josh and I walked into a manager's area one morning to discover balloons flying around. When asked what the occasion was, the manager declared, "We are celebrating chaos." Change management

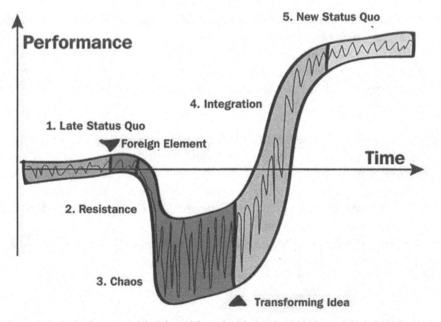

Figure 7.2 *Satir change model. Adapted from Smith, 2000, p. 96. Copyright © 2000 by Gerald M. Weinberg. Used by permission of Dorset House Publishing (www.dorsethouse.com).*

has become an industry on its own. I'm sure there are more sophisticated approaches today, but I found the Satir model both useful and simple to explain.

As a consultant trying my best to assist clients in improving performance by applying new methods, methodologies, and mindsets, my go-to reference has been Jerry Weinberg's (1985) book *The Secrets of Consulting*. His advice remains relevant today, nearly 40 years after the book's first publication. Those who attempt to change human behavior, especially mindsets, would benefit from Jerry's cautions:

Never promise more than ten percent improvement.[9]

Most of the time, for most of the world, no matter how hard people work at it, nothing of significance happens.[10]

In today's race to change, change, change, we sometimes forget we are dealing with people, and we are all slower to change than we think. Before a client engagement, or when an existing engagement bogs down, I run Jerry's cautions through my head and repeat the mantra "Patience." Looking back at the Roots of Agile era, it took me more than five years to make my own transition from structured methods to adaptive software development. Today, with the avalanche of material and consulting on agile development, the transition should be quicker, but it remains far from instantaneous.

ALISTAIR COCKBURN INTRODUCED the Shu-Ha-Ri listening or learning model, dating to Japanese Noh theater almost four centuries ago, to the agile community today and has used this extensively in his consulting practice. Alister's point was we needed to understand how people learn before we can understand how to manage change. Satir and Shu-Ha-Ri helped me through transformation efforts for a number of years.

Alistair is a great writer, so rather than try to paraphrase his work, I'll just quote his early article:[11]

---

9. Weinberg, 1986, p. 6.
10. Weinberg, 1986, p. 13.
11. A PDF of Alistair's original article can be found on www.heartofagile.com site.

"People who are learning and mastering new skills pass through three quite different stages of behavior: *following*, *detaching*, and *fluent*. People in the *following (Shu)* stage look for one procedure that works. Even if ten procedures could work, they can't learn ten at once. They need one to learn first, one that works. They copy it; they learn it."

"In the *detaching*, or Level 2, stage, people locate the limitations of the single procedure and look for rules about when the procedure breaks down. They are actually in the first stage of a new learning—namely, learning the limits of the procedure. The person in the detaching stage learns to adapt the procedure to varying circumstances."

"In the third, *fluent* stage, it becomes irrelevant to the practitioner whether she is following any particular technique or not. Her knowledge has become integrated throughout a thousand thoughts and actions. Ask her if she is following a particular procedure, and she is likely to shrug her shoulders: It doesn't matter to her whether she is following a procedure, improvising around one, or making up a new one. She understands the desired end effect and simply makes her way to that end."

ONE ISSUE THAT bothers me can be identified by the oxymoron, "prescriptive agility." Companies latch on to 12 practices of XP or 6 practices of Scrum and declare they are agile. I've used the term "prescriptive agility" to describe an organization's tendency to prescribe a set of agile practices as mandatory, rather than "adaptive agility" in which agile practices are continually adapted to each situation. How much sense does it make to build adaptable software using a prescriptive methodology?

Maybe prescribing agile practices makes sense while learning them (Alistair's "Shu" level), but if you don't move quickly to adaptive agility (the adjective should not be necessary) you might as well be using a traditional methodology. If you haven't scattered adventurous, nonconformist, adaptive people throughout your organization, you will not achieve agility. If you are not ready to embrace chaos (in the Satir model) and work through anxiety, you may be *doing* agile, but you are not *being* agile.

Alistair Cockburn has addressed this issue by defining his "heart of agile," which has only four components: collaborate, deliver, reflect, and improve. This "heart" is definitely more mindset than methodology. Embracing agility takes patience, determination, and courage. It's not easy, but that's what it takes to embrace the essence of agility.[12]

Software development

First, there were Kent Beck's (2000) *eXtreme Programming Explained* and my *Adaptive Software Development* (also released in 2000), which started a flood of agile books. By the second decade of the Agile era, there were lists of the 100 best agile books and even the 100 best Scrum books. Other authors promoted advances such as Kanban, continuous integration, DevOps, Lean, agile project management, scaling agile, and much more. These advances invigorated the agile movement.

Two other factors were impacting agile implementations at this time—one technical and the other organizational.

Transforming organizations rather than teams brought layers of difficulty. I began noticing a split in IT departments: One group was responsible for internal, legacy back-office systems, and a second rapidly growing group was responsible for web and mobile device applications, sometimes referred to as front-office or customer-engagement applications. The former stuck with Monumental Methodologies, while the latter increasingly embraced agile development. Resentment grew because the Internet groups got to work on cool new things, and therefore needed an envision–explore mindset, whereas the internal groups often struggled with 80% to 90% of their efforts going to legacy system maintenance and minor enhancements. The wider marketplace battle between traditional and agile methods took place inside enterprises as well.

Resentment between the groups was one result; clashing was another. Internet applications required accessing and updating legacy systems. Legacy groups received requests for assistance from the Internet groups, and since the agile groups were on a one- to two-week delivery cycle and the legacy groups were on months-long release cycles, the ensuing response-time clash added to the problems. One organization, two clashing mindsets. A couple of large consulting and research firms proposed a solution that merely mirrored the status quo: bimodal or two-speed IT. Rather than solve the problems, bimodal IT solidified the split. Bimodal was often the de facto structure that arose, but it worked best as a transitional strategy.

---

12. What actions define an agile person? Read on to Chapter 9.

As Internet applications became more complex, their integration with legacy systems did as well. This eventually led to painful reorganizations, reuniting the two groups, and often standardizing agile methods for the entire organization.

THE MUSTANG TEAM, Alias Systems, Sciex, and the Integrated Financial Software stories touched on the topic of technical debt. As agilists delved into enterprise agile implementations, understanding the consequences of rising debt and options to fix the problem became increasingly important. Even the most agile team advances slowly when faced with high tech debt. It presents a gnarly problem to solve.

IT and product managers, who were aware of the devastating effect of debt on their ability to maintain software, were beginning to understand the underlying issues and how to deal with them. They accepted the need for a tech debt strategy. Salesforce, whose successes were described at the beginning of this chapter, was growing rapidly in the mid-2000s, but its software delivery capabilities were faltering in the wake of that growth and tech debt. Switching to an agile delivery model and increasing its technical capabilities fueled this company's growth.

Technical debt issues are the most consequential outcome of software's intangibility. Financial debt is tangible; it shows up on the company's balance sheet. Increasing financial debt limits a company's financing options and can impact investments in innovative new products and services. Software technical debt is more insidious because it generally remains hidden, emerging only as software maintenance costs escalate and developers have less time for new products.

Two categories of tech debt occur: quality degradation and obsolescence. The primary difference between the two is whether the degradation results from internal or external forces. Quality degradation occurs when systems are poorly maintained. Obsolescence occurs when external change—client-server to Internet architecture, for example—forces a conversion effort. Technical debt can also hamper investment in new products.

What the agile methods brought to this issue was a new perspective—one of continuous delivery of value. Change the narrative, but don't pit quality against valuable features. Explain how a lack of investment in managing tech debt impacts the enterprise's stream of value delivery.

TECHNICAL DEBT

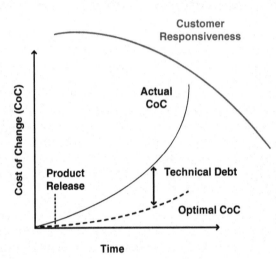

Figure 7.3 *Increasing cost of technical debt.*[13]

The bottom line for technical debt: It's expensive to fix, but much more expensive to ignore. IT organizations' ability to respond to the Internet era was compromised by technical debt (Figure 7.3).

By far, the largest technical debt event that impacted software and computers worldwide was the century transition from 1999 to 2000. This Y2K event drained resources from IT organizations at the very time they needed to focus on responding to the strategic impact of the Internet.

Tech debt caused by obsolescence (remember Windows XP?) typically results in large efforts, particularly when the decision to convert drags out. Often, these situations arise because of advances in systems software or major hardware changes. These conversion projects are prone to underestimation, in large measure, because IT departments are reluctant to admit their real costs. I once talked to a manager facing a "must do" hardware conversion estimated to keep his entire department working on it for two years—

---

13. This figure first appeared in Highsmith, 2009.

to deliver the exact same functionality as the old system, just with a new technology architecture. He was concerned about abandoning his user base for two years. He was right to be concerned.

The proverbial "kicking the can down the road" resulted in a most egregious example of tech debt. One Houston-based software company I encountered sold engineering applications to the oil industry. Its release cycle had exploded to more than two years, with a final test and integration period after "code-freeze" of 18 months! Company managers faced a daunting decision since a project to completely replace the old system was estimated to cost upward of $100 million. All of their choices at this point were bad ones. In addition, I cautioned that if they didn't address their tech debt strategy, any brand-new system would face the same degradation after a few years.

For most enterprises, fixing tech debt issues requires an incremental improvement strategy and persistence. Given the diverse software asset portfolios of big enterprises, all three of the debt reduction strategies—rewrite, systematic refactoring, and abandoning—will be required depending on specific applications.

Scaling agile

Josh Kerievsky and I showed up in China in 2010 to consult with Telecom China under the Cutter Consortium banner. Expecting a reasonably normal consulting assignment discussing issues with a few people at a time, we were surprised, and a little daunted, to encounter an audience of more than 60 people. For 10 days, we presented agile concepts and practices, answered questions, and engaged in sidebar discussions—using simultaneous translators. To one comment (I can't remember who said it since both Josh and I can be irreverent at times), the Chinese translator replied, "I can't say that!" Josh and I traded off presentations often, so the non-presenter could hurriedly figure out what he was going to say next.

Telecom China was a large equipment manufacturing firm that had implemented IBM's Phase-Gate process for product development.[14] The software division, was committed to the Capability Maturity Model (CMM). Many agilists would argue the first priority would be to get rid of both the

---

14. A Phase-Gate system is a type of Monumental Methodology often found in companies that design and manufacture industrial products. It has waterfall-like phases (plan, design, engineering drawings, etc.) and gates that are formal management control points. Gate reviews are often very time consuming.

CMM and the Phase-Gate system. However, in a large manufacturing company, ousting such embedded processes was beyond the scope of work Josh and I were tasked with. So, we found a way to imbed an agile software development methodology within its overall process[15] by using the Phase-Gate system for governance, CMM for a definitional system, and agile practices for operational development. This was an extension of what we had done with Sciex. Admittedly kludgy, it worked. It was enough to give the software division cover to introduce agile. In large agile transformations, you have to pick your battles carefully. Trying to implement agile practices in a software division of several thousand developers was daunting enough, so insisting on changing long-embedded management systems across the entire organization needed to be planned in a future phase.

One thing we learned from this engagement was the difference between an impediment and a barrier. Most agilists at the time looked at barriers as challenges to overcome and didn't recognize specific types of barriers. With large organizations, particularly those in other countries, differentiation was necessary. We defined an impediment as something that could be overcome in an agile implementation. We thought breaching a barrier was much, much harder, requiring senior executive involvement.

Would Josh and I have preferred not to work around the Phase-Gate system? Certainly. Did we have our hands full introducing agile to the thousands of software engineers already? Absolutely. Trying to fit the agile initiative into their Phase-Gate system was the only feasible way to go, at that time. One lesson I have learned from working with clients over the years is that banging my head against the wall causes headaches. I try not to do that anymore. For large agile transformations, understanding the difference between impediments and barriers is critical to avoiding headaches.

A dining adventure highlighting this trip was arranged by Guo Xiao, then managing director of Thoughtworks China (currently president and CEO of Thoughtworks). Xiao ordered a table full of Chinese delicacies that we would never have tasted on our own.

ENGAGEMENTS LIKE MY work at Telecom China and Integrated Financial Software provided further confirmation that agile practices would scale, but there were still detractors who relegated agile to small projects. Our work

---

15. I wrote about an approach to handling Phase-Gate and Agile in *ASDE* (Highsmith, 2002).

at Sciex and Integrated Financial Software saw agile scale to medium-sized companies and projects. Now came the challenge of huge organizations. At the Agile Executive Forum in 2011, I was talking to a Chinese vice president of software engineering whose staff numbered about 20,000 engineers.

"How many agile projects did you have last year?" I asked.

"Three," he replied.

"And how many do you want to tackle this year?"

"Around 200."

I was so surprised I had a hard time finishing the conversation. Maybe he knew something I didn't, but going from 3 agile projects to 200 in a year's time wasn't doable in my experience. As with any major change initiative, balancing moving too fast and moving too slow is hard, and the right approach varies greatly between organizations. Convincing IT executives of the realistic cost and time to implement agile practices was a challenge, because they often employed another form of wish-based planning—wish-based agile implementations. A few, like the ones at IFS and Sciex, better understood both the challenge and the cost.

In the Digital Transformation period, scaling agile development became a hot topic with the introduction of the Scaled Agile Framework (SAFe) and the Disciplined Agile methodologies. SAFe was developed by Dean Leffingwell and Disciplined Agile by Scott Ambler, both pioneers in the industry. Indicative of the escalating interest in scaling approaches, Disciplined Agile was purchased by PMI, and SAFe received a major capital infusion by private equity firm Eurazeo.

However, in the Courageous Executives period, specific methods for scaling agile development were just emerging and company CIOs and others were skeptical. Chapter 8 will address scaling again, first asking if we were even addressing the right questions. In this chapter, I want to offer a couple of arguments that an agile mindset should not be limited to small projects.

MY FIRST ARGUMENT comes from a brief interaction in 2002 with Sheila Widnall, an aerospace researcher and professor at MIT. She served as U.S. Secretary of the Air Force between 1993 and 1997, making her the first woman to hold that position and the first woman to lead an entire branch of the U.S. military. Dr. Widnall gave the keynote address at a 2000 Risk Management Symposium jointly sponsored by the Aerospace Corporation and the Air Force Space and Missile Systems Command.

In her talk, Dr. Widnall examined the previous year's rash of launch and vehicle failures that led to review committees and the launch industry rethinking its approach to mission reliability. Her goal was achieving a higher level of effectiveness in systems engineering and risk management.

She then mentioned my *Adaptive Software Development* book:

> I was quite taken recently with a new book by Jim Highsmith on adaptive software development. Using a mountain climbing metaphor, he traces the considerations one goes through in thinking about undertaking a risky, complex venture, where the outcome is inherently unpredictable and where one misstep can be fatal: a venture that requires considerable skill, planning, and adaptability. And again, the parallels are drawn, and comparisons made between the approach taken to climbing a mountain and that taken in developing a new and complex piece of software.

Dr. Widnall wondered about using the concepts in *ASD* to develop a similar aerospace approach, possibly called adaptive systems development. But she also cautioned that while the application to software was obvious, the application to systems was less so—something she asked the audience to "think about."

In a follow-up phone call after I learned about her keynote address, Dr. Widnall offered: "Maybe in the aerospace business, where programs to build new aircraft take 10 to 15 years, we would not be able to use weekly or monthly iterations, but even some type of say two-year iterations would benefit us." Of course, if agile/adaptive concepts could be helpful in aerospace programs, then they just might scale in software development.

THE FIRST DIGITAL camera was developed by Eastman Kodak engineer Steven Sasson in 1975. Kodak made enormous profits on the film side of the camera business, selling both film and film-processing equipment. Early digital cameras didn't have the resolution many camera buffs desired, so executives at Kodak continued to pour investments into the film business. But digital cameras also had benefits—namely, ease of use, instant viewing, and low cost. First slowly, and then more rapidly, digital cameras overcame their resolution deficiencies. The market for inexpensive digital cameras exploded, and then expensive cameras made the transition. The film business went up in smoke and Kodak declared bankruptcy.

This story suggests the constant dilemma businesses face today—when to cannibalize their existing products and when to launch new ones. The timing is tricky. Recently, the inexpensive camera market has been overtaken by smartphones that have great cameras and many other applications. Kodak was brought down by what Clayton Christensen (1997) called the "innovator's dilemma," in which a lesser product with new desirable features overtakes a market leader as the product's deficiencies are fixed in subsequent releases. In the beginning, digital cameras had low cost, no film processing, and, best of all, instant response. Their early downside was poorer picture quality. But, for a large segment of the market, instant response and not having the hassle of film processing was more important than picture quality. Then, as their picture quality increased, digital cameras intruded further into the market, until eventually film cameras were a small, specialty item.[16]

In the Rogue Teams period within the Agile era, scaling may have been an issue.[17] However, similarly to the case for digital cameras, slowly but surely that early deficiency faded. There are still detractors of digital cameras, just as there are skeptics about agile development's ability to scale, but they are proving to be on the wrong side of history.

FINALLY, IN REGARD to scaling, I ask several questions related to the values expressed in the Agile Manifesto. At what size of project do process and tools become more important than individuals and their interactions? Remember, the Agile Manifesto uses the specific word "over," meaning process and tools are important, just less so than individuals and collaborative teams.

Second, at what size of project does customer collaboration become less important than a contract? Contracts are important, certainly. But without a collaborative relationship with the customer, a contract, no matter how detailed, won't provide the desired outcome—and both parties may suffer.

You can construct similar questions for the other Agile Manifesto value statements. While larger projects require more methodology guardrails in the form of documentation, processes, and management reviews, an agile mindset still offers the best chance of success.

---

16. According to systems thinking, every solution comes with its own new problems. Now we have thousands and thousands of mostly unorganized pictures on our digital devices. Previously we had only boxes and boxes of them.

17. Scaling isn't the only agile feature that came under fire, but it will do as an example here.

Athleta

The next Agile-era period, Digital Transformation, advanced from a focus on IT agility to enterprise agility. The Athleta story was an early example of what *business* agility could accomplish and provides a lead-in to the Digital Transformation period.

Pat Reed told me this story, and I've retold it many times in conference talks and workshops because it shows what an agile mindset can accomplish. Athleta, founded in 1998 to meet the unique needs of athletic women, was acquired by GAP, Inc., in 2008. A question faced by executives was whether to keep Athleta as an Internet-only shopping experience or to open bricks-and-mortar stores. Pat related the story behind the story.

GAP executives wanted to expand the Athleta brand into brick-and-mortar stores but were hesitant about the move. To gain additional viability information, they wanted to create a prototype store to test their hypothesis. When they approached their GAP facilities management and legacy IT departments, the estimated build-out time frame was 18 months.

Working with an agile mindset and recognizing that this was an experimental probe into the market, Pat Reed's online development department assisted the GAP business leaders to open the prototype store in Mill Valley, California, in a little more than three months. When siting the store in the target market community, they didn't construct a building, but rather rented one. They eliminated the time usually taken to install corporate information systems and used QuickBooks instead. They broke corporate new-building standards, but the results were encouraging enough that the brick-and-mortar decision was made. In fairness, the facilities department's mission was to build the 20th or 50th store, not a prototype. In the IT legacy department, product experimentation was not their area of expertise—but it needed to be for the coming decade of change. The first GAP Athleta store was opened in 2011, and today there are more than 200 stores worldwide. The Athleta story illustrates the benefits of agility—both in management and in software development.

Period observations

While technical practices were honed and new practices like DevOps and Kanban emerged, the Courageous Executives era focused on implementing agile practices in organizations by changing organizational policies built on decades of waterfall thinking, hiring and retention policies, contract terms, leadership style—a seemingly endless list.

There are many impediments to change in organizations, and implementing agile methodologies ran headlong into many of them. Notably, the organizational impediments followed a pattern of reluctance to become part of agile teams. In the Rogue Teams period, agile teams consisted primarily of developers, as they faced impediments to organizational change such as audit "separation of duties" standards that kept some organizations from adding testers to project teams. As automated testing, continuous integration, and deployment pipelines emerged, they injected additional changes into the mix.

Another impediment involved product management roles. Scrum identified a Product Owner whose job was to identify, define, and prioritize product features. Companies hadn't designed this new Product Owner role, which required facetime with the development teams, and the omission created a capability gap. Internal IT departments didn't normally have product specialists (the closest role was probably the infamous subject-matter expert [SME]), while software companies typically had product management capabilities, just not enough. Problems funding and defining product roles happened frequently.

This redefinition of roles and responsibilities on teams impacted every functional group in IT and beyond—testing, operations, product management, data design and administration, and user interface design. Each area was reluctant to "go agile" and could cite multiple reasons why agile practices wouldn't work in their functional area.

Another area of conflict in agile implementations was between agile teams and project management offices (PMOs) and project managers. In IT organizations (though not as much in software companies), the PMOs wielded considerable power they didn't want to give up. Furthermore, PMOs were typically staffed by the business personnel rather than IT staff and often served as the "enforcers" of Monumental Methodologies. The project management community was probably three to five years behind in adopting agile principles. (The friction between development groups and PMOs was long-standing and didn't begin with the incursion of agile practices.)

So, the transition from rogue teams to agile organizations was a bumpy one, replete with impediment after impediment. Some companies were able to break through, while others were stymied at each roadblock. One sentence describing Gary Walker's experience at Sciex bears repeating here: "As I recall, we began to see a change in the team mindset and behavior approximately 18 months after we initiated the agile transformation." Effective organizational change takes time and patience.

My own observation is that success versus failure with organizational implementation of agile development rests with courageous executives who understand agility at their core. Ken Delcol at Sciex not only encouraged and funded their agile transformation, but also proposed such outlandish practices as forming teams from multiple engineering disciplines and restructuring workspaces to accommodate them. Barry, from another story, encouraged and funded his company's agile implementation, but he never embraced the principles. Agile teams could succeed without courageous executives' involvement; organizational agile initiatives could not.

Another observation relates to the approaches taken to effect organizational change. Agilists had enough background in change models to muddle through team-level and small-company implementations. At an enterprise level, they often needed help from organizational change experts, but didn't always get it. It made a difference when agilists did receive such assistance.

Overall, my experiences in two eras (Structured and Agile) showed the success rate for agile transformations was higher than that for earlier Monumental Methodology initiatives, although what constituted success was widely debated in the agile community. The reasons for this success were: (1) The business benefits were demonstrable; (2) agile practices appealed to developers (whereas previous methodologies had little appeal to this group); and (3) the Agile Manifesto stated a clear purpose and principles for the movement. The heavy-weight waterfall methodologies of the 1980s and 1990s were document driven and bureaucratic, and their implementation was driven from the top (management) to the bottom (engineers). Agile implementations have, for the most part, been either driven by or supported by developers.

8

Digital Transformation

(2011–Present)

> *"Since 2000, 52 percent of the Fortune 500 companies have either been acquired, merged, or have declared bankruptcy."*
>
> —Tom Siebel, *Digital Transformation* (2019)

FIFTY-TWO PERCENT GONE. In 19 years. The shifting sands of time had become a torrent of change, and this was before COVID-19, the Russia–Ukraine conflict, superstorms spawned by climate change, looming world-wide recession, and increasingly unstable geopolitics. In this topsy-turvy world, companies began articulating their digital transformation strategies as key to survive and thrive during this tumult. This chapter focuses on that transformation, my work for Thoughtworks, and our EDGE approach to transformation (an operating model linking strategy to action), a unique agile organizational model, and empathetic management. The problem now wasn't scaling agile, it was *scaling innovation at enterprise levels*, as the following story about Latam Airlines illustrates.

THERE ARE TWO alternative strategies to solving enterprise problems—do more of the same thing and expect different results or try something new. Courageous executives are required for the second strategy, and Thought-works finds them in countries around the world—one in particular in South America. I was privileged to talk about Latam Airlines' digital transformation with Ricard Vilà, the company's chief digital officer.

Latam Airlines Group S.A., an airline holding company headquartered in Santiago, Chile, has subsidiaries in Brazil, Colombia, Ecuador, Paraguay, and Peru. Latam has been buffeted by the forces released by the COVID-19 pandemic, as have all airlines and hospitality industry businesses. From the smallest mom-and-pop retail stores to cruise lines and airlines, all have traversed the violent swings from good business to no business to short-staffed business.

Latam's push into digital transformation began in 2017 with the installation of a new chief information officer (CIO), Dirk John. Its digital initiatives were split between an information and communications technology (ICT)[1] organization, which had responsibility for operational systems, and a digital organization, which assumed responsibility for all customer experience systems. At that early point, drivers for change included industry trends, fragmented ICT systems resulting from independent business units, aging ICT infrastructure, and executives viewing ICT as a service provider, not a partner.

Thoughtworks had partnered with Latam in developing software. In August 2018, David Robinson, my coauthor on the *EDGE* book (Highsmith, Luu, and Robinson, 2020), put together a team to explore a comprehensive digital transformation. Although I kept up with this project because it provided feedback for our EDGE practices, I wasn't a direct participant on David's team.

There were two initiatives. One, done by McKinsey, was the customer experience (CX)[2] initiative prework to provide a basis and motivation for selecting a technology partner. Then, Thoughtworks' 10-week effort kicked off to carry the CX initiative to the operational level. The major goals were end-to-end accountability (rather than silo accountability), simplification of business rules that had grown topsy-turvy, and a fresh modern technology architecture.

The three key findings from the project were that Latam management:

- Had little insight into effort being wasted on projects not delivering value

---

1. The name information and communications technology (ICT) has slowly been replacing information technology (IT). ICT is a better fit for today's Internet connectivity–infused world (maybe it should be information and connectivity technology), so this newer term will be used in Chapter 8, as it covers the last decade of technology advances.
2. Latam uses the abbreviation XP for customer experience. To reduce possible confusion with Extreme Programming's XP, I chose to use CX in this Latam narrative.

- Didn't have the data or review processes to stop or pivot low-value projects until it was too late
- Had no systematic way to learn and course correct at the mid-project stage

These findings corresponded to findings in other organizations that had long used waterfall style rather than iterative development, had conflicting business and digital strategies, and continued different measures of success in the business and ICT.

The onslaught of the COVID-19 pandemic was sudden and hit airlines, including Latam, hard, resulting in steep revenue reductions, cuts in staffing and other costs, rethinking of routes and services, and, for some airlines like Latam, recovery under Chapter 11 bankruptcy. But looking to the future, the Latam executives, under the leadership of a courageous CIO and visionary CEO, continued to fund digital transformation projects they knew were critical for the future. This was not just a digital initiative, but an organizational one in which overlapping lines of accountability were integrated and the chief commercial officer and CIO formed an e-business partnership. Instituting these business/technology partnerships aided their focus on high-value initiatives.

One aspect of methodology I've stressed, from the time of the Structured era up to the EDGE transformation period, is the need to adopt and adapt, EDGE not exempted. Organizations these days are too complex, too different, for any one approach to suffice. However, just like taking Extreme Programming (XP) practices and saying, "We will use refactoring, but not automated testing," you must understand the dynamics of how the parts fit together before you rearrange them. EDGE may be your starting point, but every operating model must be adapted to fit each organization.

Today, no executive lacks a digital strategy, but far fewer have made substantial implementation progress. Success requires leadership, an operating model linking strategy to operations, an adaptive organizational structure, and a portfolio management approach using value-based prioritization. Overall, innovation must be prioritized over optimization. That's easy to write, but not so easy to implement. However, Latam continues to make progress by following the EDGE roadmap David and his team developed in conjunction with Latam executives. As of mid-2022, the envisioned technology infrastructure was in place, business–ICT partnerships had evolved, and applications were coming online. A better descriptor for this evolution is *transforming*, rather than *transformation*. Transformation implies an end state, but as we all know, transforming accurately states reality.

Latam's response to the times was enterprise transformation, not scaling agile software development (although it was a part). The company realized that not only its digital infrastructure must adapt quickly, but also its business–ICT partnerships, and leadership mindset needed to change. Latam's executive management supported the effort and actively participated in it.

Thoughtworks

Throughout the first decade of the Agile era, I worked with the Cutter Consortium. During the second decade, I went to work for Thoughtworks (TW). In 1997, I met Martin Fowler, who worked for TW (and still does); bumped into and worked with other TWers in Sydney, London, and various places in the United States; and got to know Roy Singham, then CEO. After a 2010 breakfast with Roy in Orlando, Florida, I joined TW as an executive consultant. The announcement was made shortly thereafter at an agile conference in Sydney, Australia, where I was speaking.

Becoming an employee again was definitely a change. But I was certainly going to work for an adventurous company. For me, this period was marked by a change of pace. I worked on short-term engagements with customer executives and managers rather than lengthy consulting gigs. My TW portfolio included consulting on agile implementations, writing, enhancing executive communications, and working on digital transformations.

TW staff have been leading proponents of agile approaches since the late 1990s, when Martin, author of well-known books and co-author of the Agile Manifesto, joined the company. TW culture was a key factor in my decision to work there because it included software excellence, transforming IT, social action, and diversity. It gave much more than lip service to all of these areas. TW was an adventurous organization in which agile development was a core competency. For example, XP practices included pair programming (two developers co-writing code). If it was good for programmers, maybe it was good for managers, so TW experimented with pairing them. As with all experiments, some aspects worked better than others. I expected my tenure to be a few years; it lasted 10. I worked with a group of extremely gifted people—in technology, in management, and in the executive suite.

In the early years of the decade, I traveled widely to work with TW clients and speak at conferences. I worked on internal TW projects, including two that focused on communications. We developed a guideline with tips on how to improve writing skills and get ideas to stick. We tried to keep the guide simple, and light with items like these:

- Don't drape prepositions onto verbs that don't need help. Don't say "personal friend," say "friend."
- Use short words, not long ones. *Assistance* (help). *Numerous* (many).
- Most adverbs are unnecessary and add to the clutter.
- Most adjectives are unnecessary, too.

I also created a storytelling workshop with the thought, "It's not enough to have good ideas; you must make those ideas interesting and credible enough to be acted upon." Fiona Lee, Tony Maitz, Dutch Steutel, and I presented the first Storytelling workshop in San Francisco in mid-2014. The workshop's objective was "To improve your ability to influence, engage, and inspire others." Teams developed and presented their own stories and then refined them. Tony turned out to be an expert at assisting teams through their struggles. We used our own stories to illustrate various aspects of storytelling, and Chip and Dan Heath's SUCCESs framework, which says to be sticky, ideas need to be Simple, Unexpected, Concrete, Credible, Emotional, and tied to Stories.

"A credible idea makes people believe. An emotional idea makes people care. The right story makes people act."
—Heath and Heath, 2007, p. 206

In 2013, I gathered blog posts from the previous five years and published *Adaptive Leadership* (Highsmith, 2013). It incorporated what I had learned about leadership from the previous decade of collaborating with courageous executives on large agile implementations, and included the following topics:

- Examining the flow of opportunities in high-change environments
- Defining strategic, portfolio, and operational agility
- Examining in detail both the *why* and *how* of continuous flow of value
- Building an adaptive, innovative culture
- Making decisions in chaotic, paradoxical situations

My work on adaptive leadership generated my first around-the-world trip—though it lasted 2 weeks, not 80 days.[3] As I was planning a trip to Australia to speak at an agile conference and visit with several TW clients in Sydney, Roy Singham called and asked if I could present a condensed Adaptive Leadership workshop at an upcoming TW leadership meeting in Munich, Germany. I've found that you don't say no to the company CEO unless the meeting falls on your wedding date. Plus, I was excited to share my ideas with senior management. My route of travel took me from Venice, Florida, to London, to Munich, back to London, on to Sydney, a long direct flight from Sydney to Dallas, Texas, and finally home. It's more fun to look back on this type of trip than to actually experience it.

Then came a meeting that focused my remaining time at Thoughtworks.

"HOW SHOULD WE respond to customers who ask about our approach to scaling agile?" was the question that precipitated a TW meeting in 2015. Scaling approaches were gaining attention and companies were responding to this trend. Angie Ferguson, then TW's group managing director for the Asia Pacific region, initiated the meeting in San Francisco. Chad Wathington, then chief capabilities officer; David Robinson, digital transformation principal; Linda Luu, product principal; and I met to discuss TW approach to scaling.

As the San Francisco group wrestled with the question of scaling agile practices within an IT organization, we realized it wasn't really the right question. The right question was "How do we scale enterprise-wide agility and innovation?" The first was a CIO question. The second was a CEO question.

To that point, scaling agile software methods fell back on traditional practices that quickly escalated into bureaucracy, which then stifled innovation. To succeed in the era of digital enterprises, every individual, team, department, division, and executive suite needed to innovate. The key strategic advantage lies not in size scaling, but rather in innovating at scale—retaining the ability to learn and adapt not just in IT, but across the entire enterprise.

The TW group had several concerns that centered on the growing need for adaptability and an operating model and portfolio management approach that would scale without losing that adaptability. We thought the solution needed to be edgy like early agile methods, not safe like several prevailing

---

3. The "80 days" reference is from Jules Verne's 1872 book, *Around the World in Eighty Days*.

scaling approaches. What emerged was EDGE, which became a key part of TW's digital strategy and the beginnings of a book, *EDGE: Value-Driven Digital Transformation*, authored by David, Linda, and me (Highsmith, Luu, and Robinson, 2020).

"In today's era of volatility, there is no other way but to reinvent. The only sustainable advantage you can have over others is agility, that's it. Because nothing else is sustainable, everything else you create, somebody else will replicate."
—Jeff Bezos, former CEO and president, Amazon[4]

A world accelerating

Digital enterprise, the Fourth Industrial Revolution, Lean enterprise—the literature teemed with exhortations to transform from the old to something new. How were enterprises responding? Did they have a digital strategy in place? How were they going to realize that strategy? Were enterprises getting incremental outcomes in a world of exponential opportunities? Whether the goal was to become a digital enterprise, foster widespread innovation, or implement a digital strategy, was strategy being thwarted by poor execution?

This decade saw the death of the former president of South Africa, Nelson Mandela; the Ice Bucket Challenge, which raised $100 million for medical research; Malala Yousafzai, Pakistani activist, winning the Nobel Prize; and the Paris Climate Accord. In the technology realm, Apple introduced the iPad and became the first public company to surpass the $1 billion valuation mark.

In the Cynefin framework, the early half of this period would be considered chaotic, a time when novel approaches to strategy were needed. But from 2020, the world entered a time of disorder—a vast unknown, when even novel approaches may not be good enough.

In a 2017 survey conducted by the MIT Center for Information Systems Research (CISR) of senior leadership from across the globe, 413 senior executives reported that over the next five years their companies may

---

4. https://hbr.org/2021/01/in-the-digital-economy-your-software-is-your-competitive-advantage

be at risk of losing an average of 28 percent of their revenues because of digital disruption. (Weill and Stephanie Woerner, 2018)

An unstoppable revolution is now under way in our society, affecting almost everyone. The revolution is being conducted in plain sight by some of our largest and most respected corporations. It's visible to anyone with eyes to see. It's a revolution in how organizations are being run. (Denning, 2018)

We are experiencing a business event analogous to what biologists call a punctuated equilibrium (PE). Biologists have identified five PEs in the last 500 million years—the event that caused the demise of the dinosaurs was one. During PE events, Darwin's concept of the *survival of the fittest* did not matter. The fittest dinosaurs in the pre–meteor strike ecosystem (*Tyrannosaurus rex*) died when the ecosystem weather changed drastically. There were a few cold-blooded reptile survivors (crocodiles), but the new ecosystem favored those that could adapt to severe weather changes—the warm-blooded mammals.[5]

Less known than the dinosaur extinction event was the catastrophic late Permian event, 225 million years ago, when 96% of all living species vanished from earth (Gould, 2002). Hundreds of species, many superbly honed as the fittest in their environment, died in the Permian extinction. Some, barely surviving in small ecological niches, accidentally happened to have characteristics allowing them to flourish in the subsequent Triassic period.

We believe the Covid-19 crisis is likely to significantly accelerate the shift to digital and fundamentally shake up the business landscape. A world in which Agile ways of working are a prerequisite to meeting seemingly daily changes to customer behavior.

—Fitzpatrick et al., 2020

If Darwin was correct, his *survival of the fittest* explains how we adapt to normal changes in biological or economic agents. If Holland (1995) was correct, his *arrival of the fittest* concept (introduced in Chapter 4 of this book) explains how we adapt when the pace of change accelerates, and we need

---

5. In this chapter, several passages from the book *EDGE* (Highsmith, Luu, and Robinson, 2020) have been used and edited.

to pivot. If we are truly in the throes of a PE, which Snowden[6] might call the area of disorder and for which effective methods are probably unknown, then we are probably in an era of *survival of the luckiest*.

In an era of *survival of the luckiest*, what should be your response? Is your organization analogous to a dinosaur, or a mammal? Will there be a Permian equivalent? What was the key to mammalian thriving, besides luck? Adaptability, adaptability, and adaptability. What is the key to your organization's thriving? Adaptability, adaptability, and more adaptability. That should be your focus for your organization's digital transformation. Think about what happened to airlines like Latam during the COVID-19 pandemic. Instantly air traffic plummeted to record lows. Airline companies slashed variable costs, but airlines are a business with high fixed costs, so their cost-cutting opportunities are limited. Net incomes dove precipitously downward, causing bankruptcies in the worst cases. Then, as vaccines became viable and available, air travel rocketed back upward. From struggling to cut capacity, airlines began struggling to increase capacity.

In this volatile and uncertain time, an organization's ability to adapt, from the CEO's office to front-line workers, will determine success, or failure, in the future.

Digital transformation

The bulk of my last five to six years at TW was spent working on digital transformation and EDGE. After the original EDGE meeting, David, Linda, and I developed an internal EDGE workbook for TW consultants and then gathered client engagement observations on how the process was working. *EDGE: Value-Driven Digital Transformation* was published in 2020. EDGE became a component of TW's digital transformation and operations service offering. What follows is an overview of what we learned while developing EDGE and new material that has emerged since our book's publication.

We found CEOs were asking, "How can we create responsive organizations?" while CIOs were asking, "How can our organizations take advantage of our IT capability?" In the July 2022 *McKinsey Quarterly Report*, technologist Marc Andreessen answered an interview question about how to digitally transform big companies this way: "Find the smartest technologist in the company and make them CEO."[7]

---

6. https://thecynefin.co/about-us/about-cynefin-framework

7. www.mckinsey.com/industries/technology-media-and-telecommunications/our-insights/find-the-smartest-technologist-in-the-company-and-make-them-ceo

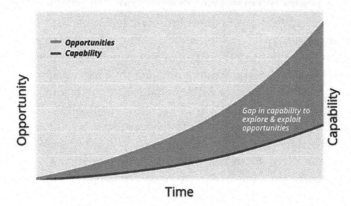

GAP IN ENTERPRISE SUSTAINABILITY

— *Opportunities*
— *Capability*

Opportunity

Capability

Gap in capability to
explore & exploit
opportunities

Time

Figure 8.1 *Gap in enterprise sustainability.*

Technological advances intensify the difference between the rate of opportunity growth and the rate at which the capabilities to take advantage of those opportunities are developed (Figure 8.1). Many enterprises faced opportunities and threats but lacked capabilities to take advantage of them. This growing opportunity–capability gap became a critical issue for executives.

CIOs and CEOs needed to rethink their organizations' IT strategy, escalating it from a function-level strategy—aligned but always subordinate to business strategy—to an overarching *digital business strategy*. The latter is defined as "organizational strategy formulated and executed by leveraging digital resources to create differential value" (Bharadwaj, 2013).

Defining a digital business strategy was easier than figuring out how to implement it. As we discovered, developing the capability of moving from strategy to action involves five areas:

- Measures of success: Digital business transformation needs modern performance measures.
- Tech@Core: Technology must be woven into the core capabilities of all leaders.
- Operating model: Transformations require a fast, effective process for determining how to implement strategy by linking it to action through a value-driven portfolio.

- Organizational model: Organizational structures must emphasize value streams rather than functions and make those structures highly malleable.
- Empathetic management:[8] Whatever name you prefer, "modern" management in the digital era must adapt.

The first three and the last area shown here were covered in EDGE: the organizational model comes from a different source.

Remember the lesson from agile projects: To change behavior and culture, you must change measures of success. The same must happen at the strategic level. Just as in project-level agile transformations, convincing executives and managers to change their measures of success proved to be sticky.[9]

AT LUNCH ONE DAY WITH staff from a prominent agile software tool vendor, one was touting their tool's ability to roll up velocity from teams to the organizational level. I was so aghast at this use of velocity I wrote a blog post titled "Velocity Is Killing Agility" (no longer available online). I wasn't prepared for the reaction—the traffic volume crashed my website.

Was James Michener a better writer than Ernest Hemingway because his books are longer? Or because he could type 20 words per minute faster? Makes sense—right? Assessing the effectiveness of writers based on per-unit productivity (activity) measures makes no sense. If your job is to write Java code "words" rather than English (or French or Polish) words, similar productivity measures make no sense, either.

Productivity measures are meant for tangible things, such as how many widgets a machine can manufacture in an hour. Productivity measures were never designed to assess intangibles such as ideas and innovations. But measuring intangibles is hard and measuring tangibles is easy, so naturally people gravitate toward what is easiest, even when it's wrong. Better to have some measure rather than nothing—right? No! Give me a fuzzy (or relative)

---

8. I've been using *empathetic management* as an encompassing term. Adaptive leadership would then be an instance of empathetic management.
9. For another comprehensive view of digital transformation with an edgy name, see Sanjiv Augustine's (n.d.) "Business Agility SPARKS."

metric of something valuable (an outcome) rather than a precise metric for something unimportant (an output) any time.

Unfortunately, productivity mania has followed us into the Agile era. Too many organizations are still obsessed with productivity measures that limit their agility. Velocity is lines of code dressed up in new clothing.[10] As many times as agilists say, "Use velocity as a capacity indicator, not a productivity measure," velocity inevitably sets teams against teams and undermines both value and quality. Velocity is a quantity measure (output), and it gets us in trouble every time.

In Jerry Weinberg's quality workshop, he would ask, "What would you pay me for an application that I guarantee has no defects that calculates the biorhythms of Stanley Jones, who worked in the Ohio Department of Motor Vehicles from 1945 to 1964?" The value of that app, for 99.99% of people, would be zero, so who cares if the development team delivered 50 stories per iteration or 3?

When we are exploring new products, services, marketing programs, or business models, productivity measures make even less than no sense. Innovative ideas, valuable stories, high-quality code, reduced cycle times—these are better measures of success in today's environment. Comparing two teams who are working on two different new products, in two different business functions, using two different technology stacks, based on their story velocities makes as much sense as using typing speed as the criterion to decide Michener is a better writer than Hemingway. There has to be a better way.

Better requires a clear understanding of the value to be derived from a given portfolio. For example, measuring progress toward a customer value goal based on customer satisfaction will drive a different behavior than focusing on return on investment (ROI).

Enterprises do need a set of internal measures of success. Revenue, profit, market share, and time to market are measures of "business benefits" desirable to an enterprise, but not something a customer sees as valuable (except they want to know their suppliers are financially viable). Business benefits are useful as "guardrails" or constraints. You don't want delighted customers and no profit, but if done correctly, improving customer value accrues business benefits as well.

And there is a third kind of enterprise measure of success—sustainability. In the past, companies have optimized supply chains to reduce costs.

---

10. Velocity is a better measure because it is relative rather than absolute, which makes it easier to determine.

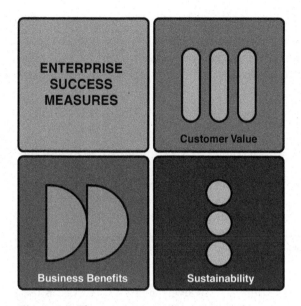

Figure 8.2 *Three enterprise agility measures of success.*

Given the geopolitical situation today, local availability may be more important than cost. Do you build multiple supply chains, at significant cost, in an effort to increase sustainability? What are your environmental sustainability goals? Waiting for something to happen and relying on your ability to adapt is one thing; building a sustainable enterprise having a greater *capability* to adapt is even better. What if you approach technical debt as a sustainability issue, rather than a quality issue?

To survive and thrive today, enterprises have to address three high-level agility measures of success, shown in Figure 8.2: consistently deliver customer value (satisfaction), foster business benefits (ROI, sales growth), and build a sustainable (adaptive) enterprise. Note the use of *agility* rather than *agile* in the preceding sentence. Agile methodologies may come and go; the need for enterprise agility will not.

In the execution age, productivity and financial measures reigned. During the expertise era, there was a transition from productivity to effectiveness measures.[11] When we look back at the steadily increasing number of

---

11. In this discussion of measures of success, I assume that financial measures are important and therefore don't delve into them.

S&P 500 companies that have been bought out, declared bankruptcy, or drastically declined, we must wonder about relying on traditional financial measures during periods of high change.

The next component in building a framework for digital transformation is Tech@Core.

Tech@Core

Tech@Core, a phrase coined at Thoughtworks, identifies the importance of technology being at the core of business.

"Tech@Core means that technology is your business—
no matter what your business."
        —Highsmith, Luu, and Robinson, 2020, p. 22

Enterprise leaders, at all levels including CEOs, must be tech-savvy. In a 2017 study (Guo, 2017), TW found that "Courageous executives know grasping the ins and outs of technology matters: 54% have developed a deep understanding of technology and a remarkable 57% have written code."

Are technology costs and efficiency important? *Of course.* Will they determine your success? *Of course not.* As you move from creating strategic goals to executing initiatives, adaptability and speed will determine success. Customer value drives your operating model. Adaptability and speed will determine your effectiveness in achieving value goals.

The case for adaptability has been made, but what about speed? Speed has been known to get people in trouble. But it is how you pursue speed that makes the difference.

If the pace of the pre-coronavirus world was already fast,
the luxury of time now seems to have disappeared
completely. Businesses that once mapped digital
strategy in one- to three-year phases must now scale
their initiatives in a matter of days or weeks.
        —Blackburn et al., 2020

It is not how fast you perform a certain task, but rather how fast you perform a series of tasks that produces customer value. There are major cycles—concept to cash—shorter contributing cycles— and weekly software delivery cycles.

The factor keeping both speed and quality high is measurement of the continuous flow of value from a product. A software delivery system needs to produce value in small increments time after time, not just at the end of a long project. While technical quality may not resonate with executives, reducing the cycle time to deliver continuous value does.

Part of my job at TW was to help convey what technology meant for executives. An example was an article on tech stack complexity.

In 2015, Mike Mason (TW's global head of technology), Neal Ford (software architect and meme wrangler), and I authored an article titled "Implications of Tech Stack Complexity for Executives" that addressed a technology issue executives needed to understand. We wrote about the expansion of that complexity in just the previous 10 years. We asked a series of questions: Which technologies do you monitor? Which ones do you experiment with? Which ones do you set aside? Which ones do you embrace? Fifteen years ago, few people anticipated the impact of cloud computing or Big Data or social media. In 2005, a software tech stack (layers of programs to accomplish specific tasks) might have 5 components. Today, these stacks often exceed 15 components. When I started, the tech stack contained an IBM 360 operating system and a COBOL compiler. In 2015, the stack might contain the following components:

- Platforms: Microsoft Nano Server, Deis, Fastly, Apache Spark, and Kubernetes
- New tools (which pop up every week): for example, Docker Toolbox, Gitrob, Polly, Prometheus, and Sleepy Puppy
- Programming languages and new frameworks: for example, Nancy, Axon, Frege, and Traveling Ruby
- Advanced techniques: Data Lake, Gitflow, Flux, and NoPSD

Tech@Core means articles like the one Mike, Neal, and I wrote in 2015 need to be on the radar of executives, who need to understand the ramifications of tech stack complexity: Single vendor solutions are outdated, team composition and organizational structures need to change, and building software delivery capabilities is increasingly difficult.

EDGE operating model

A robust digital business strategy provides direction, but where TW transformation experts found a yawning gap was between strategy and bona fide action. Enterprises lavished time on the process of creating a strategy, but then had difficulty linking it to action. We identified two factors as contributing to this puzzle—an effective strategy for linkage and organizational structure inertia.

Early in our development of EDGE, a TW team (I talked with team members but was not a member myself) worked with a telco client on its strategy-to-action process using a Lean Value Tree (LVT; shown in Figure 8.3).[12] Their assessment started with the director of digital products.

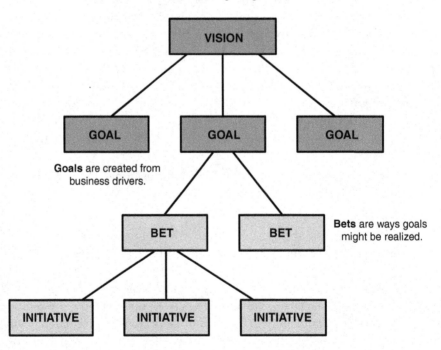

Figure 8.3 *The Lean Value Tree structure.*

---

12. This graphic and client story originally appeared in Highsmith, Luu, and Robinson (2020).

The team (TW and client members) mapped current work in progress against business goals and discovered the goals didn't indicate their importance. For example, "Drive to 20% market share" didn't express any benefit for the customer. Together, the team reframed the work into customer outcomes. For instance, "Drive to 20% market share" became "Enable customers to seamlessly view live TV and Internet TV all in one place."

The team learned three things from this exercise:

- By articulating the organizational goals in terms of customer outcomes, it became really clear what the value of each investment was and why it was important for the organization.
- By visualizing all work in flight, they could see the least important initiatives were receiving too much funding. This led to opportunities to rebalance the portfolio.
- By time-boxing the initial portfolio review, they were able to demonstrate the value of applying EDGE and build the case for continuing this work with the portfolio owners, business unit leads, and chief digital officer.

The ultimate question remained where to invest. First, the team articulated the business vision and strategy as a LVT of goals, bets, and initiatives. Second, they developed actionable, outcome-oriented measures of success that indicated progress *as the delivery process unfolded*, not at the end. Third, they used the *relative value* of those measures of success to prioritize work. Prioritizing work by calculating relative values takes less time than traditional (and typically false precision) ROI analysis and focuses on customer outcomes rather than business benefits.

The word *tree* in the LVT concept is important. Trees have branches evolving from the trunk (vision). Trees are living things that change and adapt to environmental conditions. An LVT isn't a planning document that sits on the shelf behind a desk gathering dust. Instead, it is leadership's vision of the future—from its trunk to its leaves—that everyone in the organization can point to and say, "We are going that way, and I understand why." When done well, this tool closes the traditional gap between strategic plans, is understood by the executives, and influences the decision making of the people in each value stream who steer the business on a day-to-day basis.

WATCHING THE TRANSFORMATION to a digital organization is like watching a chain reaction of dominoes: One falling domino sets off another, which sets off another, in an unending cascade. Embracing customer value as a primary business goal, and establishing speed and adaptability as required for sustainably achieving that goal, lead us to another domino called "project to product" in IT and "discrete to flow" in the enterprise.

By starting with customers, the Lean technique of value-stream mapping helped organizations analyze how to deliver value effectively. Lean concepts led from a functional view of the organization (marketing, manufacturing, accounting) to the view of a flow (a product's flow from order to shipment). Modern technology (continuous delivery) and organizational collaborations (DevOps) provide the capability to deliver applications and features continuously rather than periodically.

A product delivery team owns all aspects of the product—from the newest ideas for product enhancements to maintenance items. From the traditional perspective, projects consisted of a collection of features to be implemented and delivered and a project team assembled to complete the set of features within a period. When the project was completed, the team disbanded. Most organizations—including both IT and software companies— had maintenance groups that handled minor enhancements and bugs.

Product delivery teams may expand, contract, or change size depending on product needs, but they don't disband, as is the case with project teams. These product teams make prioritization decisions affecting the entire life cycle of the product. They are responsible for generating a continuous stream of value and managing the end-to-end customer experience, from a new customer signing up to an existing customer abandoning the product. In essence, product teams became responsible not for a specific project deliverable, but rather for a continuous stream of value—hence the switch from a project-centric view of the world to a product-centric one.

Enterprises implementing a digital strategy must follow a similar path. That is, they must think about their total experience with customers and consider how they can build a framework for continuous delivery of valuable customer experiences rather than discrete product sales.

The unFIX organization model

A transforming operating model requires a flexible, dynamic organizational model. In 2010, Jurgen Appelo published *Management 3.0: Leading*

Agile Developers, Developing Agile Leaders, a refreshing addition to the agile management literature. Jurgen had been the CIO of a mid-sized company, where he instituted Scrum. As a middle manager he hadn't found much about what management's role should be, so he wrote *Management 3.0* to fill the gap.

The Management 3.0 framework was both theoretical and practical. Through a series of workshops, appealing exercises, and a book by the same title, Jurgen showed people *how* to become empathetic leaders.

In early 2022, Jurgen released his latest entrepreneurial endeavor—unFIX—as an organic way to think about organizational design. He was concerned the currently available scaling-oriented approaches to agile development leaned hard toward traditional organizational structures that did not support adaptability (or innovation).

The unFIX model described a key piece in organizations' digital transformation efforts. Even if you have an agile mindset, how do you organize to rapidly adapt to changes? Of course, the answer to any complicated problem is Legos! Think of unFIX as organizational Legos, rather than as a framework for scaling. It is a pattern for thinking about how to grow an organization organically, but still able to respond to wide variations in sensory input.

The unFIX approach, depicted in Figure 8.4, enables versatile organizational design that encourages speed and innovation. There's no speed in classical hierarchies and matrix organizations, because only self-managed units can act fast when faced with crises or opportunities. The unFIX model offers no processes. Instead, it aims to provide organizational design patterns. Value stream crews are responsible for products or product lines, while other types of crews support them.

The Legos of unFIX are crews with names such as Value Stream, Capability, Base, Experience, and Governance. Each crew has a captain. Small organizations or projects might need only a few crew types—Base, Value Stream, Governance. As the organizations or projects grow, additional specialized crews can be added.

I want to reiterate this point: unFIX is not a process guide; it is an organizational structure guide. Two Value Stream crews in the same organization could use two different processes—Kanban and Scrum. Two different Governance crews might use different portfolio prioritization methods—or the same one.

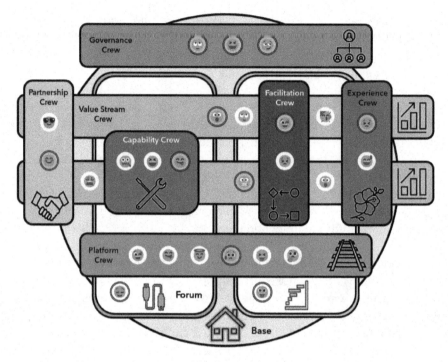

Figure 8.4 *Jurgen Appelo's unFIX organizational un-structure.*
(Courtesy of Jurgen Appelo.)

Two categories of scaling are rarely differentiated: implementing agile practices across a large organization and implementing agile practices for a large product (an autonomous vehicle product, for example). Yet each of these requires its own organizational structure. unFIX can handle both. Agile methods have long focused on building value-driven, collaborative, self-organizing, self-sufficient teams. Now we have a guide to putting together organizations that incorporate the same characteristics.

I HAD A CONVERSATION with Jurgen Appelo about his work in mid-2022.[13]

---

13. You can visit Jurgen's website at https://unfix.com/.

What was your background in software development?

I graduated with a degree in software engineering within a computer science department. While I enjoyed programming, my interests included the broader realms of finance, marketing, and general business topics. In the 1990s, I saw a need for courses targeting emerging software development topics, so I founded a company that developed and presented courseware. I get bored easily, so I enjoyed developing the material, but not so much delivering the same course time after time. I began engaging others to teach the courses as I developed new ones.

What came next?

In 2000, I became the CIO of a mid-sized company for 10 years. We started with 31 people, and it grew to 200 before I left. I had been reading all the agile books, including yours, and implemented Scrum in our department. The agile theme for middle management seemed to be "keep them out of the way," which seemed disrespectful to my position, so I started thinking about what managers' role was in an agile department. This thinking resulted in publishing *Management 3.0* in 2010. Somehow Mike Cohn learned about my book early on and invited me to publish it in his signature series, which I was ecstatic to do.

How did the unFIX organizational model evolve?

As I mentioned earlier, I get bored easily, so I sold the Management 3.0 workshop business and began casting around for the next big thing. I investigated using gamification techniques for learning and looked at organizational design. Similarly, to the evolution of [Management] 3.0, organizations were attempting to scale agility, but the available frameworks like SAFe were too structured. As organizations scaled, they lost adaptability—the very characteristic that is the core of agile. unFIX fixes that.

Where did the name unFIX come from?

That's an interesting question. While I'm not wild about SAFe, I admire their marketing. The name does well convey their mission—to stay safe. I wanted a name that would convey the right signal, a dynamic, innovative, exploring mindset. The "ix" parts of the name represent innovation and experience. I wanted the idea you could "fix" an organization by systematically unFIXing parts of it. [In Figure 8.4], the colors, and smiley faces are important also. They convey the unseriousness of a serious topic.

Where would you like unFIX to go?

I hope that unFIX becomes an alternative to frameworks like SAFe and Spotify for organizations. Holacracy is sometimes mentioned as an alternative, but it's a little far out there for most—and the name doesn't help. I want to give organizations their organizational Lego blocks so they can adapt quickly. I want to keep this as simple as possible for an organization. I want to start with the simplest thing possible and then add as necessary but not enough to interfere with innovation and adaptability. SAFe takes the opposite approach, adding too many topics and then asking users to "take away" what they don't need [Remember RUP?].

For an agile team to succeed, its members need an agile mindset, an agile process, and appropriate skills and experience. For organizations with multiple teams, you need to add "a little bit less than just enough structure." Jurgen's unFIX model offers a building-blocks way to accomplish that. You need enough structure to balance on the edge of chaos, but no more. Although I don't have firsthand experience with unFIX, I've read and talked enough with Jurgen to think he is on the right track.

Empathetic and adaptive leadership

Evolving management theories have had numerous impacts on software development throughout the years. The agile movement provided encouragement and leadership for those later changes. Since this is not a management book, I have picked out a few voices instrumental in leading the way. As you will see, we are cautiously making the transition from a traditional command-control, Theory X, optimizing view of management to an empathetic, modern one incorporating leadership-collaboration, Theory Y, unFIX, empathy, agility, and adaptive leadership.

Transformation isn't going to happen using organizational structures or culture from the industrial age. Rita McGrath (2014) identifies this new management age as one based on empathy:

Others have sensed that we are ready for a new era of business thinking and practice. From my perspective, this would mean figuring out what management looks like when work is done through networks rather than through lines of command, when "work" itself is tinged with emotions, and when individual managers are responsible for creating communities for those who work with them. If what is demanded of managers today is empathy (more than execution, more than expertise), then we must ask: What new roles and organizational structures make sense, and how should performance management be approached? What does it take for a leader to function as a "pillar" and how should the next generation of managers be taught? All the questions about management are back on the table—and we can't find the answers soon enough.

Tracy Bower (2021) writes, "Empathy contributes to positive relationships and organizational cultures, and it also drives results. Empathy may not be a brand new skill, but it has a new level of importance, and the fresh research makes it especially clear how empathy is the leadership competency to develop and demonstrate now and in the future of work." An empathetic leader can put themselves in another's shoes, providing a deep understanding of their thoughts, fears, and triumphs. An example of an empathetic leader was illustrated by an interview I had with Kent Beck in 2002.[14]

Why did you become interested in complex adaptive systems (CAS) theory?

Complex adaptive systems (CAS) theory has quite a simple explanation about how you ought to behave in the world. Find this set of rules and then act on them, measure the results, and tweak the set of rules. It's very liberating when you really take that in. You don't have to oversee everything; you don't have to make all the technical decisions. In fact, to the degree to which as a leader you are making technical decisions, you are screwing up the dynamic of the team.

But sometimes people want you to make decisions, and you must push back.

Oh, absolutely! Someone comes into your office and asks you for a decision. You ask them, "Which alternative do you think is the best?" They often respond that they don't know. "Well, if you don't know, maybe we'd better try them both and take the hit." When they don't want to take that much time, encourage them to just pick one.

---

14. This section is an edited version of the interview with Kent in my *Agile Software Development Ecosystems* book (Highsmith, 2002).

In these situations, a control-oriented manager will often use people's reluctance to make decisions to bolster their view managers must make the decisions. Pushing out decision making helps everyone learn a new way of operating.

Then came the C3 project at Chrysler, where I tried to be much more hands off. I wasn't going to make a single technical decision.

You were trying to create the right kind of environment?

Yes, Ron [Jeffries] and I were trying to set up the initial conditions and then tweak them. No heroics, no Kent riding in on a white horse, which was quite a switch in value systems for me. I prided myself on being the biggest object guru on the block. I had to deliberately give that up and just say that's not what's going to make me valuable.

I've found that one of the problems with this approach to management is success often seems almost accidental to people.

The best manager I ever had was at the Stanford linear accelerator lab. I worked in the control room. This guy spent all his time building Heathkits.[15] Everybody complained about how lazy he was and why he didn't do this or that. But everything was always on time; if you needed parts, they were there. Personality clashes got resolved instantly. I've always wished I wasn't 20 years old when it happened so I could appreciate that this guy was absolutely masterful. He kept everything running absolutely smoothly. So that's my aesthetic as a coach. If I do everything perfectly, then my contribution is totally invisible to the team. The team says, "We did this."

That's a hard thing. If your view of a leader is Teddy Roosevelt charging up San Juan Hill, braving death with the bullets flying around, then it's just impossible to operate like this. But if you have a team that's operating in this self-organizing fashion, it's disorganizing to have someone inject that kind of leadership.

Kent makes a telling point—the difference between Teddy Roosevelt charging up San Juan Hill versus his invisible, but successful manager's style couldn't be greater. The big question, which is better? If there is a "best" leadership style, why isn't it obvious? Why do we continue to have a cascade of leadership books? There isn't really one best style: Managers need to adapt their style to conditions based on an underlying set of values.

---

15. For those who started life after the 1970s, these are electronic product kits, like radios, that one assembled.

Period observations

Moving beyond implementing agile methodologies in an organization, the Digital Transformation period explored what becoming a digital enterprise meant, much like jumping from the proverbial "frying pan into the fire." We went from working with second- and third-level leaders to working with CIOs, CEOs, and McKinsey-level strategic consulting firms.

In the early years of the decade, CEOs intensified their interest in ICT and their digital enterprise strategies. Enterprise executives developed digital strategies but found their transition from strategy to operating models lacking. Looking back at previous ICT transformations, they clearly pointed out that it was time to be adventurous and nonconformist. EDGE, unFIX, and SPARKS (Augustine, "Business Agility SPARKS") were developed in response to that need—to present methods and methodologies beyond the safe and traditional.

Enterprises today should be seeking to become *digital transforming* rather than to achieve *digital transformation*. *Transformation* indicates completion of a stage, whereas *transforming* suggests a constant state of becoming. More than six decades of escalating rates, and types, of change have required organizations to constantly adapt by addressing the following areas:

- Measures of success: Performance measures can drive or restrict change.
- Tech@Core: Being digital demands a business technology partnership.
- Operating model: Linking strategy to action.
- Organizational model: Creating a quickly malleable structure.
- Empathetic management: Management suited for the digital era.

These five ideas are oriented towards action, to "doing agile." Chapter 9 identifies measurable (assessable) actions that indicate what "being agile" means for leaders.

After reducing my travel and work hours for a time, I retired from Thoughtworks early in 2021. But I now understand the quip of other TW alumni, "Once a Thoughtworker, always a Thoughtworker," as I continue to interact with former coworkers. The beat goes on, and it is still fun.

9

Prepare to Engage the Future

FOR FATHER'S DAY in 2022, my youngest daughter gave me a bright red T-shirt with a sun-drenched mountain scene and a slogan that read, "Think Outside: No Box Required." I've never quite liked the cliché "think outside the box," possibly because I don't like to think of either myself or others in a box to begin with. I do like the phrase "think outside" because of its double meaning—thinking about your next outdoor adventure or thinking outside your current thinking—it's both physical and mental.[1]

Now, in 2022, we are in a topsy-turvy punctuated equilibrium period where the higher the rate of change, the less chance we have of predicting the future. "In such conditions, we need other methods to navigate our way" (Courtney et al., 1997). To survive and thrive in the future, we must prepare for it diligently. Learning from the past is part of that diligence, as Winston Churchill said:

Those who fail to learn from history are condemned to repeat it.[2]

In the context of this book, I revised Churchill's statement:

History's role is not to help us predict the future, but to prepare us for it.

---

1. Psychologist Barbara Tversky, professor at both Stanford and Columbia Universities, offers a theory of human cognition that movement, not language, is the foundation of thought.
2. Address to the House of Commons in 1943, paraphrasing philosopher George Santayana.

Why history?

Winston Churchill's knowledge of history (his six-volume history of World War II won a Nobel Prize) shaped Great Britain's World War II strategy. General George Patton was an avid student of military history from the Peloponnesian War to World War I; he framed his World War II battles in the context of famous historical ones. Knowledge of world and military history gave Patton and Churchill a historical framework with which to make decisions about their present courses of action.

Similarly, Walter Isaacson, a well-known historian, offers an understanding of the history of two critical technologies that offer both promise and threat in the future—information technology and gene splicing. Isaacson authored both *Steve Jobs* (2011) and *The Code Breaker: Jennifer Doudna, Gene Editing, and the Future of the Human Race* (2021). Preparing for our chaotic future would be shallow without this kind of historical knowledge about information and gene splicing technologies, and the pioneering individuals who spearheaded them.

Kevin Kelley, former editor of *Wired* magazine, published an article on his website called "How to Future," in which he declared, "Most futurists are really predicting the present." If we are in a period of economic, political, and health punctuated equilibrium, then trying to predict the future seems futile. We need to move from predicting and planning for the future, to building a platform that enables us to adapt to whatever happens. The evolution of software development forms part of that platform. History offers us more than dates, names, and places; it also helps us understand why events transpired as they did. In turn, this offers us the possibility of better understanding our present and making better-informed decisions in the future.

So, what did we learn from our journey through six decades of software development? What happened during that time? What did we learn about the pioneers who created those developments? How might an understanding of those events and the pioneers help prepare us for the future? What did I learn about myself as I researched and wrote about my past?

Writing this book forced me to remember pieces of the past and attempt to put them into context. Preparing for the future challenges us to scale an agility mindset, not simply agile methods and methodologies. Changing individual and organizational mindsets defies simple approaches and canned answers. My sense is that adventurousness and nonconformity helps us meet these challenges.

What about the people who pioneered software development advances? One of my joys in writing this book was reconnecting with colleagues I hadn't talked with in a decade or three. Catching up on their lives was long overdue, and their thoughts about software development, then and now, were invaluable.

The history of software development is bumpy, not smooth, which makes it exciting. But first, is agile development here to stay?

Agile and agility

A growing contingent is now asking, "Has agile run its course? Is it time for a change?"[3] My answers are (1) "It depends on your definition of agile" and (2) "It's always time for a change." In truth, we need to ask the question about agile development's future in three ways: "Have existing agile methods become obsolete? Have agile methodologies become obsolete? Have agile mindsets become obsolete?" Agile evolved from Structured-era approaches because business problems and technology changed. Technology in the form of the Internet spurred new business models that demanded speed and flexibility. The questions about the obsolescence of agile development must also be evaluated within the context of the times. For example, would agile practices have worked in the Wild West era when input-to-output times were in the range of 12–24 hours?

The answer to the first question is relatively simple, given the advances in technology and software development platforms. Some agile methods will still be relevant; others won't. Consider Larry Constantine's Structured-era concepts of coupling and cohesion, which are still relevant 35 years later. Automation may hasten other methods' journey to irrelevance. Suppose Martin Fowler, author of *Refactoring: Improving the Design of Existing Code* (2018), created an automated refactoring tool—then subsequent generations of developers might no longer need to learn manual refactoring. Individual methods will arise and retire as the context of the times changes and may not be identified as agile methods.

Methodologies respond to both business problems and technology innovation. Someone will come up with a new methodology combining both existing agile methods and new methods that respond to technological advances. They may invent a genre with a new name and say, "The Excalibur Methodology is new, modern, and solves all the problems with agile.

---

3. For example, read "The End of Agile" by Kurt Cagle (2019).

You can utilize the latest in virtual reality and artificial intelligence to deliver high-quality software much faster." Maybe delivery will be so fast that Ken Orr's *One Minute Methodology* (1990) will come back into vogue. This will happen, bet on it. And just as agilists harped on the shortcomings of structured and waterfall development, so Excalibur proponents will harp on agile's shortcomings.

It is worth repeating a statement made in Chapter 3: As we traverse the evolution and revolution of software development, we need to remember that methods, methodologies, and mindsets all evolved to solve the problems of each era, both enabled and constrained by the technology of that time.

That leaves us with the last question, "Have agile mindsets become obsolete?", which might also be phrased as "Has agility become obsolete?" Over the six-decade span of time covered by this book, when have you noticed the rate of change in the world, in technology, in business, in culture, in music, slow down? From my perspective, change has spiraled constantly upward, not only linearly, but bordering on exponentially. I won't say the need for an agile, adaptive mindset will never change, but I just don't see it happening in the foreseeable future.

For organizations and individuals trying to become agile, one conclusion from this history is that *agility*, not *agile*, should be the goal. Agility is a mindset; agile is a type of methodology. Failure to make this differentiation has left organizations with prescriptive agile methodologies, while leaders who embrace agility have the best chance of thriving in the future. Given the unknown and unknowable from the potent combination of climate change, geopolitical unrest, COVID-19, and the Russia–Ukraine war, we may be entering a period in which Darwin's law of "survival of the fittest" gives way to "survival of the luckiest," in which case agility may be our only remaining strategic advantage.

ACHIEVING AN AGILE mindset is difficult for two reasons: It's hard to do, and it's ill defined. No one changes deeply held mental models easily and if they did, the models wouldn't be useful. Change takes more than a one-day workshop. Colleague Gil Broza, who wrote a book on the agile mindset, says, "Even when organizations and managers intend to start their Agile journey with the right mind-set, many don't realize the magnitude and complexity of the transformation" (Broza, 2015, p. xix).

Steve Denning took a stab at this mindset in a recent *Forbes* online article:

The Agile mindset is an attribute of practitioners more than theorists. It is pragmatic and action-oriented more than a theoretical philosophy. It goes beyond a set of beliefs and becomes a tool for diagnosis and the basis for action. (Denning, 2019)

While Steve's description is fine, I don't find it actionable.

Mindset has been a topic of interest to psychologists like Carol S. Dweck, author of *Mindset: The New Psychology of Success* (2006). Dweck proposes that two mindsets—fixed and growth—exist, and explains how each one affects the way we learn, perceive the world, and make decisions.

Mindset can also be viewed as a system of beliefs. If you believe in Douglas McGregor's Theory X, which assumes people are basically lazy and need to be "motivated" by managers, then that belief permeates your approach to personnel issues. Conversely, if you believe people are motivated by Dan Pink's purpose, mastery, and autonomy, then your approach to people management will be entirely different.

Searching for a simpler, actionable assessment of mindset, I recalled that history is made by people, so to understand history, you have to understand those people. But what do you need to understand about them? To evaluate agility, rather than use elusive personality traits, I categorize people's actions:

Adventurous:

- Sets courageous goals into uncharted territory.
- Accepts risks but isn't imprudent.
- Can act when conditions are ambiguous.
- Overcomes disappointment and fear.

Nonconformist:

- Challenges social, cultural, or workplace norms.
- Authentic to oneself even when outside the norm.

Adaptable:

- Senses environmental inputs and filters the relevant ones.

- Creates innovative organizational responses, by balancing at the "edge of chaos".
- Quickly acts, adjusts, pivots, or abandons initiatives.

Learning about individuals' actions in each of these areas helps assess their agility. You can observe these actions, but they are not measurable, only assessable. Climbing is similar. Decisions about routes, when to move on and when to turn back, are assessable, but they are not measurable. Entire books have been written about decisions that led to climbing disasters and successes. Climbers must select their climbing partners wisely—an assessment similar to assessing individuals for team membership at any level.

ENGINEER, DEVELOPER, business analyst, business systems coordinator, software development manager, accounting supervisor, vice president of sales and marketing, vice president of consulting, product manager, director of agile project management, executive consultant. At some point in my career, I've held each of these positions. As I look back over six decades, I realized there was a single element common to all these positions: Each was hard, extremely hard. They were all difficult in different ways—some technical, some interpersonal, and some political.

I bring this up because of the ease with which we tend to disparage others. It's easy for developers to disparage product managers, development managers to disparage project managers, and virtually everyone to disparage senior management. While this tendency may be natural, it's not helpful. As pointed out in the Portland Mortgage company story, forming cross-functional teams can bring diversity to a team, but those teams can then become isolated from each other, leading to miscommunication. I've found the issue revolves around not understanding what others actually do.

Put a software developer into a sales representative's shoes, or thrust a product manager into an executive role, and see how fast attitudes change. Having to function in another role can rapidly alter one's opinion of other role groups. Whatever job I held at the time, the common task I was given or assumed was to be a bridge builder between different groups. The most visible example was at Optima in the CASE tool era, where my job title was product manager but my tacit role was to bring two warring factions together—or at least reduce the vitriol between them. In my business systems coordinator job, I spearheaded having refinery groups find common ground. My consulting work always involved bringing groups together. One of my favorite Jerry Weinberg quotes is his Second Law of Consulting: "No matter what the problem is, it's a people problem" (Weinberg, 1985, p. 5).

I reminded myself of this quote before any client engagement because I've found it to be true. It's nearly always a people problem. Maybe the best advice comes, again, from Jerry: "Leadership is the process of creating an environment in which people become empowered" (Weinberg, 1986, p. 12).

Thinking about Jerry's quotes, the Agile Manifesto, and my own experiences, I offer the following:

> Based on six decades of experience, I think the root cause of success is people and their interactions, and the root cause of failure is also people and their interactions.

Tech@Core encourages everyone in an enterprise, from top to bottom, to better understand the technological world we live in. Software methods, methodologies, and mindsets are required to bring those technologies to life. But we can't forget that at the core of technology and software development are people and their interactions.

MY FAVORITE ADVENTURE story isn't about Sir Edmond Hillary's first climb of Mount Everest or the Italian team that was first to summit K2 (the world's second highest mountain), but rather a less well-known first scaling of an 8,000-meter peak—Annapurna in 1950. Maurice Herzog's (1952) story of that ascent is riveting, from weeks wandering around uncharted wilderness trying to find the mountain, to the backbreaking work of setting up successively higher camps, to figuring a route to follow, to the near crawl to the summit, and then a series of mishaps on the dangerous descent, which nearly ended the expedition in death. Fingers and toes were removed due to frostbite.

Although I've never attempted a climb anywhere remotely as difficult as Annapurna, reading Herzog's book inspired me to climb mountains. Although not life-threatening, ascending software development mountains offered a challenge as well. Those software challenges were climbed by a different set of adventurers, from Tom DeMarco, Larry Constantine, and Ken Orr in the Structured era to Kent Beck, Alistair Cockburn, Martin Fowler, and

Ken Schwaber in the Agile era—and by the managers and executives who took a chance on their leading-edge, and occasionally bleeding-edge, ideas.

Writing this book has been my recent adventure. It has been a challenge, comparable to my first ice climb in winter in Rocky Mountains National Park—striking out, not knowing what to expect. At some point, struggling with the interplay of the various narratives, I discussed my frustration with my goddaughter, Amy Irvine, an author (Irvine, 2018) and a faculty fellow at Southern New Hampshire University's Master of Fine Arts program for creative writing. As Amy described her environmental articles as braided narratives, I realized instantly that I had found an organizing principle to work with.

So, with fits and starts and tremendous help from a host of others, this book emerged. When I first proposed this book idea to colleagues, I quipped, "This is either the best idea I've ever had, or the worst." Which do you think it is?

Afterword

Why write this book?

I wrote this book assuming that telling readers about me, my motivations, my perspective, my personality, and the drivers that shaped my career might make the history of software development more understandable and, I hope, more enjoyable.

After family, seeking adventures—career and personal—has been central to my life. Over the course of this book, I've conveyed a bit about who I am and the overall purpose behind my work.

To revisit my goals for this book:

- Document the evolution and revolution of software methods, methodologies, and mindsets.
- Remember and honor the pioneers of software development.
- Prepare for the future, by learning from the past.
- Give my generation a vehicle to reminisce about events we lived through.
- Give younger generations a peek into events they may have missed.

Additionally, I wanted my grandkids to know something about me, to understand something about my career. I wanted to give them more than a genealogy, something beyond "great uncle Max married Greta in 1921" or "I worked for ABC company as a software developer from 1965 to 1968." As I worked on a memoir for my family, I realized my career paralleled vast changes in software and technology over six decades and I had played a part in that history. Maybe others would be interested.

Why are so many books written about the Middle Ages or the California Gold Rush? Because historians provide a unique lens through which to view the facts of the past. The facts are that Napoléon Bonaparte was a French military and political leader who rose to prominence during the French Revolution. But why have so many historians written about him? Because each historian has a particular lens or perspective to offer the reader. As I wrote about my journey through the eras of software development, I hope my stories offered a valuable perspective.

Much has changed in the six decades of my career, nowhere more than in relation to issues around diversity, equity, and inclusion (DEI). In the 1960s—while I was in high school, college, and early career—there were turbulent battles for marginalized groups' civil rights. By 2022, there were gains, such as legalization of same-sex marriage and expansion of women's roles in the workforce, but as the "Black Lives Matter" and "Me Too" movements proved, there is a still a long way to go. In 1962, when I enrolled at an agricultural and engineering university, the student body was 95% male and 5% female. Today, that university is 51% male and 49% female and has a comprehensive DEI program.

If history helps us prepare for the future, then what role can *Wild West to Agile*, or agility in general, play in preparing us for a more inclusive future? For one thing, I hope the agile movement's incorporation of collaborative, self-organizing, empowered teams and its emphasis on an empathetic management style has played an active part in furthering DEI goals. Traditionally underrepresented groups are bringing their voices and actions to the cultural-change practices of agility. As with any transformation, specific actions, systemic approaches, and changes in mindset are needed. As with any transformation, mindset is the most important.

Diversity benefits organizations in many ways, for example, "Teams make better decisions than individuals do 66 percent of the time. Age + gender + geographic—diverse teams make better decisions 87 percent of the time."[1]

In the early 2000s, a *ComputerWorld* columnist was lambasted by a reader for supporting a gay rights issue; the reader argued the column had no place in the corporate world. One of the reasons I joined Thoughtworks for the

---

1. Study by Cloverpop, "Hacking Diversity with Inclusive Decision Making," www.cloverpop. com.

last decade of my career was the company's commitment to diversity in all its forms. From its 1990s start-up, Roy Singham, founder and longtime CEO, incorporated social justice issues into the fabric, the DNA, of Thoughtworks. That embedded voice still rings loud. In 2022, 56% of executive-level positions are held by women and underrepresented gender groups (WUGM).[2,3] There is no longer any venue—corporate, governmental, religious, or nonprofit—where silence about diversity issues can be justified.

As a person of privilege, writing about an industry that has been slow to incorporate diversity, I add my voice to those calling for a mindset change. My goal is to move the bar closer to wider awareness and understanding of DEI and be an ally in the transformation process.

Purpose

In the Wild West era, career planning was simple—be hired by a big company, work until you were 65 years old, retire. It was trickier for those who chose another route. Like me, those who searched for other niches were on a spectrum from meticulous planners to random job hoppers. As the rate of change began upending major segments of the economy, even those people with a one-stop plan were thrown into a random category, for which they were often ill prepared. It took me years to articulate my own career guide was purpose, not plan. Any plan I could have conceived early on would not have withstood reality. What I needed was not a plan, but rather a purpose (an idea that companies are beginning to utilize).

I wish I could say a well-articulated purpose drove me all these years, that I was laser focused from the start, but I can't. My purpose, my *why*, has evolved in fits and starts and scrambles, with the last piece just falling in place. As I now look back over the decades, these drivers or purposes have emerged and evolved, but the core ideas have remained. I've mentioned aspects of this purpose in earlier chapters, and these four reflect my current thinking:

- Deliver valuable software
- Promote enlightened leadership
- Grow digital enterprises
- Share my stories

---

2. www.thoughtworks.com/about-us/diversity-and-inclusion/our-people
3. Many other companies have similar DEI success stories.

Or, in a little greater detail:

To enable the continuous delivery of customer value by creating advanced software and management methods, methodologies, and mindsets.

This purpose statement isn't as pithy as I would like, but it conveys concepts important to me—delivering customer value; creating new methods, methodologies, and mindsets; ensuring high technical quality software that has the ability to deliver continuously rather than discretely.

To promote an enlightened leadership style fitting the modern era—a style that empowers people and teams to break their bureaucratic log jams.

Some people's purpose is to make the world a better place. That's more than I want to tackle. I'd like to make workplaces better, but that's a stretch as well. I want my purposes to be aspirational and doable, so I will narrow the scope even further—to the workplaces of clients I've worked with and the readers of my books, articles, and blogs.

To grow digital enterprises by integrating adaptive leadership (mindset) and emerging technologies (methods).

The last 10-plus years of my career were predominantly spent working with senior managers and Thoughtworks colleagues on enterprise digital transformations—using agile software development implementations as a springboard to integrate agility (mindset) and technology (methods).

To share my stories.

I added this last purpose recently as I reflected on my writing. In each of my books, I've added a wrinkle that I hope made the narrative more appealing and satisfying—from analogies to mountain climbing, to interviews with luminaries, to client stories, to using an informal personal voice. This book contains all of these wrinkles plus a big new one—personal experience stories. It has been a stretch and a challenge.

By offering my personal stories, my career purposes, and my reasons for writing this book, I hope to encourage you to tell your own stories. The onslaught of climate change, geopolitical conflict, pandemic health challenges, technology innovation, and their accompanying social justice issues will continue. We are going to need a new generation of thoughtful, engaged technologists and leaders who can adapt to this volatile future. This leadership won't be found in an explanation of the latest and greatest technology or management theory. It needs a personal touch, personal journeys, and personal stories. Writing this book, I was constantly faced with the challenge of braiding technology together with my personal stories.

Many colleagues challenged me to stress the personal, and pushed me through my reluctance—and they were right. I hereby challenge you to tell your personal stories. I don't just want to know *what* you think, I want to know *who* you are. I reiterate the idea from Chapter 9: "*I think the root cause of success is people and their interactions.*" If this is true, and I believe it is, the better we know each other, the better our interactions can be, and ultimately the more success and well-being we can bring to the world.

Appendix

Computing Performance Improvements over Six Decades

Computing performance improvements over the decades had an enormous impact on software development methods and methodologies. From punch card input and printed outputs in the 1960s, to the Internet connected to multiple devices, to autonomous cars and virtual reality, technology capabilities have challenged software developers. This table shows those performance trends in four areas: processing speed, external storage, connectivity, and person–computer interfaces. I am indebted to colleagues Barton Friedland and Freddy Jandeleit for their research in constructing this table, but I take full responsibility for the accuracy.

TECH AREA	PROCESSING SPEED	EXTERNAL STORAGE[1]	CONNECTIVITY	PERSON–COMPUTER
Wild West **1966–1979**	From kilohertz to megahertz Intel 4004 (1971[2]): 750 kHZ[3] Intel 8008 (1972): 800 kHz[4] Intel 8080 (1974): 3.125 MHz[5] Motorola 68000 (1979): 16 MHz[6]	Magnetic cores to random access IBM "Minnow" floppy disk drive (1968): 80 KB Apollo Guidance Computer read-only rope memory (1969): 72 KB 1 KB Intel 1103 (1974) integrated circuit memory	Leveraging the phone network Bell 103A (1962): 300 bit/s[7] ARPANET (1969): 56 Kbps VA3400 (1973): 1,200 bit/s	Wild West of concepts Dynabook (1968): concept of a laptop[8] Pong arcade game (1972)[9] Xerox Alto (1973)[10] Apple II, PET, and TRS-80 (1977)[11]

1. https://www.computerhistory.org/timeline/memory-storage/
2. https://www.computerhope.com/history/processor.htm
3. https://en.wikipedia.org/wiki/Intel_4004
4. https://en.wikipedia.org/wiki/Intel_8008
5. https://en.wikipedia.org/wiki/Intel_8080
6. https://en.wikipedia.org/wiki/Motorola_68000
7. https://en.wikipedia.org/wiki/Modem
8. https://en.wikipedia.org/wiki/Dynabook
9. https://en.wikipedia.org/wiki/Pong
10. https://en.wikipedia.org/wiki/Xerox_Alto
11. https://en.wikipedia.org/wiki/History_of_personal_computers#Apple_II

TECH AREA	PROCESSING SPEED	EXTERNAL STORAGE[1]	CONNECTIVITY	PERSON– COMPUTER
Structured **1980–1989**	From 16 to 32 bits Intel 80286 (1982): 25 MHz[12] Intel 80386 (1985): 40 MHz[13] Intel 80386SX (1988): 32 bits 40MHz[14]	The sprint to GB ST506 (1980): 5 MB CD-ROM (1982): 550 MB Bernoulli Box (1983): up to 230 MB	Increasing speed Ethernet 2.94 Mbps (1983)[15] V.22bis (1984): 2,400 bit/s NSFNET T1 (1988): 1.544 Mbps[16]	Increasing mobility Osborne 1 (1981)[17] IBM PC (1981)[18] Apple Macintosh (1984)[19] Macintosh portable (1989)[20]

12. https://en.wikipedia.org/wiki/Intel_80286
13. https://en.wikipedia.org/wiki/I386
14. https://en.wikipedia.org/wiki/I386#The_80386SX_variant
15. https://en.wikipedia.org/wiki/Ethernet
16. https://www.bandwidthplace.com/the-evolution-of-internet-connectivity-from-phone-lines-to-light-speed-article/
17. https://en.wikipedia.org/wiki/Osborne_1
18. https://en.wikipedia.org/wiki/History_of_personal_computers#The_IBM_PC
19. https://en.wikipedia.org/wiki/Macintosh
20. https://en.wikipedia.org/wiki/Macintosh_Portable

TECH AREA	PROCESSING SPEED	EXTERNAL STORAGE[1]	CONNECTIVITY	PERSON-COMPUTER
Roots of Agile **1990–2000**	From MHz to GHz Pentium (1993): 60 MHz[21] Intel Pentium Pro (1995): 200 MHz[22] Xeon (1998): 4 GHz[23]	From kilograms to grams (miniaturization) IBM 9345 hard disk drive (1990): 1 GB Iomega Zip Disk (1994): 2 GB	Introduction of wireless NSFNET T3 (1991): 45 Mbps[24] 2G (1991): 40 kbit/s (5 kB/s)[25] WWW (1993): 145 Mbps[26] 802.11 Wi-Fi protocol first release (1997): 54 Mbps[27] Bluetooth (1999): Data transfer speed 0.7 Mbps[28]	NeXT (1990)[29] IBM ThinkPad (1992)[30] Apple iMac (1997)[31]

21. https://en.wikipedia.org/wiki/List_of_Intel_Pentium_processors
22. https://en.wikipedia.org/wiki/Pentium_Pro
23. https://en.wikipedia.org/wiki/Xeon
24. https://www.bandwidthplace.com/the-evolution-of-internet-connectivity-from-phone-lines-to-light-speed-article/
25. https://en.wikipedia.org/wiki/Wireless_network#Wireless_networks
26. https://en.wikipedia.org/wiki/Wireless_network#Wireless_networks
27. https://en.wikipedia.org/wiki/Wireless_network#Wireless_networks
28. https://en.wikipedia.org/wiki/Bluetooth#History
29. https://en.wikipedia.org/wiki/History_of_personal_computers#Next
30. https://en.wikipedia.org/wiki/History_of_personal_computers#Thinkpad
31. https://en.wikipedia.org/wiki/History_of_personal_computers#IBM_clones,_Apple_back_into_profitability

TECH AREA	PROCESSING SPEED	EXTERNAL STORAGE[1]	CONNECTIVITY	PERSON-COMPUTER
Agile **2001–2021**	From single to distributed processing on a chip, Moore's law no longer applies Intel Core 2 Duo (2006): 1.86 GHz[32] Intel Core I7 (2008): 2.67 GHz[33] Intel Core I9 (12 chips on a chip) (2017): 2.9 GHz[34]	Transition to cloud Amazon Web Services launches cloud-based services (2006): EC2 and S3 First 1 TB hard disk drive (HDD) (2009)	From speed to compression Bluetooth 3.0 (2009): transfer speed 23 Mbit/s[35]	Interaction via touch 64-bit computing (2003)[36] Apple iPod Touch and iPhone (2007)[37]: Introduction of a touch phone SIRI (2010)[38]: voice commands XBOX Kinect (2010)[39]

32. https://en.wikipedia.org/wiki/Intel_Core#Core_2_Duo
33. https://en.wikipedia.org/wiki/List_of_Intel_Core_i7_processors
34. https://en.wikipedia.org/wiki/List_of_Intel_Core_i9_processors
35. https://www.androidauthority.com/history-bluetooth-explained-846345/
36. https://en.wikipedia.org/wiki/History_of_personal_computers#64_bits
37. https://en.wikipedia.org/wiki/IPhone
38. https://en.wikipedia.org/wiki/Siri
39. https://en.wikipedia.org/wiki/Kinect

References

Anthes, G. H. (2001, April 2). Lessons from India Inc. *Computerworld*, 40–43. www.computerworld.com/article/2797563/lessons-from-india-inc-.htmlhe article

Appelo, J. (2010). *Management 3.0: Leading agile developers, developing agile leaders.* Boston, MA: Addison-Wesley.

Arthur, W. B. (1996). Increasing returns and the new world of business. *Harvard Business Review*, 74(4), 100.

Augustine, S. (n.d.). Business agility SPARKS: Seven SPARKS to build business agility. http://businessagilitysparks.com/

Austin, R. D. (1996). *Measuring and managing performance in organizations.* New York, NY: Dorset House.

Bach, R. (1970). *Jonathan Livingston Seagull.* New York, NY: Macmillan.

Bayer, S., and J. Highsmith. (1994). RADical software development. *American Programmer*, 7, 35–41.

Beck, K. (2000). *eXtreme programming explained: Embrace change.* Boston, MA: Addison-Wesley.

Bharadwaj, A., O. A. El Sawy, P. A. Pavlou, and N. V. Venkatraman. (2013). Digital business strategy: Toward a next generation of insights. *MIS Quarterly*, 37(2), 471–482.

Blackburn, S., L. LaBerge, C. O'Toole, and J. Schneider. (2020, April 22). Digital strategy in a time of crisis. *McKinsey Digital.* www.mckinsey.com/capabilities/mckinsey-digital/our-insights/digital-strategy-in-a-time-of-crisis

Boehm, B. (1988, May). A spiral model of software development and enhancement. *IEEE Software*, 21(5), 61–72.

Booch, G. (1995). *Object solutions: Managing the object-oriented project.* Reading, MA: Addison-Wesley.

Brooks, F. (1975). *The mythical man-month: Essays on software engineering.* Reading, MA: Addison-Wesley.

Brower, T. (2021, September 19). Empathy is the most important leadership skill according to research. *Forbes*. www.forbes.com/sites/tracybrower/2021/09/19/empathy-is-the-most-important-leadership-skill-according-to-research/?sh=70cc6a9b3dc5

Brown, S. L., and K. M. Eisenhardt. (1998). *Competing on the edge: Strategy as structured chaos*. Boston, MA: Harvard Business Press.

Broza, G. (2015). *The agile mind-set: Making agile processes work*. CreateSpace Independent Publishing Platform.

Cagle, K. (2019, August). The end of agile. *Forbes*. www.forbes.com/sites/cognitiveworld/2019/08/23/the-end-of-agile/?sh=2c2e74132071

Carr, N. G. (2003, May 1). IT doesn't matter. *Harvard Business Review*. https://hbr.org/2003/05/it-doesnt-matter

Christensen, C. M. (1997). *The innovator's dilemma: When new technologies cause great firms to fail*. Boston, MA: Harvard Business School Press.

Collier, K. (2012). *Agile analytics: A value-driven approach to business intelligence and data warehousing*. Boston, MA: Addison-Wesley.

Constantine, L. (1967, March). A modular approach to program optimization. *Computers and Automation*.

Constantine, L. (1968). Segmentation and design strategies for modular programming. In T. O. Barnett and L. L. Constantine (Eds.), *Modular programming: Proceedings of a national symposium*. Cambridge, MA: Information & Systems Press.

Constantine, L. (1968, February). The programming profession, programming theory, and programming education. *Computers and Automation*, 17(2), 14–19.

Constantine, L. (April 1968–January 1969). Integral hardware/software design [Ten-part series]. *Modern Data Systems*.

Constantine, L. (1968, Spring). Control of sequence and parallelism in modular programs. *AFIPS Conference Proceedings*, 32, 409ff.

Constantine, L., and J. F. Donnelly. (1967, October). PERGO: A project management tool. *Datamation*.

Constantine, L., W. P. Stevens, and G. Myers. (1974). Structured design. *IBM Systems Journal*, 13(2), 115–139. Reprinted in special issue, "Turning Points in Computing: 1962–1999." (1999). *IBM Systems Journal*, 38(2&3); P. Freeman and A. I. Wasserman (Eds.). (1977). *Software design techniques*, Long Beach, CA: IEEE; and E. N. Yourdon (Ed.). (1979). *Classics in software engineering*, New York, NY: Yourdon Press.

Constantine, L., and E. Yourdon. (1975). *Structured design*. New York, NY: Yourdon Press.

Courtney, H., J. Kirkland, and S. P. Viguerie. (1997). Strategy under uncertainty. *Harvard Business Review*, 75(6), 67–79.

DeMarco, T. (1978). *Structured analysis and system specification*. New York, NY: Yourdon Press.

DeMarco, T. (2001). *Slack: Getting past burnout, busywork, and the myth of total efficiency*. New York, NY: Dorset House.

DeMarco, T., and T. Lister. (1987). *Peopleware: Productive projects and teams*. New York, NY: Dorset House.

Denning, S. (2018). *The age of agile: How smart companies are transforming the way work gets done*. New York, NY: Amacom.

Denning, S. (2019, August 13). Understanding the agile mindset. *Forbes*. www.forbes.com/sites/stevedenning/2019/08/13/understanding-the-agile-mindset/?sh=2eff46145c17

Drucker, P. (1954). *The practice of management*. New York, NY: Harper Business.

Dweck, C. (2006). *Mindset: The new psychology of success*. New York, NY: Random House.

Edmondson, A. C. (2002). *Managing the risk of learning: Psychological safety in work teams*. Cambridge, MA: Division of Research, Harvard Business School.

Fitzpatrick, M., I. Gill, A. Libarikian, K. Smaje, and R. Zemmel. (2020, April 20). The digital-led recovery from COVID-19: Five questions for CEOs. *McKinsey Insights*. www.mckinsey.com/capabilities/mckinsey-digital/our-insights/the-digital-led-recovery-from-covid-19-five-questions-for-ceos

Fowler, M. (1999). *UML distilled: A brief guide to the standard object modeling language*. Reading, MA: Addison-Wesley.

Fowler, M. (2018). *Refactoring: Improving the design of existing code*. Boston, MA: Addison-Wesley.

Fowler, M., and J. Highsmith. (2001, August). The Agile Manifesto. *Software Development Magazine*, 28–32.

Friedman, T. L. (2016). *Thank you for being late: An optimist's guide to thriving in the age of accelerations*. New York, NY: Farrar, Straus and Giroux.

Gane, C., and T. Sarson. (1980). *Structured systems analysis: Tools and techniques*. Hoboken, NJ: Prentice Hall.

Gell-Mann, M. (1995). *The Quark and the Jaguar: Adventures in the Simple and the Complex*. New York, NY: Macmillan.

Gilb, T. (1988). *Principles of software engineering management. Vol. 11*. Reading, MA: Addison-Wesley.

Goldratt, E. (1984). *The goal: A process of ongoing improvement*. Great Barrington, MA: North River Press.

Goldratt, E. (1997). *Critical chain*. Great Barrington, MA: North River Press.

Gould, S. J. (2002). *The structure of evolutionary theory*. Cambridge, MA: Harvard University Press.

Guo, X. (2017, July 20). The next big disruption: Courageous executives. *Thoughtworks Insights*. www.thoughtworks.com/insights/blog/next-big-disruption-courageous-executives

Haeckel, S. H. (1999). *Adaptive enterprise: Creating and leading sense-and-respond organizations.* Boston, MA: Harvard Business Press.

Heath, C., and D. Heath. (2007). *Made to stick: Why some ideas survive and others die.* New York, NY: Random House.

Herzog, M. (1952). *Annapurna.* Boston, MA: E. P. Dutton and Company.

Highsmith, J. (1987, September). Software design methodologies in a CASE world. *Business Software Review*, 36–39.

Highsmith, J. (1998). Order for free. *Software Development*, 80.

Highsmith, J. (2000). *Adaptive software development: A collaborative approach to managing complex systems.* New York, NY: Dorset House.

Highsmith, J. (2000, August). Retiring lifecycle dinosaurs. *Software Testing & Quality Engineering*, 22–30.

Highsmith, J. (2001). History: The Agile Manifesto. http://agilemanifesto.org/history.html

Highsmith, J. (2002). *Agile software development ecosystems.* Boston, MA: Addison-Wesley.

Highsmith, J. (2009). *Agile project management: Creating innovative products.* Boston, MA: Addison-Wesley.

Highsmith, J. (2013). *Adaptive leadership: Accelerating enterprise agility.* Boston, MA: Addison-Wesley.

Highsmtih, J., and A. Cockburn. (2001, September). Agile software development. *IEEE Computer*, 120–122.

Highsmith, J., L. Luu, and D. Robinson. (2020). *EDGE: Value-driven digital transformation.* Boston, MA: Addison-Wesley.

Highsmith, J., M. Mason, and N. Ford. (2015, December). The implications of tech stack complexity for executives. *Thoughtworks Insights.* www.thoughtworks.com/insights/blog/implications-tech-stack-complexity-executives

Hock, D. (1999). *Birth of the Chaordic Age.* San Francisco, CA: Berrett-Koehler.

Holland, J. H. (1989). *Emergence: From chaos to order.* Reading, MA: Addison-Wesley.

Holland, J. H. (1995). *Hidden order: How adaptation builds complexity.* Reading, MA: Addison-Wesley.

IBM Corporation. (2010). Capitalizing on complexity. www.ibm.com/downloads/cas/1VZV5X8J

Irvine, A. (2018). *Desert cabal: A new season in the wilderness.* Salt Lake City, UT: Torrey House Press.

Isaacson, W. (2011). *Steve Jobs.* New York, NY: Simon & Schuster.

Isaacson, W. (2021). *The code breakers: Jennifer Doudna, gene editing, and the future of the human race.* New York, NY: Simon & Schuster.

Johnson, G. (1996). *Fire in the mind: Science, faith, and the search for order.* New York, NY: Vintage Books.

Katzenbach, J. R. (1992). *The wisdom of teams: Creating the high-performance organization.* Boston, MA: Harvard Business Review Press.

Kelly, K. (2022, June 17). How to future. www.llrx.com/2022/06/how-to-future/

Kerievsky, J. (2005). *Refactoring to patterns.* Boston, MA: Addison-Wesley.

Kerievsky, J. (2023). *Joy of agility: How to solve problems and succeed sooner.* Dallas, TX: Matt Holt.

Kidder, T. (1981). *The soul of a new machine.* Boston, MA: Little, Brown.

McGrath, R. G. (2013). *The end of competitive advantage: How to keep your strategy moving as fast as your business.* Boston, MA: Harvard Business Review Press.

McGrath, R. G. (2014, July 30). Management's three eras: A brief history. *Harvard Business Review*, 2–4. https://hbr.org/2014/07/managements-three-eras-a-brief-history

McGrath, R. (2019). *Seeing around corners: How to spot inflection points in business before they happen.* Boston, MA: Houghton Mifflin.

McGregor, D. (1960). *The human side of enterprise.* New York, NY: McGraw-Hill.

McMenamin, S., and J. Palmer. (1984). *Essential systems analysis.* New York, NY: Yourdon Press.

Orr, K. (1981). *Structured requirements definition.* Topeka, KS: Ken Orr and Associates.

Orr, K. (1990). *The one minute methodology.* New York, NY: Dorset House.

Pink, D. H. (2011). *Drive: The surprising truth about what motivates us.* New York, NY: Penguin.

Ries, E. (2011). *The lean startup: How today's entrepreneurs use continuous innovation to create radically successful businesses.* New York, NY: Crown Business.

Royce, W. W. (1970). Managing the development of large software systems. In *Proceedings of IEEE WESCON*, 8, 328–338.

Schwab, K. (2016, January 14). The fourth Industrial Revolution: What it means, how to respond. *World Economic Forum.* www.weforum.org/agenda/2016/01/the-fourth-industrial-revolution-what-it-means-and-how-to-respond/

Schwaber, K. (1996, March 31). Controlled chaos: Living on the edge. *Cutter IT Journal.* http://static1.1.sqspcdn.com/static/f/447037/6485970/1270926057073/Living+on+the+Edge.pdf?token=0d8FV9%2FHU

Schwaber, K., and J. Sutherland. (1995). Scrum development process. In *Proceedings of the Workshop on Business Object Design and Implementation at the 10th Annual Conference on Object-Oriented Programming Systems, Languages, and Applications (OOPSLA'95).*

Senge, P. M. (1990). *The fifth discipline: The art and practice of the learning organization.* Sydney, Australia: Currency.

Siebel, T. M. (2019). *Digital transformation: Survive and thrive in an era of mass extinction.* New York, NY: RosettaBooks.

Smith, P. G., and D. G. Reinertsen. (1997). *Developing products in half the time: New rules, new tools*, 2nd ed. New York, NY: John Wiley & Sons.

Smith, S. M. (2000). The Satir change model. In G. M. Weinberg, J. Bach, and N. Karten (Eds.), *Amplifying your effectiveness: Collected essays*. New York, NY: Dorset House.

Takeuchi, H., and I. Nonaka. (1986). The new new product development game. *Harvard Business Review*, 64(1), 137–146.

Tate, K. (2005). *Sustainable software development: An agile perspective*. Boston, MA: Addison-Wesley.

Thoughtworks. (n.d.). Lens two: Evolving the human-machine experience. *Thoughtworks Insights*. www.thoughtworks.com/en-us/insights/looking-glass/lens-two-evolving-the-human-machine-experience

Thoughtworks. (2018, October). The word that took the tech world by storm: Returning to the roots of agile. *Thoughtworks Perspectives*. www.thought-works.com/en-us/perspectives/edition1-agile/article

Waldrop, M. M. (1993). *Complexity: The emerging science at the edge of order and chaos*. New York, NY: Simon and Schuster.

Weill, P., and S. Woerner. (2018, June 28). Why companies need a new playbook to succeed in the digital age [Blog post]. *MIT Sloan Management Review*. https://sloanreview.mit.edu/article/why-companies-need-a-new-play-book-to-succeed-in-the-digital-age/

Weinberg, G. M. (1971). *The psychology of computer programming*. New York, NY: Van Nostrand Reinhold.

Weinberg, G. (1985). *The secrets of consulting: A guide to giving and getting advice successfully*. New York, NY: Dorset House.

Weinberg, G. (1986). *Becoming a technical leader: An organic problem-solving approach*. New York, NY: Dorset House.

Weinberg, G. (1992). *Software quality management: Vol. 1: Systems thinking*. New York, NY: Dorset House.

Weinberg, G. (1994). *Software quality management: Vol. 3: Congruent action*. New York, NY: Dorset House.

Weinberg, G. M. (2001). *An introduction to general systems thinking (Silver Anniversary ed.)*. New York, NY: Dorset House.

Weinberg, G. M. (2006). *Weinberg on writing: The Fieldstone method*. New York, NY: Dorset House.

Wheatly, M. (1992). *Leadership and the new science*. Oakland, CA: Berrett-Koehler.

Yourdon, E. (1972). *Design of on-line computer systems*. Upper Saddle River, NJ: Prentice-Hall.

Yourdon, E. (2001, July 23). Can XP projects grow? *Computerworld*, 28.

Bibliography

Greenleaf, R. K. (2002). *Servant leadership: A journey into the nature of legitimate power and greatness*. Mahwah, NJ: Paulist Press.

Grint, K. (2022, January). Wicked problems in the Age of Uncertainty. *Human Relations*, 75(8). https://doi.org/10.1177/00187267211070770

Highsmith, J. (1981). Synchronizing data with reality. *Datamation*, 27(12), 187.

Highsmith, J. (1987, September). Software design methodologies in a CASE world. *Business Software Review*, 36–39.

Highsmith, J., and A. Cockburn. (2001, September). Agile software development. *Computer*, 120–122.

Kanter, R. M. (1983). *The change masters*. New York, NY: Simon & Schuster.

Kanter, R. M. (2001). *E-volve!: Succeeding in the digital culture of tomorrow*. Boston, MA: Harvard Business School Press.

Kernighan, B. (2019). *UNIX: A history and a memoir*. Kindle Direct Publishing.

Larson, C. (2003). Iterative and incremental development: A brief history. *Computer*. www.craiglarman.com/wiki/downloads/misc/history-of-iterative-larman-and-basili-ieee-computer.pdf

Tversky, B. (2019). *Mind in motion: How action shapes thought*. London, UK: Hachette UK.

Index

Also available from Jim Highsmith

Jim Highsmith's career spans six decades of rapid technology and business change. He coauthored the Agile Manifesto, cofounded the Agile Alliance, was first president of the Agile Leadership Network, and coauthored the Declaration of Interdependence for project leaders.

EDGE
ISBN: 978-0-13-526307-5

Your guide to using EDGE, a set of fast, iterative, adaptive, lightweight, and value-driven tools to achieve digital transformation

Adaptive Leadership
ISBN: 978-0-13-359865-0

Learn to extend agility across the enterprise with this guide on agile and lean methodologies for a management audience

Agile Project Management, 2nd Edition
ISBN: 978-0-321-65839-5

Best practices for managing projects in agile environments for even the largest projects and organizations

Adaptive Software Development
ISBN: 978-0-13-348946-0

Available as an eBook, this award-winning book helped launch the Agile movement in 2000

informit.com/highsmith

Pearson

Register Your Product at informit.com/register

Access additional benefits and save up to 65%* on your next purchase

- Automatically receive a coupon for 35% off books, eBooks, and web editions and 65% off video courses, valid for 30 days. Look for your code in your InformIT cart or the Manage Codes section of your account page.

- Download available product updates.

- Access bonus material if available.**

- Check the box to hear from us and receive exclusive offers on new editions and related products.

InformIT—The Trusted Technology Learning Source

InformIT is the online home of information technology brands at Pearson, the world's leading learning company. At informit.com, you can

- Shop our books, eBooks, and video training. Most eBooks are DRM-Free and include PDF and EPUB files.

- Take advantage of our special offers and promotions (informit.com/promotions).

- Sign up for special offers and content newsletter (informit.com/newsletters).

- Access thousands of free chapters and video lessons.

- Enjoy free ground shipping on U.S. orders.*

* Offers subject to change.

** Registration benefits vary by product. Benefits will be listed on your account page under Registered Products.

Connect with InformIT—Visit informit.com/community

 twitter.com/informit

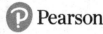 Pearson

informIT

Addison-Wesley · Adobe Press · Cisco Press · Microsoft Press · Oracle Press · Peachpit Press · Pearson IT Certification · Que